Stirring the Pot

STIRRING THE POT

The Kitchen and Domesticity in the Fiction of Southern Women

Laura Sloan Patterson

McFarland & Company, Inc., Publishers
Jefferson, North Carolina, and London

Earlier versions of two chapters of this book appeared as journal articles. "Sexing the Domestic: Eudora Welty's *Delta Wedding* and the Sexology Movement" appeared in *The Southern Quarterly*, 42 (Winter 2004). Copyright © 2004 by The University of Southern Mississippi. Reproduced by permission. "From Courtship to Kitchen: Radical Domesticity in Twentieth-Century Southern Women's Fiction" was published in *Women's Studies: An Interdisciplinary Journal* 32:8 (December 2003) [also see www.informaworld.com]. Reproduced by permission.

LIBRARY OF CONGRESS CATALOGUING-IN-PUBLICATION DATA

Patterson, Laura Sloan, 1974–
    Stirring the pot : the kitchen and domesticity in the fiction of southern women / Laura Sloan Patterson.
        p.   cm.
    Includes bibliographical references and index.

    ISBN-13 978-0-7864-3523-4
    softcover : 50# alkaline paper ∞

    1. Domestic fiction, American — History and criticism.
    2. American fiction — Women authors — History and criticism.
    3. American fiction — Southern States — History and criticism.
    4. American fiction — 20th century — History and criticism.
    5. Feminist fiction, American — History and criticism.
    6. Domestic relations in literature.   7. Kitchens in literature.
    8. Home in literature.   9. Women in literature.   10. Southern States — In literature.   I. Title.
    PS374.D57P38   2008
    813'.5 — dc22   2008029316

British Library cataloguing data are available

Cover image: Kate Irwin ©2008

Manufactured in the United States of America

McFarland & Company, Inc., Publishers
  Box 611, Jefferson, North Carolina 28640
  www.mcfarlandpub.com

To Michael

ACKNOWLEDGMENTS

I am thankful for the mix of prodding, encouragement, empathy, listening, research assistance, and financial support I received while working on this book.

Many of the ingredients in this recipe were provided by friends, family, and colleagues. My husband, Michael Sims, a full-time writer, helped me get started with gentle prodding just as I finished graduate school. His initial question — "When are you going to write your book?" — made it seem possible. He was willing to read early drafts and offer invaluable critique. Perhaps more important, he kept up a steady stream of encouragement, peppered with empathy about the difficulties of finishing a big project. Unfortunately, writing about domesticity sometimes means neglecting one's own domestic environment, and there's no way to offer enough thanks for all he does.

My mother, father, and sister, Bill, Rhonda, and Sarah Patterson, have supported this project from its origins, willingly listening to me on the days when I talked more than I wrote. My mother in particular never failed to ask, "How's the book?" I'm grateful for such consistent support and good humor.

Vanderbilt provided a delightful environment for the start of this project, including generous financial support. I'm indebted to Michael Kreyling for sparking my imagination in his Southern Literature seminar during my first semester of graduate school, directing my dissertation, and, above all, treating me as a colleague from the beginning. Thanks to Jay Clayton, Carolyn Dever, and Cecelia Tichi for reading and critiquing early drafts, and for sound advice. Ronnie Steinberg and the Vanderbilt Women's Studies Program provided financial and emotional support (you too, Gayle Parrott). I'm also thankful to Deandra Little, who listened to me ramble on about this topic, especially when we shared an office, and to Lisa Barnes and Julie Hipp, who provided friendship and support as I worked on early versions.

For the past three years, I have worked on this project in my new academic home, Seton Hill University in Greensburg, Pennsylvania. I thank John Spurlock, Mike Arnzen, Dennis Jerz, Al Wendland, Lee McClain, Christine Cusick, Stephen Honeygosky, and Terry Wansor for camaraderie and for listening to a displaced southerner go on about all things southern. Wendy Lynn keeps us all on our toes and equipped with everything we need. Maureen Vissat, Susan Eichenberger, and Kim Pennesi have offered listening ears and emotional support on many occasions. I thank Mary Ann Gawelek, our provost, for enthusiastic support for this project and for generous research and travel funding. Karissa Kilgore was every researcher's dream assistant: prompt, thorough, cheerful, and intellectually engaged. The staff of Reeves Library, especially Kelly Addleman, Judith Koveleskie, and David Stanley, diligently helped me track down research materials. Finally, I thank my students, and in particular my Southern Women Writers class in the fall semester of 2007. Your enthusiasm for the material makes it all worthwhile.

TABLE OF CONTENTS

PREFACE

The kitchen has been called the heart of the American home, and it is often the first place that comes to mind when we consider the term "domesticity." The kitchen, however, is not always a pretty place. In the romanticized version, played out in countless television commercials for food and cleaning products, the kitchen shines and sparkles, disinfected, somehow remaining emotionally warm and smelling buttery and sweet. But in many homes, the kitchen serves as playground, dog pen, homework center, craft corner, computer work station, breakfast nook, and more. The kitchen may show more about personal and familial identity than any other room in the home. For these reasons, within this study of twentieth-century southern American literature, I have chosen the kitchen as a special area of focus in the home.

But within the spectrum of perfect televised kitchens and their less-than-ideal real counterparts, where does the literary home — and contemporary literary domesticity more generally — fall? What does a fictional kitchen reveal about its inhabitants' interactions with technology and feminism? How can homes unlock the essence of a particular time and place? More specifically, what happens when we focus such an investigation on a region known for its affiliation with domesticity, kitchen labor, and food — the American South?

In her memoir *My Kitchen Wars* (1999), Betty Fussell comments on the near-constant state of chaos in this part of the home: "It's always this way, because a kitchen is in the middle of things, in the middle of life, as I'm living it now, this moment, the detritus of the past heaped like a midden everywhere you look" (4). The opening of Fussell's memoir suggests the importance of the location of the kitchen, both as a physical space and as a marker of historical and current identities. As a physical space, the kitchen may act as an entryway to the home, but, when its owner allows the opening of cupboards and drawers, as Fussell does, the kitchen is a signifier of a bond. Only one's intimates are allowed to see the mess of the kitchen. Yet Fussell subverts the mannerly notion that the cook should hide her mess by calling attention to it, by giving it both historical and cultural weight, not as mere clutter, but as the "detritus of the past."

Perhaps the most striking feature of Fussell's narrative is its odd mix of comfort in the physical space, in the handling of its gadgets, combined with a vague sense of apologia, a need to explain, if not the mess, at least one's own presence in the kitchen. Yet Fussell is clearly unwilling to give up her kitchen life even if it remains embedded in the past, even if she must view her own time in the kitchen as a series of wars fought on her own turf, between World War I and the Vietnam War. Fussell's meditations bring to mind another series of questions: What is it about the kitchen that would persuade a woman to occupy it, despite her sense of feeling at war with it? What is the kitchen war about? Why does she need the artillery of gadgets? Are these technological innovations helpful, bothersome, or merely decorative? Do they change her perceptions of her own role in this space? Further, what are the forces that provoke a need to explain a kitchen life? And how did the kitchen come to occupy its space — as a collection of cultural detritus, and, simultaneously, as a shorthand expression of its inhabitants' identity?

While the historical changes in the physical space of the home offer some answers to these questions, domestic texts provide far more information than contemporary advertising, recipes, or floor plans alone. Often, the twentieth-century domestic novel incorporates versions of all these elements, lending it a kind of hypertextual or postmodern pastiche feel. The reader moves between a letter, a recipe, an advertisement for domestic goods, a conversation about household duties, and a personal meditation on what it means to feed others.

Each strand of this type of pastiche offers important cultural information in its own right, and the construction of the narrative may offer implicitly political statements about what it means for a woman to work within her own kitchen at a particular nexus of class, racial, gender, sexual, regional, and temporal locations. When domestic novels are read in conjunction with contemporary cultural material — an important part of my methodology throughout this work — we may realize larger changes in the narratives of domestic novels that have political implications, usually incorporating the feminist ideology and gender imagery of the time period. It is also important to note, however, that no novel within this study, even in combination with relevant cultural material, can offer a full picture of a particular point in twentieth-century domestic life. It is my intention, rather, that the studies of novelists from the early, mid, and late twentieth century, as well as the hypertext writing of the late twentieth and twenty-first centuries, question the feminist implications of domestic narrative patterns. I argue that in these texts, the home, and its nexus, the kitchen, operates not only as a physical space, but also as an ideological tool for investigating larger cultural and historical issues. The decision to write a domestic text does not indicate, as presumed by many literary critics of the past and present, a lack of historicity — whether this lack is perceived as experiential or ideological — but a recognition of the richness of the domestic experience as a tool for understanding a cultural moment.

The issue of region is indispensable to the question "Where is the twentieth-century kitchen, and where has it been?" Considering this question in terms of region not only adds layers of tradition and folkways to domestic practice, but adds ideological problems as well. In the American South, gender stereotypes often die hard, as evidenced by phenomena such as debutante balls and magazines such as *Southern Living*. Because of a seemingly longer shelf life for gender stereotypes, southern women (and especially southern women who identify themselves as feminists) may be faced with an exacerbated gender identity politics when they choose to enter (or to re-enter) the kitchen as domestic providers. A southern feminist might feel disinclined to embrace the kitchen because it would link her to a variety of traditions that she does not wish to support, ranging from non-egalitarian marriage to domestic servitude to slavery. Yet at the same time, the middle-class southern woman may also feel the social pressures of a highly codified and constructed identity — pressures to prepare elaborate meals or to entertain in a certain way according to the community's standards. Because of these often unspoken pressures still felt by many southern women, and because of the lacuna that seems to exist in southern feminist scholarship, I have chosen as my focus for this book the southern home as represented in domestic literature.

Critics of domestic fiction often downplay regional differences, focus on the nineteenth-century New England domestic novel as the American model, or interrogate southern domestic novels solely as products of lingering racial tensions in the South. These approaches deny the domestic its full relevance as a category for study within twentieth-century literature, preferring to view twentieth-century domestic novels as women's fiction or as local color. Within the field of southern literary studies, some scholarship relegates domestic novels to a sub-category of southern fiction rather than viewing domestic novels as southern fiction proper. Critics such as Fred Hobson typically point to the southern domestic novel in contrast to works by male authors (Faulkner most notably), citing the domestic novel's tendency to disengage from larger historical themes.

In contrast, *Stirring the Pot* seeks to valorize the category of southern women's twentieth-century domestic fiction, and, more specifically, to recognize the feminist discourse within such works. In the mode of recent critics of women's media, including Marian Meyers, Carolyn Lin, and Nancy Walker, I examine the fractured nature of many of the images of women in domestic literature. The portrayals of women within southern domestic novels appear fractured, like those in magazines and television advertising, in that they are frequently neither wholly stereotypical nor wholly progressive. Further, within each chapter I explore the ways in which the domestic-feminist discourse of a specific historical moment is influenced by its newest modes of technology, whether in the field of medicine, transportation, or electronic communication. Unlike Hobson, I do not see the domestic as a private arena separated from the progress of cultural and historical events. The characters within the narratives I examine often seek out new technological developments (even those seemingly far removed from the kitchen, such as railway lines and the sexology movement). They use these developments to enhance their own roles within the home and to establish a sense of domestic community that extends far beyond their own neighborhoods.

Despite the notion that feminism and femininity were and are mutually exclusive within the South (and throughout much of the country), southern domestic novelists frequently use guises of femininity to promote feminist ideals. Yet some critics have overlooked these guises, as Rebecca Mark notes in her introduction to *The Dragon's Blood*. Mark claims that critics have ignored Welty's wide variety of cultural critiques "not only because no one could imagine a nice southern lady doing such a thing, but primarily because no one has consistently applied a close feminist textual and intertextual analysis to this collection of stories" (4). Mark correctly identifies the second part of the problem of southern femininity and feminism. If no one can "imagine a nice southern lady doing such a thing," then it is likely that no one will apply feminist criticism (or, for example, Marxist criticism) to her work. Many readers seem to take the code of southern femininity at face value, refusing to see beyond all that is "nice" about southern novels. I witnessed this phenomenon first-hand while teaching southern literature on both sides of the Mason-Dixon line, as students accustomed to careful close reading and interpretation suddenly balked at the idea of "reading so much into" what they perceive as a nice or simple story. This view perpetuates a mythology of the literary South, as the all-too-familiar land not only of moonlight and magnolias, but also of a band of scribbling, yet consistently nice southern ladies. Many southern women writers are therefore cut off from the prospect of subverting their own cultural norms not by virtue of what they have actually written, but on the personal reputation assigned to them by their readers and their critics.

The real scene of southern women's literature holds much more complexity as well as its own internal historical patterns. For instance, within this book, I will identify what I see as a domestic narrative pattern that continues throughout the twentieth century, a pattern that corresponds with the physical changes of the kitchen's shape, space, and position within the home. Physically, kitchens and homes have expanded spatially throughout the twentieth century. By the 1880s and 1890s, the kitchen was no longer a separate outbuilding, but an integral part of the home, usually located on the first floor. Innovations such as gas lines and electricity, combined with a shortage of domestic workers (due to industrialization and the migrations of African Americans), meant that more and more middle-class white women found themselves working in the kitchen; it became a unified part of the home for them, rather than a workspace for a class or racial Other. Yet this trend often left the middle-class white "lady of the house" in her kitchen alone and isolated. It is important to note, however, that African American women would have had an entirely different relationship with the home and the kitchen during this period, due to the association of domesticity with slavery and domestic work for hire. As we will see in chapter five, African American domesticity, in opposition to these associations, seems to hold the potential for increased community-building and pride, especially when contrasted with working in the kitchen of the Other.

Domestic narratives by white women from this period, including the work of Ellen Glasgow, examined in the second chapter, contain overtones of isolation as well as a claustrophobic form of third-person narration that, though technically omniscient, rarely turns from the physical and mental toil of its homemaker protagonist. Moreover, Glasgow herself seems particularly attuned to the isolated homemaker's plight although she rarely acted as a homemaker in her own life. I would argue that Glasgow's hearing disability isolated her socially, giving her a remarkable ability to recognize women afflicted with what I term "domestic deafness," that is, an inability to understand the role of one's family in the larger fabric of community, region, or nation, because of a preoccupation with practical, domestic details. Ultimately, however, Glasgow condemns domestic deafness, because isolated homemaker characters, far from being idolized by family and friends, often find themselves neglected and in despair as they age.

In the third chapter, I follow the myth of the "nice southern lady" into the 1920s through the 1940s. During these years, the boundaries of the kitchen and the home more generally continued to expand, through newer and better household "conveniences," and also through new home designs, such as the bungalow, a design intended to place the home in direct communication with its natural surroundings. The kitchen itself lost much of its isolating character, as whole families entered the kitchen and food preparation took on a more communal aspect. Eudora Welty characterizes this type of movement in her novel *Delta Wedding*, as in the scene in which Ellen, the family matriarch, invites the youngest and most recent addition to the family into the kitchen to bake a cake. While this scene is often noted for the ways in which Ellen's personal narrative and her recipe blend as dual texts, far more is at stake. Much of Ellen's meditation while she bakes the cake, and throughout the rest of the novel, is about the changing sexual mores of the period.

Although it is often overlooked as an issue directly related to domesticity, the sexuality of each family member infuses domestic practice as they prepare, separately and together, to marry a daughter, Dabney, to a field hand, Troy Flavin. Much of the cross-class conflict of the marriage is evident in differing domestic standards, as when Troy makes a marriage present of his mother's handed-down quilts, while Dabney decides to dress her bridesmaids as shepherdesses, outfitting them with crooks special-ordered from Memphis. Dabney must simultaneously navigate both class differences and her own changing sexual status within the family, and Welty frequently condenses both of these issues into highly codified domestic scenes. The multiple modes of sexual discourse and sexual practice within the novel reflect the changing climate of sexuality, as well as the increasing body of work available on the topic due to the new sexology movement.

The sexology movement started in earnest with the formation of the Committee on Maternal Health, in the same year *Delta Wedding* is set, 1923. Though perhaps euphemistically named, the committee's purpose was to examine the psychological effects of sexual activity, both within and outside of marriage, on women, and more important, to advance the use of birth control within the United States. Welty explores the sense of changing sexual and domestic roles for women in the structure of her narrative. Far from Glasgow's claustrophobic patterns of narration, Welty creates a blended sequence of multiple feminine narrators, drawing comparisons between the sexual and domestic habits of generations of women.

Chapter four moves from the Delta to the Appalachian mountains, a region often linked to "local color" rather than to southern literature proper. Lee Smith has been characterized as a local colorist, but I argue that her work provides an important chronicle of Appalachian life and of larger national changes in domestic practice, namely the standardization of domesticity in even the most remote, rural areas. The time period of Smith's settings — the 1930s through the 1970s — captures this region in a state of flux due to coal mining. Writing during the 1980s, Smith captures one element of the mining boom that had a particular effect on Appalachian domesticity: the unification of national railway lines.

Though the unification project began just after the Civil War, many coal lines were not integrated with regular passenger and transit lines until the late 1930s. This development aided standardized delivery of the U.S. mail. In turn, mail-order catalogues for domestic goods took off during this period. Suddenly, mountain coal miners and farmers had access to every kitchen implement available in Chicago or New York. Even if the impoverished mountaineers lacked the money to buy these goods, they were exposed to them, not only through the catalogue, but also through women's magazines. The train also brought new modes of domestic life. With expanded railway service, visitors to the region, many of them coal investors, missionaries, and teachers, became far more common. To house these visitors, entrepreneuring women established boarding houses, as Smith's characters do in both *Oral History* and *Fair and Tender Ladies*. Boarding houses meant that one's kitchen could expand to feed not only the family, but also travelers who brought with them new, foreign foodways and domestic practices.

In these ways, the kitchen expanded not only as a single-family unit, but also as an ideological concept. With trains running through the yard, the Appalachian homemaker might now see herself as a link in a national chain of homes, with similar goods and information available in any kitchen that could afford them. Isolated homes were no longer individual centers for production. Instead, each home became a part of a network connected to the train as the supplier of its most basic goods. Yet the concept of a network invades Smith's novels not only through their images of the train, but through their narrative structures as well. Unlike Welty's use of a fused narrative structure, with one narrative blending into the next, Smith's narratives stand alone as distinct sections, mimicking the structure of a community of independent rural homes linked primarily by the railroad and the provisions it might bring. Smith's novels are often broken down into highly compartmentalized narratives, each labeled with its narrator's name, or else, each contained within an epistolary format, complete with identifying dates and salutations. Each narrative stands alone, but within an undeniable network, much like the railway stations linking hundreds of small southern towns. Like Glasgow and Welty, Smith creates her own innovation alongside the domestic changes she catalogues by using new kinds of narrative patterns not previously associated with sentimental or domestic literature.

Toni Morrison has always been known as an innovator in contemporary fiction, and the narrative styles of *Jazz* (1992), *Paradise* (1997), and *Love* (2003) offer no exceptions to this reputation. But unlike Glasgow, Welty, and Smith, Morrison is sometimes overlooked in the categories of domestic and southern fiction. As Thadious Davis and others have argued, this omission can be traced to racism in literary canon and sub-group formation. Because Morrison is African American, some critics and readers assume that her race serves as a kind of over-arching identifier for her work, to the exclusion of other identifiers such as "southern" or "domestic." I want to purposefully include Morrison in this project as a way of questioning the boundaries of these categories and investigating the assumptions that go with them. Her work exposes domestic spaces and ideologies, and her fiction depends upon the homes within it not only to *tell* but to *act*, as if the homes were characters themselves. The trope of the home as character is most obvious, of course, in *Beloved*, but I argue that the homes of *Jazz*, *Paradise*, and *Love* also take on subtler, but no less essential, personae. Further, Morrison qualifies as southern because of her focus on the long view of life after slavery, and because of her ongoing status as a figure of comparison to more traditionally recognized southern novelists. Her novels set outside the South show clear links to the region through the histories of her fictional communities. In chapter five, I argue that her work must be recognized in relation to other southern and domestic novels in order to resist marginalization or strict race-based categorization.

While *Beloved* has achieved high popular and critical praise for its haunted domesticity (a *New York Times* poll in the summer of 2006 named it America's best work of modern fiction), *Jazz* and *Paradise*, the next two novels of the same trilogy, along with *Love*, were judged less accessible by many readers. Yet Morrison does more than expose the horrors of slavery; she also takes the long view of slavery's effects when she looks toward the home spaces haunted by Reconstruction, separatist ideologies, and the move to urban areas and urban economies in *Jazz*, *Paradise*, and *Love*. Here, I will focus on *Jazz*, *Paradise* and *Love*, her most recent novel, precisely because of their less-examined "haunted" domesticity.

Beyond the twentieth century, what is next for the home? How far can these expansive patterns continue? In the final chapter, I argue that the patterns of expansion of domestic practice and domestic narrative continue into the twenty-first century, using the technology of the Internet to afford many homemakers a chance to author their own kitchen stories. Kitchen-themed hypertexts, including web sites and weblogs, or blogs, locate the kitchen in a new and wholly different way. If, until this point, the kitchen has existed simultaneously within domestic literature as both a narrative pattern and a physical space, then the innovations of electronic media point to a new kitchen in the form of communities shaped by shared domestic practices but not tied to a specific location, neither a single kitchen, nor an entire region. Yet the problem of regionality within the online kitchen seems to create a great deal of anxiety, particularly among southerners unwilling to align themselves with, say, the homemakers of New England or the Midwest. This type of anxiety appears as hyper-southern-ness, with the earlier online kitchens tied to larger structures such as the "Southern Belles Web Ring" or the "B.R.I.T.s" (the Belles Raised in the South). Even in their names, these organizations promote very specific criteria for the southern homemaker, or, to put it more accurately, the southern cyberdomestic. Yet interestingly, and particularly in their initial rise during the late 1990s, these groups did not promote or even emphasize a high degree of technological skill. Instead, many of the sites contain what can only be called a technological apologia. The creators seem compelled to explain their need to promote themselves online at all. Unlike the online communities in which self-promotion and boasting are the norms, the southern cyberdomestics cling to a down-home "just folks" ethic. They often cite the dire consequence of recipes that might be forever lost as their reason for entering the showy online world. They put up web sites in the name of "tradition," negating their own subversive power to unite women who might otherwise remain isolated in their real-life kitchens and homes. Interestingly, the lure of a virtual South (complete with "authentic" recipes, but minus the humidity) has not been lost on the corporate online world. I compare the types of Souths promoted by commercial and personal web sites, and the roles (whether virtual or biological) available and unavailable to women within these structures.

Stirring the Pot looks closely at a wide variety of twentieth-century portrayals of southern domesticity. Although often assumed to be monolithic in content but narrow in scope, southern domestic narratives warrant further attention. Far from being married to the old ways of doing and thinking in the kitchen, southern women remain eager to try new forms of domesticity and to mold new methods and ideologies to fit their own complex needs. To assume that the "nice southern ladies" only meant to entertain themselves and their peers with their stories is to ignore a vital component of American women's cultural history. Similarly, to assume that the southern domestic texts and American feminism are at odds is to miss the often delightfully subversive voices from within the kitchen. In the words of Betty Fussell, "the kitchen condenses the universe" (5).

Chapter One

FROM COURTSHIP TO KITCHEN

Radical Domesticity in Twentieth-Century Southern Women's Fiction

> The dinner too in its turn was highly admired; and he begged to know to which of his fair cousins, the excellence of its cookery was owing. But here he was set right by Mrs. Bennet, who assured him with some asperity that they were very well able to keep a good cook, and that her daughters had nothing to do in the kitchen. He begged pardon for having displeased her. In a softened tone she declared herself not at all offended; but he continued to apologise for about a quarter of an hour [Jane Austen, *Pride and Prejudice* (1813) 58].

In the case of the Bennet daughters, Jane Austen's heroines have "nothing to do in the kitchen." The mere suggestion that her daughters might be responsible for a fine meal is considered degrading to Mrs. Bennet, especially when the suggestion is made by a "pompous" and unfamiliar dinner guest (56). Her daughters' domestic duty, as she explains it in the novel, is simply to make good and favorable matches that will bring honor to the family. And indeed, the "duty" that Mrs. Bennet decrees throughout the novel is the accepted literary notion of domesticity for young middle-class women in the late eighteenth and early nineteenth centuries.

Other domestic occupations for middle- and upper-class young women of this period included painting, drawing, and music (under the heading of "accomplishments"), as well as walking and traveling for amusement. Yet none of these accomplishments and diversions became an end unto itself. As the reader of Austen knows, accomplishments made a woman marketable for marriage because they allowed her to entertain men and, if necessary, to teach her own future offspring the delicate arts. Walking and traveling, in contrast, were considered acceptable means of meeting one's beloved by chance, although the hopes of these meetings were usually hidden from one's traveling companions. Direct flirting, however, was strongly discouraged, not so much because it might lead to a sexually compromising position, but because it dampened the overall reputation of a family, thus leading to a less favorable match for the flirt herself, as well as for any of her female relations. In short, domestic activities, even those with tangible products, such as embroidery, were deemed productive only if they led to successful marriage.

In *Desire and Domestic Fiction: A Political History of the Novel*, Nancy Armstrong argues that domestic novels (which existed in the eighteenth and early nineteenth century as courtship narratives) were engaged in larger projects as well, that they "seized the authority to say what was female" (5). This move, in turn, led to a reevaluation of "proper" femininity that would resist the former ideal of aristocratic femininity on the grounds that it led to waste, pride, and vanity. The image of the ideal woman evolved throughout the nineteenth century to favor "essential qualities of mind" (such as modesty, thrift, generosity, and patience) over title, status, and wealth (4). Yet these "essential qualities of mind" would, in the nineteenth century, remain just that — a certain set of values rather than an applied work ethic. As Armstrong notes in a chapter on conduct books, "The frugal domestic economy that these conduct books idealize in their educational program for women was one fueled by interest from investments rather than by labor" (73). The domestic woman was in charge of preserving extant lines of "invisible" income through thrift in activities such as furnishing a country home. She was not, in contrast, responsible for producing goods and foodstuffs for household consumption.

It is important to note that the newer, less aristocratic nineteenth-century ideal of the domestic woman did not develop overnight, nor did it develop into a coherent, monolithic identity. In *Uneven Developments: The Ideological Work of Gender in Mid-Victorian England*, Mary Poovey charts the uneven rise of this ideal, as well as the constructed notions of gender surrounding it. Poovey argues that rather than functioning as governing forces, our notions of Victorian sexual "repression" and Victorian femininity were constantly being constructed throughout this era, especially in the arenas of law, medicine, education, and literature. Similarly, figures such as female midwives, nurses, litigants, governesses, and writers often openly contested contemporary gender and sexual strictures.

Poovey claims that "the middle-class ideology we most often associate with the Victorian period was both contested and always under construction;

because it was always in the making, it was always open to revision, dispute, and the emergence of oppositional formulations" (3). Yet even in Poovey's "border cases" of women who contested and constructed social norms (15), the radical work (in both labor and ideological function) these women perform remains separate from household productivity. Even the women who enter the homes of other families to work, such as the governess Jane Eyre, are primarily concerned with psychologically reforming themselves and others so that they might be fit for marriage, not with contributing to their own finances or to the material economy of another household. These ideas of reform involve establishing moral, not financial or creative, strength and independence.

Resistance to the feminine ideal of the time — on the part of both fictional characters and actual women — usually takes place outside one's own home, often in the semi-private areas of someone else's home. The radical nature of what might happen if the lady of the house treated her own home as a system or a business with its own economy, employing herself as the chief worker, is not examined until the very late nineteenth and early twentieth centuries. It is as if labor in one's own kitchen remains the untouched frontier — for either conforming to or contesting the Victorian domestic ideal. It is difficult to know what role critical perceptions have played in the marginalization of the kitchen within eighteenth- and nineteenth-century domestic literature and history. Nonetheless, it is safe to say that until the late nineteenth century a domestic novel was usually centered around a courtship plot, not a kitchen.

Critics of nineteenth-century American literature have acknowledged women's place in the home, largely resisting the once-dominant notion of separate spheres. Even in mid–nineteenth-century American literature, middle-class women were mostly absent from their own kitchens. Instead, during the nineteenth century, common concerns included managing the overall workings of the home and instilling spiritual and moral values in children. Yet women did eventually begin to enter their own kitchens as productive laborers, in both Britain and America at the end of the nineteenth century for the reasons noted by Poovey and Armstrong: a focus on the individual woman and her "essential" qualities, a push for frugality as an ideal middle-class characteristic, advances in health care and hygiene, the downfall of the aristocracy and the rise of a homogenous middle class, the desire of women to effect political change through work, and mass industrialization and resulting servant shortages.

American women who entered their own kitchens during the twentieth century with a focus on material productivity were likely to face a matrix of practical and ideological concerns. These included managing "emotional" time spent with the family versus "productive" time spent on family concerns, balancing activities within and without the home, coping with emotional isolation, grappling with feminist ideologies versus "kitchen" lives, and many more issues. Yet despite the intricacies of these concerns, critics of twentieth-century literature often fall into a pattern of identifying the twentieth-century domestic novel with its earlier counterpart, which they characterize as the sentimental novel rather than as a different type of domestic novel. This slippage of signifiers risks critical confusion, especially because it takes the British sentimental novel as a kind of unstated ideal, even when the point of comparison is as far removed as a domestic novel with feminist overtones written in the American South during the twentieth century. Using the sentimental novel as an ideal or model precludes the recognition of evolving types of domestic novels as important cultural artifacts. Some critics have tended to view southern domestic fiction as a shadow of its more "noble" British, and then Victorian American, predecessors, rather than as its own genre with valuable cultural implications and radical political import.

Other critics categorize domestic novels as "novels of manners," thus reducing their cultural significance to the documentation of social structures. These approaches ignore the textual richness of twentieth-century domestic novels and divorce them from the breadth of their political, cultural, and historical concerns. To slight the concerns of the domestic novel is to ignore the value of its permutations, including the cultural information imparted about a region by looking not only to its broad landscapes, but into even its smallest of kitchens. This project seeks to relocate twentieth-century domesticity within the kitchen and to call for an exploration of the historical and political links between the southern home and American culture at large in the twentieth century.

Defining the Southern Feminist

In a review of Susan Goodman's *Ellen Glasgow: A Biography* (1998), Jonathan Yardley sanitizes and polishes Ellen Glasgow's experiences to fit his notion of her as a "mannerist." He remarks that she "was able to support herself on her writing" although Goodman points to various financial burdens.

Yardley also casts her as "a canny student of publishing practices who knew how to make her publishers pay handsomely," neglecting to mention that her first experience with a publisher involved an unwanted sexual proposition as well as a sexual assault. The "unknown literary adviser" noted that Glasgow was "too pretty to be a novelist" (41).

In many ways, Yardley's review reconstructs a romanticized notion of the South as a romanticized *literary* South, with little regard for Glasgow's struggles with financial matters as well as publication, struggles made clear by Goodman in her biography of Glasgow. With the label of "mannerist," Yardley also ignores Glasgow's well-known politics, including the feminist politics at work in her novels and her activism against cruelty to animals. Instead, Yardley remarks that Glasgow "was a feminist ahead of her time, but she liked men and was liked by them in return" (X03). Seemingly biased by his own conception of Glasgow as a "novelist of manners" (a distinction Goodman's biography works to dismantle), Yardley makes this comment after positioning Glasgow in the biographical context of an unhappy, wealthy Virginia family, as if her family background easily explained her ideology and her sexual preference.

Embedded in these remarks are two implications. The first, that the terms "feminist" and "heterosexual" are somehow at odds, represents the type of claim that infuriated feminist activists as well as socio-historic feminist literary critics in the 1970s. That Yardley makes this claim unchallenged in 1998 might be traced to the second implied notion — one that prevails throughout the review — that southern women writers, as well as their readers, biographers, and critics, remain largely unconcerned with and unimplicated in feminist politics.

Ironically, by divorcing himself from the feminist politics of the biography and its subject, Yardley elides the more troubling details of Glasgow's life. Yet he claims that Goodman seems faced with the problem of "not having much of a story to tell" because Glasgow "spent her life at her writing desk." Here, at the conclusion of the review, the reader encounters a third implication about southern literary women: that a story that takes place within the home is not much of a story at all, whether it arrives in the form of a novelist's life or her novels themselves.

While Yardley would deny the domestic the power to entertain, critics of domestic literature, such as Anne Romines, argue that housekeeping must be read as a vital "common human language" while analyzing domestic rituals as "rituals performed in a house, a constructed shelter, which derive meaning from the protection and confinement a house can provide" (*The Home Plot* 296, 12). Using texts by southern women, including much of Eudora Welty's fiction, Romines points out both the positive and negative connotations of "constructed shelters" while also paying attention to the subtle tensions between confinement and protection erected within many works of domestic fiction. In *Domestic Novelists in the Old South: Defenders of Southern Culture*, Elizabeth Moss focuses less on the home and its tensions, and more on the women writers who argued for "the importance of home influence in securing the future of Southern civilization" (2). Similarly, Anne Goodwyn Jones explores the literary manifestations of "ideal" southern womanhood and notes the significance of writing as the only profession open to southern women of "good" families (*Tomorrow Is Another Day*). Each of these studies valorizes the southern domestic genre. Romines illuminates potential meanings for specific domestic rituals; Moss politicizes the act of writing a domestic novel in the mid–nineteenth-century South; Jones stresses the conflict between the ideal southern womanhood role and the role of the southern woman writer.

Yet because of these foci—domestic ritual in literature, domestic novels within the narrow context of a specific historical period, and domesticity as it relates to a particular image of womanhood—these studies do not necessarily contextualize the southern domestic novel within the broader paradigm of changing ideological concepts of domesticity. In addition to calling for more critical attention to the radical politics of southern domesticity, I would argue for an exploration of what I view as a spatial and narrative explosion of domesticity. Literary representations of the domestic expand to encompass multiple physical centers of domestic activity, and writers forge a corresponding expansion of the limits of southern domestic *narrative*. That is, not only do we find a radical politics in southern women's domestic fiction, we also find radicalized narrative patterns at work when the old narrative structures (including the sentimental courtship narrative) may no longer be enough to contain the multivalent new forms of domesticity.

For the purposes of defining domesticity in the southern novel of the twentieth century, I will refer briefly to M.M. Bakhtin's notion of the chronotope: "We will give the name chronotope (literally, "time space") to the intrinsic connectedness of temporal and spatial relationships that are artistically expressed in literature" (*The Dialogic Imagination* 84). The notion of the chronotope is helpful because it unites both the spatial and the narrative strategies used to examine the domestic realm by southern writers such as Ellen

Glasgow, Eudora Welty, Lee Smith, and Toni Morrison. My project is to trace the increasingly fragmented physical locations of domesticity (not just the kitchen, but domesticity as it spreads through entire landscapes) along with increasingly temporally fragmented narrative patterns (from one narrator to several fused narratives to a distinct, delineated sequence of narrators in multiple historical settings) and to note how these patterns reveal the positioning of domesticity in women's lives. To varying degrees, Glasgow, Welty, Smith, and Morrison craft feminist revisionist histories of what it means to be domestic, to work within a domestic realm. Yet, like Yardley, critics of southern literature have often abandoned detailed accounts of the feminist politics of southern domestic writing, choosing instead to use the southern domestic novel to support some version of a monolithic South, often a romanticized environment for both women writers and their characters.

Feminist critics of southern literature seem to fall (often unwittingly) into a similar trap when they face a literary South invested in maintaining a status quo that holds out William Faulkner as the exemplum of all things both southern and literary. The corresponding literary model, based on none other than Quentin Compson, features a heroic male who leaves the South but feels compelled to return to it again and again, psychologically as well as physically. But as Michael Kreyling remarks in *Inventing Southern Literature*, "the heroism and cultural eminence of Quentin and his clones is learned behavior, style rather than substance" and "feminist critics are not unanimous on an alternative to the Quentin thesis" (106).

Kreyling's comments highlight a meta-question behind the question of why feminist theory and southern literary practice often seem to be at odds: What does it mean to be a southern(ist) feminist? Why is the regional distinction important? My answer to this question is that southern women writers have faced the double bind of gender-role confinement and a suppression of their narratives of struggle (witness Yardley's review) in favor of a romanticized notion of the South. In this mythical region, women are sometimes languid (in the manner of planters' wives) and sometimes industrious (in the manner of Reconstruction housekeepers), but they are always family- and home-centered and *happy* about it.

This notion of the home-centered southern woman extends to southern women writers, particularly when critics try to contextualize southern women writers in a Faulknerian literary tradition known for "big novels" "concerned with the sweep of history" (Hobson 78). In *The Southern Writer in the Postmodern World*, Fred Hobson writes,

Whether this is because the male, particularly in southern society, was usually conditioned to think more ambitiously, that is, to ponder history and politics in which
he, after all, could more easily participate — or whether it is because the vision of
the male writer has tended for other reasons to be more abstract, less attentive to
everyday truths and concrete details than that of most women writers — is debatable. I tend to think it is something of both. But a development of some interest
and, I believe, consequence in the 1980s was that the kinds of novels written by
southern men and those by southern women were no longer so easy to distinguish
[78].

Constructed upon false dichotomies, Hobson's "question" might be reformu-
lated by asking for a more precise definition of the "big novel." When we look
at southern literary history with the hypothesis that southern women did not
write "big novels," does the question Hobson poses not become a self-fulfilling
prophecy? Are "abstraction" and "everyday details and concrete truths" always
at odds? Are history and politics the only subjects worthy of ambitious
thought? While I agree with Hobson that southern novels written in the 1980s
are less distinguishable along gender lines, I would contest the logical model
he constructs to arrive at this point. The "everyday details" of domesticity do
not preclude large-scale historical thought.

In *Virginia*, the story of a woman who suffers for her choice to follow
an older domestic ideal in a changing cultural climate, Ellen Glasgow's
narrator remarks on maintenance of the community status quo by town leaders such as Cyrus Treadwell. Glasgow writes, "For in common with other
men of his type, he stood equally for industrial advancement and domestic
immobility" (273). In cataloguing Treadwell's ideology, Glasgow does
more than paint a portrait of the richest man in Dinwiddie; she ironically
charts a historical and philosophical position: that industrial progress, no
matter how useful, must not be allowed to enter the realm of the home. She
suggests that Cyrus's ability to change the physical and financial landscape
around him is rooted in his knowledge that nothing within the confines of
his home will change without his permission. Throughout the novel, Glasgow subtly theorizes that established community leaders (men) can craft new
moralities, art forms, and technologies only through a dependence on the stability of the home. In this scenario, similar to others throughout Glasgow's
work, the home represents far more than a quotidian set of "truths" and
"details"; the home is the basis of modernization, even when the home *seems
immutable.*

Beyond the Kitchen

By the twentieth century, many domestic protagonists did work within their own kitchens, reflecting a historical shift in home labor practices, but it is important not to allow the literal kitchen to become the entire critical focus. The simplified form of separate-spheres, kitchen-centered domesticity criticism reinforces the sharp gender divides of a romanticized, monolithic South constructed by some literary critics of southern novels. Moving domesticity beyond the kitchen consists of a process of locating the spaces that a writer defines in domestic terms. The spaces defined by domestic terms are those in which eating, drinking, preparing/storing food, health-oriented ministrations, family entertainment, or *meditation on any of these processes* occur. For just as Harvard becomes a significant setting for Quentin Compson's construction of his notions of the history of the South, so does a woman's study or bedroom or lone forest retreat become an important place where she may construct an ideology of the domestic, including the (sometimes ironic) meditations on the importance of domesticity in her own life.

In an examination of the gendered processes of reading African-American literature, Deborah McDowell addresses the issue of the kitchen, along with its representational possibilities, in reference to Darryl Pinckney's review of Ishmael Reed's novel, *Reckless Eyeballing*:

> The male readers of this debate [the "conspirational theme" against black men in African-American literature], whose gazes are fixed on themselves, seem to have entered a fictional territory marked by unreadable signs. Pinckney refers to this territory as the kitchen. He remembers when "Black women's concerns had belonged to what was considered *the private*, rather than the public, as if the kitchen range could not adequately represent the struggle. But it turned out that the concerns of the kitchen were big enough to encompass the lore of struggle and survival" [400].

McDowell notes that twentieth-century black women writers have deconstructed the public-private division, "for they understand the operations of power within intimate domains, operations captured in that now familiar axiom 'The personal is the political'" (400–401). The southern kitchen's close historical association with slavery may account for the dominance of the pattern of deconstruction that McDowell notes in the literature of African American southern women writers. A connection to slavery may also account for the critical attention to "kitchens" as important political arenas in the criticism of these authors' works. Toni Morrison in particular uncovers the home's position as a repository for cultural memory in *Beloved*. In *Beloved*, as in Glasgow's "Dare's Gift," a home holds the memory of a violent act.[1] In many ways, these appear to be traditional hauntings, but in both stories, the home itself, not a ghost, takes central stage. Interestingly, these particular memory-haunted homes suggest that the horrors of slavery have the power to infect homes for years, and also that women who spend much of their time in the home are as much in contact with the "outside" cultural and political world as their husbands.

Pinckney's use of the term "kitchen" as somehow representative of the struggle between public and private realms implies that "kitchen" can be shorthand logic for a private, centralized node of domesticity. Here I should add that I often intentionally stretch the term "domestic novel" to examine texts such as Lee Smith's *Oral History*, which has been categorized as a "local color" or "Appalachian fiction" novel by many critics. Similarly, I will argue that Toni Morrison should be considered as a southern writer in her own right, not merely a counterpoint to more recognized southern writers. To limit the definition of what qualifies as a southern domestic novel seems to fall into one or more kinds of marginalization: gender-role confinement, the suppression of narratives that detail home-centered struggles, racism, and/or classism. Novels that depict home-related concerns (which may or may not take place within the confines of a protective shelter) are domestic, and at the same time often politicized and replete with meta-narratives on women's places in the realms of finance, education, and the production of both history and art.

The process of defining the domestic, both its genre and its physical location in a text, poses the sub-question, "To what extent have women writers deconstructed the public-private division?" And further, "Why has little feminist attention been paid to domesticity in southern literature?" As evidenced by critical collections such as *Haunted Bodies: Gender and Southern Texts*, edited by Anne Goodwyn Jones and Susan V. Donaldson, criticism of southern literature in the late 1990s seems to be more about gender studies and less about earlier modes of feminism. Has the moment for feminist criticism of domestic novels bypassed southern literature? And if so, why? How can African American feminist criticism shed light on domestic texts? If a lacuna in southern feminist criticism can be charted, then what are the future ramifications for the discipline? Southern literary criticism seems to be largely missing the late 1970s to mid-1980s moment of socio-historical feminist criticism, and this lacuna may explain the scant amount of psychoanalytic feminist studies in relation to southern literature today.

20

At this point in the history of literary theory and southern literature, it would be fruitless to return to a feminist mode that might be broken down into several (admittedly oversimplified) lines of critical work. It does seem fruitful, however, to examine briefly two of these critical modes, in the interest of a better understanding of a potential future for feminist-southernist domestic criticism. One branch of 1970s and 80s socio-historical American feminist literary criticism consisted of valorizing the feminine — general praise (sometimes approaching deification) for both female characters and female writers. This critical trend often resulted in a second mode, the work of recovery — proving that domestic novels, often from the early nineteenth century, did indeed have "a story to tell." Critics of nineteenth-century American literature seem to have dominated the discourse of domesticity in a manner that does not typically overlap with the fields of southern literature, twentieth-century American literature, or a combination of these two categories.

American Literary Criticism, Feminism, and Domesticity

To posit theories of why this lacuna exists, I will sketch the pattern of criticism surrounding domestic issues in nineteenth-century American literature. In the opening chapter of *Home Fronts: Domesticity and Its Critics in the Antebellum United States*, Lora Romero writes,

> Feminist rereadings of literary historical periods often proceed from the assumption that women writers were excluded from the production of the canon. In the construction of the antebellum canon, however, "deployment" rather than "exclusion" better describes the fate of women's fiction. Traditional literary histories of the period do not ignore women writers so much as use them as the other which endows the "classics" with their identity.
>
> Challenging the oppositional logic through which women have been simultaneously written out of and written into this cultural history requires a complex set of critical strategies. As H. Ross Brown's vision of female masses in military formation indicates [*The Sentimental Novel in America*], the opposition is richly sedimented, not just with the proprieties of gender and assumptions about mass culture but also with convictions about hegemony and resistance [11].

Romero resists Brown's 1940 formulation of women's dominance in the sentimental field by mid–nineteenth-century. She argues that while women sold their novels in impressive numbers, the process of critiquing nineteenth-century domesticity often reaffirms a set of binaries regarding separate spheres — namely that women ruled the home (and consequently the home novel) while men controlled a separate, public sphere unavailable to women.

Romero also points out that this type of "separate spheres" criticism often leads to the dangerous assumption that male authors consciously formed our literary canon through "deviating from prevailing norms of manhood," a deviation that resulted in the American Renaissance (Leverenz, qtd. in Romero 18).

In opposition to critics who valorize male "classic" authors, often for their countercultural characteristics, Lora Romero positions herself within a context of feminist criticism of domesticity. She faults the late 1970s to mid–1980s period of "first-wave feminist attempts" (including critics such as Nina Baym and Jane Tompkins) for its tendency to position domesticity simply as a subversive tradition (19). This line of thinking supports (through reversal) the kind of binary structures Romero works to dismantle. She traces this pattern of strict binaries through the later school of revisionist domesticity, in which critics such as Laura Wexler comment on the ways in which sentimental novels have been used for racial and economic control. And while Romero does oppose any sort of strict masculine-feminine binary within the realm of domesticity, she carefully notes that domesticity need not be synonymous with feminism. She finds the fictional domesticity of this era to be almost always antipatriarchal, yet rarely radical (19–20).

Romero's work points out not only the importance of domesticity to *all* nineteenth-century literature, but also the importance of theorizing the history of domesticity and its critics. In *Home Fronts*, the meta-critique of the progression of critical approaches to domesticity is just as important as formulating new critical methods that allow for a (somewhat Foucauldian) non-binary approach to texts.

I trace Romero's argument not to suggest that critics of twentieth-century southern literature must jump onto any particular bandwagon, but simply to point out what seems to be a stalled moment in the intersection of southern literary criticism and feminism, and to suggest some preliminary hypotheses for this stall. It goes without saying that the criticism of southern literature has always been somewhat behind the curve when it comes to literary theory and feminist theory in particular. Partially excusing the relative lack of feminist criticism of southern texts, Carol Manning points to the relative youth of southern literature as a field and states that

It was not until the 1980s — with works by scholars such as Anne Goodwyn Jones, Louise Westling, Kathryn Lee Seidel, Helen Taylor and Minrose Gwin, and with special issues on Southern women writers by *The Southern Quarterly* (see Prenshaw) — that feminist murmurs about Southern literature began to be heard [2].

Manning explains that southern literature "escape[d] the feminist critique for so long" because southern women have been associated with and even defined by their relationship to the canon. Hence the myth that we do not need a revision of the canon arises (2). Yet even when critics such as Manning resist this sort of myth-making, they often define southern women writers by their chronological relationship to the Southern Renaissance, which might qualify as a kind of myth-making in itself. Classifying southern women writers as pre-renaissance, renaissance, or post-renaissance, without reference to the male-centered and culturally constructed nature of such movements, similar to David Leverenz's manner of responding to the nineteenth-century American Renaissance, seems to perpetuate a distancing effect between southern literature and feminism.

Manning comments extensively on the process of nineteenth-century southern canon revision. She positions the early 1990s stage of revision as somewhere between "subversion" feminism and "revisionist" feminism. I should point out, however, that these terms are my own rather than Manning's, derived from the general movement that Romero charts, but implied by Manning without respect to domesticity specifically. Addressing scholarship on twentieth-century texts, Manning laments the criticism (sometimes voiced as extensive praise) of consistent and unified "feminine" traits in southern women writers. While Manning's study is infinitely valuable in terms of initiating a discourse on the tension between feminism and southern literature, she does not address domesticity at length. In ignoring domesticity as both a dominant topic and an important ideological, spatial, and narrative tool, feminists face the danger of reiterating the message that domesticity is "women's work" and therefore, not significant.

Particularly in the scholarship on twentieth-century texts, domesticity is not addressed, and is even considered a non-topic, hence the rarity of the term "twentieth-century domestic fiction." In a post–*Feminine Mystique* era, does twentieth-century domesticity lose its relevance or even its appeal? Of course, my reply to this question is in the negative, but within that reply two basic assumptions arise and should be interrogated. Domesticity in twentieth-century literature by southern women has been ignored, first because of the myth that all southern women write *from within a domestic perspective*, even if they are not specifically engaged in the process of writing domestic novels. This assumption precludes the possibility that women may write about domesticity (within the form of a novel) satirically, allegorically, or as an ideology that informs not only women's lives but also their cultural milieu (their

23

books, magazines, web sites, web logs, films, television shows). A second assumption — that all domesticity is basically the same — precludes the possibility of domesticity criticism based on regional or historical divisions, as well as the possibility of a project such as this one, which proposes to identify emerging patterns within the literary discourse on domesticity.

The central patterns of twentieth-century southern domesticity that I will identify are a shift in the location of the spatial and ideological center of the home and a corresponding freedom to experiment with narrative form and historical time frames. Beginning with the early twentieth century, we find in novels such as Ellen Glasgow's *Virginia* (1913) a smothering, claustrophobic domesticity confined to dusty rooms hidden by dark draperies, as well as a conventional third-person narrator whose omniscience extends mainly to the mind of Virginia. The narrator's deep probing of the title character's mind implies that years of drudgery and confinement have made Virginia as readable as the furniture. Later, at mid-century, in Eudora Welty's *Delta Wedding*, domesticity becomes diffused, its centralized location mirroring the movements of the family members beyond the plantation's boundaries and across the Delta. Along with these multiple centers of domesticity comes a narrative style that moves cryptically among seven female characters, implying that there is no "one way" to live at home, to facilitate domesticity. In the 1980s, Smith's *Oral History* continues this detailed view of domesticity with sharply delineated, subtitled shifts between narrators. Similarly, the location of domesticity expands to fill an entire mountain range as women, and to a lesser extent men, envision households that encompass communities. Smith also self-consciously defies stereotypes of paranoid, self-contained Appalachian families. In the course of putting up pickles, her women are likely to meditate not only on the topic of family history, but also on the struggle between artistic creativity and household duties. In the late twentieth and early twenty-first century, Toni Morrison explodes the locations and narrative structures of domestic novels even further, giving us multiple points of view in chapters titled with characters' names (*Paradise*), unidentified omniscient narrators who see all and know all, often within multiple urban homes (*Jazz*) or within both public and private living spaces (*Love*). In Morrison's work, home takes on a symbolic meaning of safety, but not safety from the outside world (as in the novels of many white domestic writers). Morrison's characters seek safety *in* the world, in a reversal of racist oppression. Pushed into a particular region, neighborhood, type of home, job, or stereotype for too long, many of Morrison's characters seek a kind of transcendent home, one that allows for open physical and ideological interchange with the rest of the world.

Repositioning Domesticity: Glasgow, Welty, Smith, Morrison and Online Homes

I have chosen these four authors because they represent distinct moments in the history of southern domestic literature and because they span the twentieth century. Therefore, this selection offers not only three different historical moments in terms of narrative, but also demonstrates several different ways that women writers have conceptualized domesticity.

In her introduction to Ellen Glasgow's *Virginia*, Linda Wagner-Martin notes a mix of genres in the novel:

> In some ways, *Virginia* is a classic "domestic" novel, our attention riveted throughout on the woman and the home and family she cares about. But it is also a poignant *Bildungsroman*, for the first forty percent of the book deals with Virginia as she grows up: her "formal" education, her intimacy with the modern and forceful Susan Treadwell, her restricted life as daughter of the downright naive Pendleton family in the small Virginia community. What she "becomes" as a result of all of this instruction is clear only after she marries. Marriage and the change of location that act mandates serves as Virginia's journey to the inimical city, as well as her crucial sexual experience — both ingredients of the traditional male novel of development [xii].

While Wagner-Martin implies a connection between these generic types — the bildungsroman and the domestic novel — her division of the text into these categories focuses on the masculine/feminine, public/private divide. In this schema, Virginia's only option for coming of age is a masculinized narrative of her contact with the "public" (the city and post-marriage sexual encounters) outside the home, implying that Virginia's education (both in school and at home) is nothing more than a means to achieve her goal of becoming a married, public woman.

It seems unnecessary to graft the masculine bildungsroman tradition onto the novel, splitting it into two parts divided by the event of marriage. The beginning of the novel also acts as a primer in domesticity and a meta-commentary on how Virginia absorbs the lessons of what "good" homes are like. After all, Virginia never really "goes public"; she spends most of her life in suffocating homes, without ever coming of age in her ability to express herself or to value her own opinions. Yet Glasgow herself goes public by expressing the inner workings of domesticity in the form of a novel: as readers, we gain access to the ideology behind domesticity.

For Virginia, home extends as far as the boundary of the front yard. From an early age she defends this ground and claims it as a type of fortress: "Ever since Virginia could remember, she had heard threats of cutting down the paulownias because of the litter the falling petals made in the spring, and ever since she could lisp at all she had begged her father to spare them for the sake of the enormous roots, into which she had loved to cuddle and hide" (21). Virginia the child has not yet been indoctrinated into the emotional and physical "messes" that surround homes; she sees only the comfort and privacy of the home, represented by the border of her play area. Yet we read this snapshot of Virginia's childhood in the context of the teenaged Virginia's conversation with her best friend, Susan Treadwell. Susan assures Virginia that her parents will not cut down the trees because they know how much she likes them. Yet Virginia possesses an intimate understanding not only of her parents but also of the politics of domesticity. She responds to Susan by saying, "Oh, of course they wouldn't [cut down the trees], but as soon as I was out of sight they might persuade themselves that I liked it" (21). Virginia demonstrates her knowledge that the currency of the household is happiness; both her mother and father have trained her to recognize that only a constant exchange of pleasantries and polite babble indicates a successful home. She has also learned the family's method of managing any crisis, no matter how small: a manipulative new narrative must be constructed so that the exchange of happiness can continue, as in "Virginia would have wanted us to cut down those old trees anyway."

Just as Glasgow cuts to the heart of the manipulative art of home and familial management, she also comments on the suffocating nature of homes for women. Rather than conferring any sort of public or private status, home often dominated a woman's life as the mediating ground for issues such as politics, geography, and her own body and its changing forms. In the first chapter, "The System," told from the point of view of the town, ostensibly filtered through the mind of Miss Priscilla Batte, the school teacher, we realize the conflation between the name of the novel's protagonist and her home state. Miss Priscilla reflects on the town's attitude toward various kinds of changes:

> Already she felt the breaking of those bonds of sympathy which had held the twenty-one thousand inhabitants of Dinwiddie, as they had held the entire South, solidly knit together in a passive yet effectual resistance to the spirit of change. Of

the world beyond the borders of Virginia, Dinwiddians knew merely that it was either Yankee or foreign, and therefore to be pitied or condemned according to the Evangelical or the Calvinistic convictions of the observer [11].

This passage works in the manner of a camera that pans the landscape before zooming in on the subject of a film. Like the protective paulownia trees, the South stands in as a kind of shelter around the shelter, the home of the home. Southerners are "knit together," not bound or chained, "passive," usually not unpleasant, and able to manage the southern homefront effectively. The phrase that describes the horrors "of the world beyond the borders of Virginia" suggests both a threatening landscape as well as an unfamiliar territory beyond the familiar human body that occupies the house — Virginia herself, her physical form. In other words, women's bodies are only safe when they are doubly contained within the home and within the confines of the South.

Virginia absorbs these teachings, then carries them to an extreme as she falls in love and begins a family. As Virginia prepares for the party where she will meet her future husband, the narrator remarks that for a woman "love and life were interchangeable terms" and that love constitutes a woman's "single field of activity.... The chasm between marriage and spinsterhood was as wide as the one between children and pickles" (111). With this final comparison, the narrator breaks a pattern of high-blown sentimental prose, in what seems like Glasgow's own sense of irony breaking through the oppressive ideology of love on which Virginia's claustrophobic version of domesticity will thrive. Success at the party will lead to children for Virginia, yet this "accomplishment," despite its distance from the horrors of "spinsterhood," will become as sour as the delayed gratification and scant nourishment provided by the pickling process.

Once pregnant, Virginia slips into near agoraphobia. In a letter, she tells her mother that the doctor believes she will become ill if she does not get some exercise outdoors. Yet Virginia uses her domestic heritage to justify her defiance of the doctor's recommendation: "But you stay in the house all the time and so did grandmother, so I don't believe there's a word of truth in what he says" (173). Interestingly, this is the only instance when Virginia is able to defy masculine authority successfully. Her refusal suggests that the forces of this claustrophobic domesticity are powerful enough to override even the voice of medical authority. Virginia prioritizes the home and the privacy it provides even above the health of her own body.

The details of minor crises that follow Virginia's marriage and the birth of her first child also become couched in domestic terms. When Virginia fears that her husband is having an affair with a female fox-hunter, she accompanies him on a hunt to ward off the threat of infidelity. But once she is on the hunt, it is the landscape, rather than any feeling of jealousy, that overwhelms Virginia in its strangeness: "Today both the horn and the familiar landscape around her had grown strange and unhomelike. For the first time since her birth she and the country were out of harmony" (246). She is momentarily revolted by the sight of a huntsman eager for a kill, but her eye quickly focuses on an even more threatening expansive landscape: "Behind him, like a low, smoldering fire, ran the red and gold of the abandoned field" (246). Virginia crafts this landscape, in contrast to the safe nest of her house, into a container for all of her rage and her fears of abandonment. She convinces herself that it is not the unfamiliarity of her own husband with another woman that frightens her, but the spectacle of the hunt and the outdoors.

In all of Virginia's attempts to isolate herself within her home, we find a South that Glasgow viewed, somewhat satirically, as opposed to change. Although Virginia represents the domestic ideal of her time and place, her husband abandons her. He ultimately leaves her for another woman. To make matters worse, in Virginia's mind at least, her rival is an actress from New York City. Through Virginia's fears of her own changing, pregnant body, her borderline-agoraphobic relationship to the outdoors, and the novel's isolating pattern of a third-person eye trained on Virginia, Glasgow paints domesticity as a politicized arena. Through this "merely" domestic novel, Glasgow calls for the South to change its ways or be doomed to failure in its traditional pastimes, its morals, its art, and its economic structures.

In contrast to *Virginia,* the domestic setting and the narrative patterns of Eudora Welty's *Delta Wedding* offer a more spatially, narratologically, and ideologically expansive view of domesticity. Unlike Virginia's claustrophobic, dark home, the Fairchilds inhabit the entire Delta, equally at home in kitchens or on horseback through the forest. The Fairchilds live together in the most literal sense, allowing their bodies and their narratives to become entangled and even enmeshed.

Both novels open with bird imagery, suggesting the possibilities for and the limitations of feminine freedom. *Virginia* begins with the following sentence: "Toward the close of a May afternoon in the year 1884, Miss Priscilla Batte, having learned by heart the lesson in physical geography she would teach her senior class on the morrow, stood feeding her canary on the little square porch of the Dinwiddie Academy for Young Ladies" (3). Here, a common domestic bird lives in a carefully contained environment, circled by the cage, and "squared" by Miss Priscilla's "little porch." Additionally, the bird is mapped onto Miss Priscilla's routine, crammed between the memorization of a lesson in "physical geography" for "young ladies" (vaguely suggesting, yet never delivering, the topos of a human body) and late-afternoon social calls. The bird remains trapped both by its enclosed environment and its dependence on Miss Priscilla's carefully regimented life.

In contrast, shortly after her arrival in the Delta, Laura Fairchild imagines the Fairchild cousins as a group of birds in a less restricted environment. Commenting on the Fairchilds' ability to exist as a family in a constant state of flux, Laura imagines

> a great bowerlike cage full of tropical birds her father had shown her in a zoo in a city — the sparkle of motion was like a rainbow, while it was the very thing that broke your heart, for the birds were caged all the time and could not fly out. The Fairchilds' movements were quick and on the instant, and that made you wonder, are they free? Laura was certain that they were compelled — their favorite word. Flying against the bad things happening, they kissed you in rushes of tenderness. Maybe their delight was part of their beauty, its flicker as it went by, and their kissing of not only you but everybody in a room was a kind of spectacle, an outward thing [18].

Unlike Glasgow, Welty openly interrogates the notion of an enclosed sense of domesticity, particularly in her question "are they free?" Laura's question, as written by Welty at mid-century, pushes the domestic bird imagery beyond Glasgow's canary in a cage, into the updated and more expansive image of the exotic tropical birds in a larger group environment in a cosmopolitan setting — a zoo in a city. These birds cannot escape, but unlike Miss Priscilla's bird they demonstrate a degree of agency — they are compelled, although we are not told what they are compelled to do, only the importance of this sense of agency, movement, and beauty to their collective self-image.

In the middle of the twentieth century, domesticity loses its connotations of entombment while retaining a certain amount of tension regarding its boundaries and limitations. Shellmound's women and its versions of domesticity are numerous and mobile: Dabney is departing (into class-inappropriate marriage and off to visit on her horse); Robbie Reid is arriving (at Shellmound and also at an understanding of the clan). And meanwhile, Shelley encloses herself in her own bedroom *willingly*, away from the chaos of domesticity, to follow her own creative journey through the pages of her journal. Some critics have argued that Ellen acts as the stable, maternal force throughout the novel, reporting on the activities of the Fairchilds from a narratively convenient position of insider/outsider. She is an outsider because she has married into the family, but an insider because she is responsible for the physical conception of the children, a fact reiterated by the announcement of yet another pregnancy at the end of the novel.

But in a contrasting light, Ellen might be said to represent the non-domestic or resistant domestic woman. Rather than calming children with bedtime stories, Ellen puts Bluet to sleep with the retelling of a dream laden with sexuality:

> Mama dreamed about a thing she lost a long time ago before you were born. It was a little red breastpin, and she wanted to find it. Mama put on her beautiful gown and she went to see. She went to the woods by James' Bayou, and on and on. She came to a great big tree. Hundreds of years old, never chopped down, that great big tree. And under the tree was sure enough that little breastpin. It was shining in the leaves like fire. She went and knelt down and took her pin back, pinned it to her breast — to her breast and wore it — away — away [83–84].

Ellen narrates the loss of the breastpin — her own unbridled, non-domestic sexual self, gone long before Bluet's birth. She goes to "see," endowing herself not with the mission to find a sentimental family treasure, but instead endowing herself with the privileges of male spectatorship as she enters the woods and follows the masculine "James" bayou "on and on." The phallic tree, combined with the fiery pin buried in leaves, completes and consummates the fantasy. If Welty, however, has allowed her current narrator to explore a sexual fantasy in front of a child, she also forces Ellen to bring herself back to her domestic reality of the Delta. She attempts to re-pin herself, or to reassert an independent sexual identity within the Delta, only to narrate the dream's ambiguous ending of having taken her "pin back, pinned it to her breast and wore it — away — away" (83). In a sense, Ellen can only imagine her autonomous sexual self in dreams or "away" from the Delta.

Despite Ellen's later ability to make an actual journey into the woods where she sees a young, wild girl (a doppelganger for her own lost sexual self), Ellen has "worn away" any sexual function of her own breasts; they exist to feed and to comfort the ever-enlarging clan. The real journey fails in its mission to find the pin as well. Instead, Ellen attempts to mother and scold the lost girl she finds, yet she acknowledges the import of her words when she realizes the girl's race. The girl is white, but had she been black, Ellen might have expected her to walk through the woods alone — whether running away or on a household errand. Yet with the discovery of the girl's whiteness, "a whole mystery of life opened up" (90). Ellen recognizes a white girl, a female that she cannot entirely distance as racial Other, who has willingly taken the sexual risk of wandering the woods alone and at night. As a result, the Delta appears to Ellen in the "whole mystery of life" that opens up, as a more expansive, less rigorously maternal-domestic realm, and one that, for others, may be compatible with a variety of sexual activities and identities.

If Welty begins to crack the notion of a monolithic domestic persona by featuring a domestic mother who envisions alternate modes of life, Lee Smith fractures this type of persona completely in *Oral History* through a self-conscious separation of narrators, achieved through sub-headings and a wide-ranging topographical notion of domesticity. In short, of these three novelists (Glasgow, Welty, and Smith), Smith presents the most complicated and satirical view of domesticity, often explicitly choosing the social and cultural changes in domesticity as her subject.

Like the contrast reflected in her name, Granny Younger, a classic folk healer figure, expresses a contradiction between her purported ideology of the domestic and her own domestic activities. Early in the novel, she lectures her grandson Almarine on the benefits of finding a bride: "What you need is a girl.... What you need around here is some children on this land, and a woman's touch in the house" (36). Here, Granny's own terminology sheds light on the community's attitudes. The girl is not a woman until she has given birth, the children become a subset of the land, not their parents, and a house is somehow lacking without a "woman's touch." Yet Granny's own touch extends far beyond her own home, and always has. She travels inhospitable mountain terrain to assist in births, illnesses of all types, and deaths. She exceeds the bounds of both her own homeplace and the life cycle itself through her duties as a healer. Smith carefully constructs Granny's physical mobility in conjunction with her sense of premonition. After recommending that Almarine take a wife, she comments, "Later I wished I'd of bit off my tongue. Sometimes I know the future in my breast" (36). Unlike Ellen's struggle between the sexual and the maternal breast, Granny employs her own breast as a site of prediction, and a way to prepare for the healing she will later perform.

The wife that Almarine chooses following Granny's encouragement violates the domestic norms in other ways. As a witch, Red Emmy becomes the unholy anti-domestic woman, dissatisfied with her inability to run a home. As Granny Younger notes (about a scene she did not witness), "She looked like all the sadness in the world was in her heart. She knowed it couldn't happen, that is why" (49).

Yet Emmy puts on her best performance as the envied wife of the handsome and well-traveled Almarine. She resolves the tension of her double role by "riding" Almarine during the night, using his body as a source of energy and a vehicle for her nighttime jaunts. Again, Granny Younger, another alternative to the traditional domestic woman, comments freely on Emmy's performance:

> All that being so nice in the daytime was moren Red Emmy could take, what I think. She had to go hell for leather all night to make up for them long, sweet days. Almarine was wore out all the time, of course. He laid in the bed and slept most of the time while she worked his farm and then she'd come in and get in the bed. He was servicing her, that's all, while she liked to rode him to death. Red Emmy, she worked all day and she rode all night and she never slept. But a witch don't need no sleep [53].

Red Emmy represents far more than a traditional folk or fairy tale character; she is domesticity run amok, showing the problems of an unbalanced, prescribed household role. Smith remarks on the domestic detail of "being nice" and "smiling," duties which, for Emmy, are far harder than her new role as farm laborer. Emmy must also contend with the lack of a clear sexual role that can be reconciled with "pleasant" domesticity, represented by Emmy's vampiristic "riding" of Almarine.

Granny Younger and Red Emmy represent problematic domestic women: they are expected to function productively in a tightly knit community, but each woman's talents fall outside traditional domestic roles. In this way, Smith critiques such traditional roles while also revising domestic fiction through an Appalachian lens. Not all women perform domesticity in the same, untroubled manner in the late 1800s, nor do mountain women represent a unified, coherent identity that can be easily captured and preserved by an outside ethnographer. Smith includes such an ethnographer figure in the novel, in Richard Burlage, only to show his bumbling, intellectual mannerisms and his deep misunderstanding of mountain women as a "type." Even Richard's running commentary on Dory's body and his own thoughts about their physical relationship reveal his unending need to craft a stable identity for the women of the mountain: "To my surprise, she wears no brassiere! Or maybe none of these mountain girls do" (146). Richard fails both as ethnographer and as a member of the community; he cannot make Dory into a "safe" woman, nor can he incorporate her into his own world.

A final type of problematic domestic woman appears in the character of Pearl, who yearns to find creative outlets in her rural world. Some critics have read Pearl as a biographical stand-in for Smith herself, the artist smothered by her native Appalachian environment. For another reading of Pearl, we might return to one of her most overtly troubled creative attempts, as well as to the metaphorical area of pickling. While the pickles of *Virginia* are a figurative expression for the sour, tightly enclosed, sanitized world of spinsterhood, pickles in Smith's work come to represent domesticity's potential to destroy creative possibilities.

As Pearl helps the ever-practical Ora Mae prepare red and green peppers for pickling, she has a sudden inspiration for their arrangement. Pearl wants to layer the rings in red and green rows of stripes, asking, "Wouldn't that be pretty?" Yet Ora Mae resists, calling the project a "waste of time" (252). Pearl defends her idea by claiming that the family could give away the red and green jars as Christmas presents, and Ora Mae responds, "Give them to *who*?"

In this passage, Smith documents a 1920s moment of the "outside" world colliding violently with traditional Appalachian domesticity, which has been, up to this point, strictly a process of survival: cooking, canning, farming, and doing one's best to avoid disease. Yet Pearl has read *Life* magazine; she has cut out pictures of stormy plains and fashion models: in essence, anything that her world will not provide. Unlike authors who depict the commercialization of Appalachia as a solely destructive process, Smith points to the tension between this type of commercialization and domesticity itself. Pearl asks if domesticity can be a decorative art form, as it is in the pages of *Ladies' Home Journal*, and receives a sharply negative answer. In this case, the domestic woman becomes problematic because of her creative urges, and must leave her region, crafting her own version of domesticity in the city.

Unlike Welty and Glasgow, Smith points to specific types of domestic women in specific historical moments. She portrays the failures of those who cannot fit the mold as a kind of tragedy, using a historical scope that even Hobson might designate as a "big" novel. Yet Smith's work is founded on the work of those before her. Through her uses of narrative patterns and through *Virginia*'s unhappy end, Glasgow critiques southern domesticity by showing that it could be suffocating. For Virginia, the town's teenaged darling, domesticity simply didn't pay — it killed. At mid-century Welty continues to mark the losses associated with domesticity by exploring Ellen's lost sexual self as well as the sexuality of several other female characters. Domesticity also physically expands its boundaries: the field hand Troy will be allowed in the family and through the front door of the home. The women spend most of their time out of the kitchen and are free to roam the Delta on their own, but only because there are African American domestic workers in the kitchen. Welty depicts the growing freedoms and remaining oppressions of 1920s domesticity at mid-century, perhaps commenting on the need for new domestic roles and social structures, even in the less repressive atmosphere of the 1940s. Her multivocal narrative, with portions of the story told through the eyes of several different women, calls for a non-homogenous domestic role. These authors historicize fictional domestic practices as they build a growing critique of confined or isolated domesticity through their use of shifting narrative patterns, discontinuous domestic identities, and expanding domestic landscapes.

Toni Morrison continues the pattern of ever-expanding domesticity, using the South as an ideological and historical home for characters living across the United States in her three most recent novels: *Jazz* (1992), *Paradise* (1998), and *Love* (2003). I choose to examine these three novels because, although they deal with domesticity and the ideology of homeplace directly, the homes of these novels have not received the attention allotted to *Beloved*'s haunted home. Just as Morrison expands the physical parameters of southern domestic practice, so does she examine the changing state of domestic identity across multiple time periods, using settings in the 1920s, 1970s, and 1990s.

Women in Morrison's texts frequently find the events of their own lives so fractured that they reflect this inner turmoil through domestic practice. Upset after her husband's affair and his subsequent murder of his lover, Dorcas, Violet allows her household to slip into mild disarray. After disrupting Dorcas's funeral, Violet returns home to "free" her pet birds, "including the parrot that said, 'I love you.'" (3). Like *Virginia* and *Delta Wedding*, *Jazz* opens with caged bird imagery that seems to prefigure the caged nature of the domestic life. But unlike Miss Priscilla's caged birds living in a tightly regimented world, or even Laura Fairchild's imagining of her cousins as zoo birds living within a somewhat larger arena, these birds are abruptly forced out of the only home they've known, signifying the total disruption of traditional or stereotypical domesticity within the novel and echoing their owners' migration north. Even when Violet plans to try to love her husband again, she finds domestic practice difficult to resume: "Washing his handkerchiefs and putting food on the table before him was the most she could manage" (5). This description of the difficulties of domesticity directly precedes an account of the "poisoned silence" (5) husband and wife share, highlighting domesticity as an indicator of the mood of the home and as evidence of deep disruption that cannot be fixed by going through the motions. *Jazz* also comments on the perils of southerners trying to make a home in the urban North during the 1920s. Tensions arise between the older, more communal modes of domesticity and newer, individualized domestic practices.

That Violet cannot force herself to perform these traditional tasks also seems to indicate that the two must find new, alternate ways of living together as they age in their urban home. This idea is supported near the end of the novel, when Joe and Violet have crafted a more peaceful relationship by trying to understand the nature of the tragedy they've survived. Within their revitalized relationship, new and different domestic practices emerge: they give up sleeping at night in favor of short naps during the day, they have decided to tear a quilt "into its original scraps," and they plan to replace the quilt with a satin-hemmed wool blanket (224). The quilt they plan to tear represents a communal product typically sewn by more than one person with materials provided by many. In contrast, they imagine how their own bodies will look and feel beneath the new blue blanket, casting it as an intensely personal artifact hidden from community reach. In these ways, Joe and Violet give up traditional household practices in favor of those that suit their own needs. Violet also adopts an ailing bird and nurses it back to health, undeterred when special food does not make the bird eat. Deciding that the bird "wasn't lonely" (224), Violet intuits its need for music and cures it by taking to the roof to hear the local musicians. Like themselves, the bird has needs beyond a caged, predetermined life. As Joe and Violet reunite, they reject community standards for domestic practice. With these gestures, Morrison seems to point toward the dangers of over-conformity to and toward the personal freedoms from community standards gained through transgressive behaviors.

Similarly, in *Paradise*, the women who turn to the Convent for protection or solace forsake certain types of domestic practice while they attempt to heal themselves emotionally and physically. In the opening of the novel, several men from the community have come to the Convent to kill these "strange" women, ostensibly to remove the threat they pose to the community. The men prepare for this mission the same way they prepare for a game hunt. Yet even on a focused, planned killing mission, they still take the time to judge the women's domestic lapses: "Slack, they think. August is just around the corner and these women have not even sorted, let alone washed, the jars" (5). The men rule the bedrooms "normal" but "messy — the floor in one of them is covered with food-encrusted dishes, dirty cups, its bed invisible under a hill of clothes" (8). The commentary on sorting and washing jars prefigures the men's own mission: they intend to sort out the righteous and the non-righteous, performing their own cleansing ritual through a witch hunt, a process that allows them to place the blame for their own failures squarely on the Convent women. The state of the bedrooms both confounds and affirms their judgments. They are surprised to find normalcy in the bedrooms, having anticipated evidence of sexual indiscretions, but they reaffirm their opinion of the women by cataloguing the domestic disarray.

In *Love*, Christine crafts beautifully prepared meals using ingredients such as shellfish that she knows her former friend Heed does not eat: "Then she assembled the rice, the shrimp, the sauce, layering each meticulously, artfully, in the casserole. It would remain warm while she tossed a light salad. Then she would arrange it all on a silver tray, take it up three flights of stairs, where she hoped it would choke the meanest thing on the coast" (24). Like a traditional horror film, the description of Christine's meal preparation begins in a way that seems all too common. As if she is in the pages of a women's magazine, she layers the casserole "meticulously, artfully." The food is carefully described and carefully arranged in a build-up that exacerbates the impact of the final phrase: "where she hoped it would choke the meanest thing on the coast." Unlike Violet and the Convent women, Christine is far too proud of her domestic skills to ever allow a lapse, although she believes she lives under the constant threat of losing her home. Instead, she creates an ironic domestic perfection as she serves her enemy: the food will look perfect, but Heed cannot eat it because she links the smell of shellfish to her lower-class past.

In these scenarios, Morrison quickly conveys to the reader that the women live outside certain community standards. She allows other characters, more firmly rooted in traditional domestic practices, to judge the outlying women. The scene of Christine's meal preparations, for instance, is preceded by a family meal at the Gibbons household. At their table, Vida describes the Cosey women as "hincty, snotty girls" and warns her grandson not to eat "off her stove" (17). Instead of using domestic practice as an immutable force that individual women struggle against, Morrison portrays domesticity as fluid, as a shorthand indicator of characters' inner worlds and as measure of their acceptance within their communities. Even though she sets some portions of her novels in the same time periods as Welty and Smith, in many ways Morrison offers a more detailed and nuanced representation of domesticity's function within a community, rather than focusing on the effects of domesticity on the individual woman. I will argue that this type of African American community-based domesticity has roots in resistance to slavery in the American South and resistance to domestic labor within the homes of white women.

It is also interesting to note that Morrison offers direct, sustained commentary on the concept of racial, family, community, creative, bodily, and other types of homes, as well as an over-arching "Home" that might encompass all of these. In her essay "Home," she conceives "a-world-in-which-race-does-*not*-matter ... as home" (3). Similarly, the narrator of *Jazz*, in a section recounting the details he/she "missed" in the story, longs for the ancestral home of Wild, which seems to take on the weight of a larger, more symbolic homeplace that many of the characters lack: "I want to be in a place already made for me, both snug and wide open" (221). In *Paradise*, Reverend Richard Misner meditates aloud in front of Pat: "But can't you even imagine what it must feel like to have a true home? I don't mean heaven. I mean a real earthly home ...— there, right there where you know your own people were born and lived and died" (213). Because many characters and their ancestors have fled one or more homes in the face of dire racism, the search for "true home" pervades Morrison's work. Domestic practice, even in a temporary or less-than-ideal home, remains bound to the idea of creating or finding the true home, and thus carries added symbolic weight.

Where might this pattern of ideologically, spatially, and narratologically expanding domesticity take us now, at the beginning of a new millennium? This pattern is not limited to southern novels, and an examination of genres beyond the novel adds popular culture and consumer perspectives to this study, illuminating the ways in which the corporate world both borrows from and shapes popular ideas of domesticity. I will examine the new medium of domestic hypertext, focusing on its rise in popularity at the turn of the twenty-first century.

Hypertext knows neither spatial nor temporal boundaries. It is always already happening, and it promotes the idea of multi-leveled, multi-pathed narratives, in that any document containing a series of hyperlinks may be navigated in an infinite number of ways. In short, hypertext offers southern women (sometimes characterized as slow to use new technologies) a forum not only for writing an ironic discourse about domesticity, but for using domesticity as a platform for worldwide communication.

The current trends in home design hail new kitchen technologies not only in terms of individual appliances, but also in terms of intra-home systems. Internet-compatible refrigerators offer to order the family's food from online grocery providers, and even to provide recipes based on the contents of the refrigerator, using barcode scanning to identify specific products. In a press release, Bob Lamson, CEO of CMI Worldwide, acknowledges the significance of the kitchen as a part of his sales pitch: "We know that the kitchen is the heart of the home, and the area that has the most activity, the highest traffic and the place that some of the most important and meaningful occasions occur" ("A True Internet Appliance," *AllNetDevices*). The danger, here, seems to be that the kitchen may be re-made under corporate control, then repackaged and sold to families in ways that reinforce traditional domestic gender roles.

Yet when home managers author their own domestic-themed web sites, they open the possibility of redefining such traditional roles in a multitude of ways. Because of the potential for home managers (and others) to connect from a physical kitchen to a web site (often containing, ironically, a graphic representation of the interior of a kitchen) that offers access to the theory, information, and practice behind literally millions of other kitchens worldwide, the physical kitchen is now the ultimate site for the expansion of domestic narratives. And these narratives proliferate, not only in the form of recipe-sharing, but in intensely personal meditations on what it means to feed others and to preserve vital cultural history (even while utilizing technology) through various methods of producing goods in the home. Rather than chronicling minutiae, a charge often leveled at domestic novelists, these writers, taken collectively, can be seen as writing a valuable cultural history, one that feminist theorists cannot ignore.

In short, the work of southern domestic writers deserves to be read in more connected ways. As Thadious Davis writes, "If authors are uncovered or recovered and simply left in virtual isolation from discourses on theory, discussions of movements, trends, patterns, schools, traditions, and so forth, then in the next century they could well return to the ranks of the dead, buried, and ignored" (16). Although many of the authors in this study have never needed this type of recovery, readings of their works often suffer when they remain in isolation. Such isolation can take many dangerous forms, including isolated readings of single southern domestic novels, or readings that are isolated from feminist theory, or isolation of these works from larger national, historical events. Rather than resorting to facile labels that romanticize not only the land and people of the South but also the literary South, I want to read these works as a vital tradition within the fields of American literature, southern literature, and women's studies. Because these works offer unique cultural perspectives, they construct a part of the fabric of seemingly "non-domestic" issues of both southern and American identity. Glasgow, Welty, Smith, and Morrison, like many other domestic novelists, do not center their works on the physical kitchen or even the physical home. Rather, each invites us into a home, not to establish a tightly knit world of home comforts, but instead to offer the domestic as an entry point to a larger social, political, cultural, and historical fabric.

Chapter Two

ELLEN GLASGOW'S "SACRED INNER CIRCLE" OF DOMESTIC ISOLATION

"Wounded and Caged": Disability and Domesticity in the Work of Ellen Glasgow

In her early twenties, Ellen Glasgow found herself contemplating a total loss of hearing. She describes the beginning of this period with images of her illness as an animal on the hunt: "Morbid sensitiveness was tracking me down, like a wolf waiting to spring" (*The Woman Within* 118). Later, with her auditory capacity more fully impaired, Glasgow changes her imagery; she begins to see herself not as a wolf's prey, but as a caged bird. In her personal writing, she confesses her hidden emotions in response to an aurist's remark that she does not seem particularly depressed by her impairment: "If only anyone in the world could know! That I, who was winged for flying, should be wounded and caged!" (139). Still later, Glasgow couples her will to live a full life with the same image of entrapment: "For I was young; I was ardent for life; I was tremendously vital; I was wounded and caged" (152).

Similar entrapment imagery appears in Glasgow's fiction. The image of the caged bird recurs on the opening page of *Virginia* (1913), as Miss Priscilla Batte "stood feeding her canary on the little square porch of the Dinwiddie Academy for Young Ladies" (3). When Miss Priscilla looks beyond "the wire cage, in which the canary spent his involuntarily celibate life," she sees two students, Susan Treadwell and Virginia Pendleton, opening the rusty gate to enter the garden and speak with her. The double nature of this image, with the "rusty gate" echoing the "wire cage," casts Susan and Virginia as little more than two more celibate birds "with carefully held flounces" (4) who have come to feed at Miss Priscilla's nutritionally bereft fountain of knowledge. Glasgow herself pushes this comparison, commenting on the "earnest exhortations of the teacher on the joys of cage life for both bird and lady" (5).

Disability and Identity

Glasgow lays bare the entrapment inevitable in both roles — that of the disabled young woman novelist, and that of the upper-middle-class young woman confined to a poorly run, single-sex academy that specializes in training girls for a life of home service. Not surprisingly, critics have become attuned to the self-pitying nature of both types of entrapment imagery. Yet only recently in the critical work on Glasgow have class status and deafness been united as significant to understanding her work. In "Ellen Glasgow's Disability," Linda Kornasky notes, "Rather than stressing the significance of deafness, Glasgow's critics and biographers have attributed her pessimism, anger, and despair to her status as an unmarried woman or as a member of the upper-middle class. From Adrienne Rich to Elizabeth Ammons, critics have tended to focus on the supposedly extreme self-pity Glasgow displays in the autobiography" (284). Kornasky links the critical struggles over Glasgow's "self pity" with the current struggles of middle-class white feminists to acknowledge their perspectives on employment and education as non-universal and to include the perspectives of ethnic and racial minorities as well as disabled women. In other words, to assume that Glasgow's tone is replete with self-pity is to ignore what Kornasky identifies as her "master status" as a disabled woman — a status that overrides her sexuality, her gender, and most of all, her class (286).

In concluding her essay, Kornasky offers a close reading of Glasgow's *The Sheltered Life* with a focus on the novelist's heightened sense of vision. In particular, she notes, "The visual images of shadows, and temporarily welcoming shades of red and purple, ultimately changing to darkness, brilliantly parallel George's manipulation of Jenny Blair into believing that his sordid, commonplace betrayal of his wife is a mysteriously beautiful adventure" (291). In Kornasky's reading, a disability becomes an almost extra-sensory *ability*. That is, without her own hearing disability, Glasgow would not have been able to use her own heightened visual perception to create a "re-visioning" of an extra-marital affair. Further, without her own disability and corresponding ability, Glasgow would not have been able to capture a young woman's disillusionment so fully.

Using a different perspective, Nancy Walker also casts a somewhat positive light on Glasgow's disability in her feminist reading of the autobiography, "The Romance of Self-Representation: Glasgow and *The Woman Within*." Walker remarks that Glasgow's deafness serves as metaphor for her "web of silences — veiled allusions rather than revelations" (39).[1] Yet far from casting these silences as entirely deceptive and self-serving, Walker emphasizes "an understanding of the value and the necessity of self-creation in a world that did not readily bestow selfhood on women writers" (41). In Walker's reading, Glasgow productively uses deafness as a metaphor for navigating the dual forces of disclosure and repression inherent in the autobiographical tradition.

Interestingly, Kornasky and Walker are not in agreement on their approaches to Glasgow's deafness. Kornasky resists reading the hearing loss as any type of metaphor; she wants to read the bodily effects of deafness (i.e., the enhanced sense of vision) onto Glasgow's work. Walker, on the other hand, is intrigued by deafness as a metaphor for the politics of self-representation. Yet within both approaches, deafness directly affects writing. I would argue, however, that Glasgow incorporates deafness into her writing not only in visual imagery and in her own politics of self-representation, but also as a tool for unlocking the unspoken isolation and despair of another realm: that of domesticity.

The field of disability studies[2] in general, and the work that has been done on deafness in particular, proves helpful in understanding not only Glasgow's politics of self-representation, but also her interest in the body and home, as well as the specific positioning of the middle-class white body in the southern home during the late nineteenth and early twentieth century. The current focus in disability studies is to resist models or readings that emphasize pity, empathy, or even "sensitization," and instead to focus on the kind of political, social, cultural, and historical theory that has developed around race, class, gender, and sexuality, as not "problems," but as discursive entities (Lennard Davis 3). As many feminist scholars have noted, feminism and disability studies become particularly resonant when employing feminism's preexisting discourse on the body as a political entity and as a material experience (Wendell 261). As Rosmarie Garland Thomson asserts, "Both the female and the disabled body are cast within cultural discourse as deviant and inferior; both are excluded from full participation in public as well as economic life" (279). Further, disability studies sheds light on gender roles (and vice versa), because "exempted from the 'male' productive role and the 'female' nurturing one, having the glory of neither, disabled women are arguably doubly oppressed — or, perhaps, 'freer' to be nontraditional" (Asch and Fine). In this chapter, I will argue that Glasgow's exemption from these gender roles, due to her disability, led her to reexamine them in a critical light, focusing on the often disabling effects of the role of homemaker when that role was taken to its most repressive and isolated extreme.

Deaf Identity: Manualism, Oralism, and Deaf Culture

An examination of the history of deafness and education for the deaf reveals the battles that raged over postbellum nationalism — conflicts that contested, constructed, and reconstructed the very meaning of deafness. In the early nineteenth century, deafness was viewed as a "tragedy" that precluded the "afflicted" from hearing God's word. Manualism, also know as sign language, was the recommended means of enlightenment. With properly trained interpreters and sign language instructors for the deaf, the Bible as well as sermons could be manually translated (Baynton 128). In the 1860s, however, a second group of reformers, concerned that deaf persons living in communal living spaces and residential schools were isolated from "the life of the nation," sought to eradicate the use of sign language entirely. This movement continued into the twentieth century, and goes on today in the form of the debate over "special" or "integrated" education (Baynton 129), as well as in the cochlear implant debate. These nineteenth-century reformers, known as "oralists," advocated lip reading and speech therapy programs for the deaf, with no supplementation through sign language. In short, oralism viewed American citizenship as residing in a linguistic identity (Baynton 138).

As Glasgow's own deafness began in the 1890s, she too questioned which of the losses resulting from deafness she found most significant. Rather than focusing on the traditional answers of "God's word" or "national life," Glasgow turned her sharp eye toward the multivalent losses associated with domesticity, including the social capital lost with the attainment of "true womanliness." Even with its guise of cheerful "ableness," the embodiment of the feminine ideal acted as a physical and emotional disability. When a woman became "the angel in the house," she also became deafened to the concerns outside her home, and, in extreme cases, to all but the physical concerns of those living with her. As Glasgow's own hearing disability worsened, she began to make this comparison more frequently and more explicitly within her fiction.

43

The debate over deaf identity — in the form of manualism versus oralism — continued, and continues today, as a more fundamental questioning of whether deafness constitutes a disability at all. The oralists, those who favored lip reading, constructed deafness as a bodily problem or disease, one that could be "fixed" through lip reading rather than made "worse" or "more noticeable" through sign language. The twentieth-century incarnation of the oralist defines deafness as a strictly physical disability. On the other side, the manualists, or proponents of sign language, evolved into an opposing group in the twentieth century. This group rejected (and still rejects today) the construction of deafness as a disability. They argue that the use of sign language, combined with a strong set of traditions and cultural practices within the Deaf[3] community, makes deaf persons living within this community a *linguistic and cultural minority*, far more similar to an ethnic group than to the physically disabled (Lane 154–155). Glasgow became deaf during a crucial point in this debate, when oralists had curbed much of the educational use of sign language. Because of the time period of her hearing loss (prior to the Deaf Community movement), and because she was born with hearing and only became deaf later in life, Glasgow was encouraged to view her deafness as a disability by the many aurists and other medical professionals she saw.

The Home-Body Connection

Although physically and chronologically excluded from Deaf culture, Glasgow, like the manualists and proponents of the later "linguistic minority" concept of deafness, did deal with her own deafness linguistically. Her social realm — that of a middle-class, southern white woman, with its emphasis on active socializing — led Glasgow to view herself as both a linguistic and social minority, as one who could not speak socially because she could no longer hear the subtle social cues of her environment. It seems no accident that Glasgow found more and more success in her writing career as her hearing worsened. Cut off from the social realm of the hearing, Glasgow began a private examination of just what there was to be heard within her world, including its recognized and unrecognized social problems. Similarly, she explored the question of who could and could not hear the cry of these social ills. In a parallel with the debate over deaf education, Glasgow criticized an educational system that both caged and deafened young women

44

to all concerns beyond a social life and the pursuit of a husband, as she does in *Virginia's* harsh portrayal of the Dinwiddie Academy for Young Ladies.

Because of her own discomfort in social settings such as dinner parties and visits with neighbors in her home or theirs, Glasgow was keenly aware of the subtleties of polite communication within the southern home. She often feared that her own deafness meant missing a crucial word or two, perhaps a euphemism, that contained an entire explanation of the family's plight. In this way, Glasgow found a common tie between herself and the woman of the house, especially if that woman acted in strict accordance with the ideal of the feminine homemaker. Both Glasgow and the family homemaker missed vital details of family life—Glasgow because she could not hear them, the homemaker because she was too busy preparing the next meal, or cleaning up after the one that had just been served. Deafness enabled Glasgow to identify a type of "domestic deafness" caused by the home's confinement, a deafness that developed when an attention to practical tasks precluded all else, including the family's emotional well-being.

In this context, it is important to note the often subtle acknowledgment within the field of disability studies that the home and the body are inextricably linked, as well as the idea that a secure home is the logical extension of a sound body. Conversely, a body in pain may be linked to the lack of an appropriate domestic shelter, physically, psychologically, and metaphorically. In *The Body in Pain: The Making and Unmaking of the World*, Elaine Scarry posits that the rooms of a house, in their protection of the body from the elements, act as base units of civilization (39). Thus, when the contents of a room are made into instruments of pain, as they are in many instances of political torture, those objects, and the concept of human civilization at large, begin to disappear. Using the example of a refrigerator that is used to bludgeon the head of a torture victim, Scarry writes that "in the conversion of a refrigerator into a bludgeon, the refrigerator disappears; its disappearance objectifies the disappearance of the world (sky, country, bench) experienced by a person in great pain.... The domestic act of protecting becomes an act of hurting" (41). While Glasgow did not experience anything akin to this kind of torture, her "master status" as "a person in great pain" likely unmade much of her physical world in the theoretical manner that Scarry describes. Throughout her work, Scarry stresses that the experience of pain is, in effect, an unmaking of the material world; as the victim ceases to be conscious of anything other than the physical pain itself, pain becomes a form of linguistic and cultural destruction. Because Glasgow worked and lived (and was in pain) within a domestic environment, the unmaking of this very world led her to a closer examination of the theoretical concept of domesticity as well as of the body's relationship to the domestic, particularly when that relationship became either physically or psychologically unhealthy.

Glasgow's own pain within a domestic environment, as well as her sense of social loss because of her deafness, led her to examine the ways in which the domestic realm could become disabling, even to otherwise "able" women. Glasgow chronicles the plight of middle-class women who were forced to re-enter their own kitchens in times of economic hardship or social change. Without hired domestic help, these women took on far more household labor than usual. While working in one's own kitchen does not typically constitute a hardship, for many women it did represent a marked change in the social structure of the family. What a mother once would have overheard in a moment of leisure — a budding courtship or a family quarrel — could easily be missed when she was confined to the kitchen or to other isolated household tasks. These women subsequently lost a sense of "emotional hearing"; they missed the cues of family crises such as infidelity, domestic abuse, or "inappropriate marriage."

In this way, living one's life in the kitchen becomes a plight linked to the isolation and interiority of losing one's hearing. In many of her novels Glasgow suggests that the cage of the home traps and confines women to such an extent that they lose an awareness of their families' interactions with the outside world. This loss of emotional hearing results in physical and emotional catastrophe. Unlike other writers of her time, Glasgow does not reward her female characters for an overabundance of self-sacrifice. To sacrifice the self unreasonably invites betrayal, as Virginia learns when her husband has a long-term affair while she manages the house and raises three children alone to support his career as a playwright. Glasgow explores the same principle in *Life and Gabriella*. When the Carrs take in fancy sewing to maintain an old family name's dignity, Mrs. Carr becomes so concerned with hiding the evidence of work within the home that she overlooks her daughter's physically abusive marriage. In Glasgow's fictional world, becoming the ideal home-maker does not make a woman a saint. Instead, it frequently makes her the last person to know a key piece of information or an important sign of danger in her family circle.

"The System": Systematization of the Home and the Body

It was a historically accurate choice for Glasgow to position the women of middle-class families as having re-entered the kitchen. *Virginia* is set in 1884, while *Life and Gabriella* begins in the early 1890s. After the economic depression of 1873–1878, many middle-class families faced reduced circumstances, while at the same time new job opportunities in factories and service professions began to attract young women who might have formerly served as domestics (Plante 110). During this period, young African Americans who had worked as slaves — or, later, as paid domestics — began to leave the South in large numbers for better economic and social prospects in the North. Also, centennial celebrations of 1876 "reinforced and renewed for many the American spirit of independence and cast an unfavorable light on domestic service" (113). This period marks the beginning of the New Woman movement, which encouraged self-sufficiency and independence for (most commonly, white) women. Despite the connotations of the label "New Woman," many of the educational changes during this period focused on training middle-class women to be, first and foremost, self-sufficient in the home and, if necessary or desirable, in the workplace. This new educational emphasis was a profound change from finishing schools that taught accomplishments, such as lace-making (Marks 58), rather than practical skills such as the organization of an efficient kitchen.

The difficulties of domestic self-sufficiency were pronounced enough to inspire the advertising of new kitchen gadgets such as potato chippers, revolving slicers, and rotary flour sifters as the new "servants" for the kitchen (105). In addition to newfangled gadgets, the 1880s and 1890s ushered in easy-to-clean enameled cookware, the widespread use of the icebox, gas-powered stoves and light fixtures, indoor plumbing, iron pipes, and organized city water services (85–93). In retrospect, it becomes easy to imagine this period as an earlier model for Friedan's late-1950s era of the feminine mystique, when women began to notice that all the household conveniences added up to long, isolated hours using, maintaining, and consuming the modern home's amplified bounty.

By 1880, the physical placement of the kitchen within the house had also changed. Blueprints show that in the early 1870s some homeowners still isolated the kitchen in the basement or even in a separate building, but by the end of the 1870s the kitchen was firmly fixed within the main body of the house, usually on the first floor (Plante 85). These three factors — the loss of domestic help, the introduction of additional kitchen gadgets, and the more central location of the physical kitchen — worked together to place the kitchen as an integral part of the middle-class home, rather than as a separate space relegated to the class and/or racial Other. Increasingly during the 1880s and 1890s, being the lady of the house also meant being the lady of the kitchen.

Medical science of the period underwent a similar movement toward unification, and at the turn of the century a focus on specific body parts gave way to an emphasis on connected systems within the body. General developments in medicine at the end of the 1800s contributed to this trend. In 1861 Pasteur discovered bacteria in the air and Broca located the center of speech in the brain. In 1867 Lister introduced antiseptic surgery, a breakthrough that allowed for new and wider varieties of surgical procedures (Stevenson 4). Politizer, the most famous otologist, or ear specialist, of the late nineteenth and early twentieth century, remarked that the "essence of medicine could be summed up in the words 'everything is connected with everything'" (Stevenson 114).

As the lady of the house accustomed herself to a variety of housework, so did the medical specialist learn to focus on the interconnected nature of bodily systems. And just as doctors began to treat the ear not in isolation but as part of larger bodily systems (*otology* would eventually become *otolaryngorhinology*), so did homemakers treat the kitchen as a part of the *system* of the home. During the late nineteenth century, "kitchens were being given as much thought as the rest of the home in regard to convenience (of special interest to the wife who had to assume a greater portion of household chores)" (Plante 90). The language of the home, as represented in domestic science manuals and home guides, referred to "economy" and "system" in housekeeping. Glasgow reflects this emphasis in *Virginia* by titling the first chapter "The System." In "The System," Glasgow paints an ironic picture of the so-called education of her protagonist. The narrowness of this education has prepared her to fail, even as a complacent housekeeper and mother, because of its lack of useful information, let alone skills.

While general theories of medicine as well as the systematization and "hygienic" sterilization of the kitchen progressed, much of the knowledge of the anatomy and treatment of the ear remained decidedly primitive. The medical understanding of hearing was still in its early stages at the time of Glasgow's birth in 1873. Scarcely a decade earlier Hermann von Helmholtz had written his seminal article on acoustics, "Sensations of Tone." Called the piano theory, Helmholtz's theory of hearing noted the semblance of the strings of a piano to the cochlear fibers "and proved of the greatest value in otology" (Stevenson 57). Helmholtz asserted that the cochlear fibers, "which are all connected with different nerve fibres, must be differently tuned, and their proper tones must form a regularly progressive series of degrees through the whole extent of the musical scale" (Helmholtz 145).

The treatment of the ear still remained experimental at best at the turn of the century. Politzer, the preeminent specialist and founder of the world's first university aural clinic (Stevenson 113), recommended his own brand of treatment, Politzeration, which consisted of forcing air into the nose through a rubber bag and hose device while the patient swallowed water. As late as 1904, bloodletting by way of leeches was still recommended as a treatment for ear problems (Roosa and Davis 257) and a 1907 text proclaimed the advantages of the nasal speculum when diagnosing problems of the Eustachian tube, combined with a spray of 4 percent cocaine and followed by a spray solution of adrenaline chloride (Barnhill and Wales 176). The treatment of ear problems at the time suggests that Kornasky is quite correct when she asks critics to rethink their evaluations of Glasgow as somehow self-pitying and insensible to the hardships of others because of her own medical difficulties. Not only would such treatments be physically uncomfortable or painful, they probably would have remained unmentionable in polite turn-of-the-century conversation. An aural patient would experience a triple layer of isolation — first, through the inability to hear clearly; second, through the embarrassment and physical pain of the treatments; and third, through the resulting inability to discuss the treatment socially.

We can assume that Glasgow experienced some or all of the treatments because she states, "Twice a year I went on to be treated by one aurist or another, and as soon as I received a sufficient income from my books, I began a pilgrimage all over the world, as patient as, and more hopeless than, the pilgrimages to shrines of saints in the Dark Ages" (*The Woman Within* 138). Given the nature and the expense of the treatments themselves, the metaphor of a Dark Age pilgrimage may be seen as more long-suffering and less self-important. Glasgow was disappointed when, after she consulted several specialists, none of them offered much help or hope. She discusses her social isolation and embarrassment during this time at length in the autobiography; it would be several years before she would resign herself to using a primitive electrical hearing device known as an ear trumpet, a large trumpet-shaped object inserted in the ear to amplify sound. Goodman remarks that "the instrument was so crude, however, that when dining with friends, she had to keep one hand to her ear to hold the attachment in place. With the other, she ate like a 'hummingbird' in the only way she could manage" (113). Though Glasgow was finally able to hear dinner conversation, the clumsy apparatus drew attention to her and impaired other social functions, such as eating. New technologies for the body, such as Glasgow's hearing aid, paralleled the rise of new technologies for the home. In the rise of both bodily and domestic technologies, the ideology of systematization would play a key role.

At the turn of the century, the systematization of both body and home led to new kitchen and medical gadgetry and tools. In medicine, the knowledge that the ear was connected to the nose and throat led to indirect treatments such as Politzer's method and various new medical tools such as a variety of nasal speculums for ear treatment. In the domestic arena, the idea of a healthy, "systematized" home led to an isolated household worker who, increasingly, was also the lady of the house. In this realm, too, gadgetry was introduced as a possible solution to a housewife's new woes. Yet in many ways the systematization of both the body and the kitchen ignored the individual. Just as Politzer recommended his treatment for a variety of hearing ailments, so too in *American Woman's Home: Principles of Domestic Science* (1869) did Catherine Beecher and Harriet Beecher Stowe recommend the same white-washed kitchen walls for all homes, to "promote a neat look and pure air" (371). Thus, homemakers and medical patients alike were left with feelings of anonymity and isolation as they attempted to adapt their homes and bodies to current medical and domestic "cure-alls."

Domestic Deafness and Feminine Hardness in Virginia *and* Life and Gabriella

Doctors referred to Ellen Glasgow's problem as a "hardening of the Eustachian tube and the middle ear," a common diagnosis of the time for cases of partial deafness (*The Woman Within* 138). From the official "hardening" diagnosis, Glasgow continues: "[T]here was no cure to be found anywhere. Science has failed my body as ruinously as religion had failed my soul. Both quests, physical and spiritual, had ended in disillusionment. My only prop, a strong one, was a kind of humane stoicism. I could bear what I had to bear, but I could not pretend it away" (138–39). In this way, Glasgow implies that a hardening of the entire body and spirit — with its stoicism and capacity to bear pain—followed the hardening of the middle ear. It is as if the diagnosis of the ear comes to represent the diagnosis of her entire being and her attitude toward life. She seems to cling to this diagnosis of hardness as an element of her personality, continually connecting her strong will to live with a kind of emotional hardness as a means of self-preservation. During this time, approximately 1902, Glasgow also brings this sense of hardness to her female characters, imbuing them with the stoicism she had begun to feel.

Feminine hardness, a tangible physical condition that resonates with inner qualities of stoicism, reserve, and determination, marks many of Glasgow's female characters. The phrase "vein of iron" echoes through not only the novel of the same name, but through several other novels and short stories as well. Glasgow seems to employ her much-noted irony with this phrase, incorporating yet resisting her father's cold Calvinism and playing on his career in the Tredegar Iron Works, while also making a muted reference to her own disease as yet another "vein of iron." Julius Raper notes the influence of this theme on Glasgow's later work, notably *In This Our Life* (1941) and *Beyond Defeat* (1966) (*Without* 250). Yet Glasgow seems to promote this type of feminine hardness much earlier in her work when she depicts a life marred by softness in *Virginia*. Virginia suffers for her softness, particularly when her husband publicly conducts an affair and she feels unable to confront him on the subject. Her friend, Susan Treadwell, while less beautiful than Virginia (Susan is described as having "the face of a woman who could feel strongly" [22]) and unmarried for many of her childbearing years, develops a kind of strength that even the young Virginia recognizes as valuable. Foreshadowing her own downfall, Virginia turns to Susan in the first chapter, asking, "Can't you make him careful, Susan?" in reference to Virginia's future husband, the rash and headstrong Oliver Treadwell (18). Instinctively, Virginia knows she will never have any measure of control over the man she loves, but she recognizes Susan's strong will and persuasive capacities, the very qualities that isolate Susan in youth but bear her up in later years. Virginia, on the other hand, only grows "hard with the implacable hardness of grief" much later in the novel, after Oliver leaves her for a famous actress.

The conflict between the feminine vein of iron and the feminine ideal of self-sacrifice continues in *Life and Gabriella*. The opening chapter of the novel calls attention to an emotional economy in which each member of the family is allowed to offer up an opinion on the continual crisis of the daughter, Jane, whose husband drinks and abuses her. Mrs. Carr, the mother, suggests bringing in a male advisor, Cousin Jimmy Wrenn. Jane rejects this suggestion because she wants to keep the crisis within the immediate family circle, despite the failure of this method in the past. When Gabriella reminds Jane that "everybody knows anyway," Jane calls attention to Gabriella's own value within the family by saying, "You can never understand my feelings because you are so different" (6–7). Mrs. Carr confirms this estimation of Gabriella's views, but stresses the real reason that the family cannot "hear" Gabriella: "'Gabriella is not married,' observed Mrs. Carr, with sentimental finality" (7). Gabriella has not made the kind of financially profitable marriage the family desires, and thus her family devalues her within its emotional economy.

The Carrs are forced to take in "fancy sewing" from relatives to make ends meet. Despite her matriarchal position, Mrs. Carr is all but useless in the pursuit of income: "Though Mrs. Carr worked every instant of her time, except the few hours when she lay in bed trying to sleep, and the few minutes when she sat at the table trying to eat, nothing that she began was ever finished until Gabriella took it out of her hands" (7). The Carr family is not only deaf to Gabriella's opinions because of her unmarried status. They are unaware of the double standard they establish when locating her familial usefulness in economic productivity rather than in matters of the heart. Glasgow implies that because Gabriella transitions fluidly from public to private, and resists marriage and class-consciousness, she becomes the most economically viable (and reasonable) member of the family, despite the family's resistance to her suggestions. As in *Virginia*, Glasgow recommends a certain feminine hardness, aligning it with reason. At the same time, she aligns an over-sensitivity to class preservation, home, and family with an isolating domestic deafness, an inability to comprehend the world beyond one's home.

The family's domestic deafness continues as Cousin Jimmy fails to hear Gabriella's proposition that she work outside the home in order to sustain her family. His refusal brings out Gabriella's own "Berkeley conscience, that vein of iron which lay beneath the outward softness and incompetence of her mother and sister" (30). Like the author herself, Gabriella allows an inner hardness and strength to emerge in the face of tangible hardship. Glasgow exposes the irony of the line drawn between bringing work into the home and physically leaving the home to go to a place of employment. After the family summit on Jane's problems, the home itself takes on a decidedly different appearance.

> The scraps of cambric had been gathered up from the threadbare arabesques in the carpet; the chairs had been placed at respectable distances apart; the gas-jets in the

chandelier were flaming extravagantly under the damaged garlands; and the sewing machine had been wheeled into the obscurity of the hall, for it would have humiliated Gabriella's mother to think that her daughter received young men in a room which looked as if somebody had worked there [33].

Therefore, it is the *appearance* of work — its public acknowledgment — that brings shame, rather than the work itself. Glasgow's writing style in this passage reflects the familial ideology: she describes the work with a string of passive verbs, implying that the preparations made for guests occurred through invisible, nameless hands. The shame over "inside" work predicts the Carrs' response when Gabriella takes a job in a hat shop. With her employment, they find further reasons to ignore her advice; she is thrice removed from them through marital, employment, and class (or the *appearance* of class) status. Glasgow ultimately evaluates "soft" work within the home as far more dangerous and isolating than "vulgar" outside jobs. Without the drive to maintain social appearances by continuing to work only within the home, Gabriella is free to witness situations both inside and outside the family more realistically than her relatives.

Though Gabriella resists her family's ignorance of the outside world, largely disregarding the opinions of her mother and sister, *Virginia* implies that domestic deafness, like some forms of physical deafness, can be inherited. In Chapter II of *Virginia*, "Her Inheritance," the reader meets Virginia's mother, Mrs. Pendleton, the rector's long-suffering wife. Used to stretching the family means, Mrs. Pendleton "[begins] to talk in the inattentive and anxious manner she has acquired at scantily furnished tables." Yet the reader is never allowed to hear what Mrs. Pendleton actually says over her table, as Glasgow launches into a description of her idealism, later returning to the "soft, apologetic murmur of Mrs. Pendleton's voice" (29). In this passage, Glasgow implies that only the narrator can impart additional information about the character of Mrs. Pendleton; the character's own words merely provide a hum of background noise. Unlike other characters such as Susan, Mr. Pendleton, and even Miss Priscilla, the under-qualified school teacher, Mrs. Pendleton is not allowed to introduce herself with a piece of dialogue. Instead of her words, we hear the *sound* of her voice as we learn that she has become quite deaf both to her own babbling speech and to her family's reduced financial circumstances. Her voice "was intended to distract attention rather than to impart information" (29). Unfortunately, Mrs. Pendleton's own deafness is indeed inherited by Virginia; although she realizes that her mother has "had what is called 'a hard life,'... this knowledge brought no tremor of apprehension for herself, no shadow of disbelief in her own unquestionable right to happiness" (25). Virginia refuses to hear the message that, if she continues the course she is on, she is likely to inherit her mother's isolated life of household worry.

In Book Second, "The Reality," the inevitable occurs and Virginia and Oliver, now married, move to Matoaca City, West Virginia. Glasgow depicts the common hardship of the time — "that it is impossible to get servants for love or money" (161). The servant Virginia does procure must be fired for sweeping trash under the rug and changing only the top sheet on the bed (163). Telling herself that she will keep house out of love for her husband and to keep herself occupied, Virginia soon takes on the role of full-time housekeeper, in sharp contrast to the role of full-time lady and wife she had imagined for herself:

> At first Oliver hated dreadfully to have me do everything about the house, but he is beginning to get used to it now, because, of course, I never let him see if anything happens to worry me or if I am tired when he comes home. It takes every minute of my time, but, then, there is nothing else here that I care to do, and I never leave the house except to take a little walk with Oliver on Sunday afternoon. Mrs. Midden says that I make a mistake to give a spring cleaning every day, but I love to keep the house looking perfectly spick and span, and I make hot bread twice a day, because Oliver is so fond of it [163].

Virginia's particular brand of domestic deafness keeps her from hearing the cries of her own mind and body. The kitchen in this home never becomes a site of bonding with other women; instead, she ignores Mrs. Midden's advice that she relax her cleaning practices. She makes her husband a co-conspirator in her deafness, just as Mrs. Pendleton did with her own immediate family, by covering want and worry with pleasant, meaningless, words. Finally, Oliver becomes complicit in Virginia's kitchen entrapment through his consumption of the twice-daily hot bread. The bread indirectly leads to the couple's first fight. Oliver insists on performing the manly task of making the morning's first fire. He cannot understand why Virginia gets up earlier than he but hates to wake him. What she cannot tell him is that she wakes up "with the bread on [her] mind" (163). In her near-complete isolation within her home, Virginia focuses on the details of domestic life to the exclusion of any other subject, even Oliver. Although she had vowed to serve him happily in their new home, Virginia begins to serve for the sake of service, refusing to acquiesce to Oliver's wishes that she let him start the fire. Deaf to others' concern for her and mute on the subject of her own well-being, Virginia reveals the complete domestic narrative to her mother, and therefore, to the reading audience, only through her letters.

Perhaps because of the problem of inherited domestic deafness, Virginia does not tell her mother her troubles in person. Chapter II of the second book is entirely epistolary, the only chapter of its kind in the book. The confessional tone of the letters and the first-person narrative they create provide a jarring contrast to the ironic, third-person omniscient narration that comprises the remainder of the novel. Through this shift, Glasgow implies that only a housekeeper's own meditation on her acts can tell the full domestic story. Additionally, she implies that the experience of taking on the role of housekeeper is, ironically, Virginia's first and only independent act, meriting a writing voice of her own. A third implication is that the two women have become "deaf-mute" in their narrow focus on domestic detail, and can communicate to one another only in the visible form of letters. Yet only Virginia's letters to her mother are printed; we never receive her mother's replies. The lack of reciprocation (and Glasgow's choice of omission) builds on the earlier idea of Mrs. Pendleton as voiceless. Similarly, the one-sided correspondence depicts Virginia as thoroughly isolated socially, emotionally, intellectually and physically.

The narrative shift to the epistolary format highlights the extreme change in Virginia's physical surroundings. While the Pendletons are not well off, they are able to retain their links to the past in a tangible way, through the blended customs of neighbors who remember both the elder Mr. Pendleton, a Confederate hero, and Mr. Pendleton, the rector, with gifts of food. Virginia, however, loses such kitchen-to-kitchen contact when she moves to an industrial city full of new "ugly" homes (160). She refuses to abide by her neighbors, noting the "very few people of our class." Virginia describes Mrs. Payson, the manager's wife as not "just exactly what I should call ladylike": She wears a red feather in her hat and even "makes speeches when she is in the North." Yet Virginia ultimately couches her refusal to make friends in terms of the domestic:

> I doubt if I'll ever want to have much to do with anybody that I've seen. It doesn't make a bit of difference, of course, because I shan't be lonesome a minute with the house to look after and Oliver's clothes to attend to; and besides, I don't think a married woman ought to make many new friends. Her husband ought to be enough for her [160].

Here Virginia veers toward a personification of her house as a character that will save her from becoming lonesome. Like the house itself, Oliver's clothes are positioned as having a life of their own, as needing Virginia's attendance. The declaration that she will simply attend to Oliver's clothes rather than become lonely resonates strangely with the next statement that a woman's husband should be "enough for her." Virginia seems to create a ghostly double for Oliver through his clothes, and to imagine herself interacting with this representation when the actual Oliver is unavailable. Through this passage, as well as the negative description of Mrs. Payson, Glasgow implies that the home and the domestic labor it provides act as a comfortable barrier between Virginia and her new town. Because the law of the social order is on her side, Virginia can block out any thought of a new kind of life by keeping herself indoors and enacting the domestic role she has learned from her mother.

Virginia also loses the heavy, dimly lit atmosphere of her childhood home, with its "prim set of mahogany and horsehair furniture, with its deep, heavily carved sofa midway of the opposite wall and the twelve chairs which custom demanded arranged stiffly at equal distances on the faded Axminster carpet" (25). She is able to escape, in part, the heavy, dark, and oppressive physical nature of this home. Yet the Matoaca City home, surprising in its newness, does not suit Virginia either. She describes her house for her mother:

> And now I must tell you about our house, for I know you are dying to hear how we are fixed. It's the tiniest one you ever imagined, with a front yard the size of a pocket handkerchief, and it is painted the most hideous shade of yellow — the shade father always calls bilious. I can't understand why they made it so ugly — but, then, the whole town is just as ugly as our house is. The people here don't seem to have the least bit of taste. All the porches have dreadful brown ornaments along the top of them, and they look exactly as if they were made of gingerbread. There are very few gardens, and nobody takes any care of these [213].

Virginia employs a certain tone of resignation in her depiction of the house. She writes to her mother about how they are "fixed," and Virginia does seem to feel fixed in Matoaca City for the time being, resigning herself to her ugly surroundings accordingly. The details she offers reveal her true feelings; she relates the outside of the home to images of deeply hidden interiority. The front yard, the most obvious foreground of the home, is like a "pocket handkerchief," an intimate object worn close to the body and kept, for the most part, hidden. The color of the house itself, its primary identifying feature, is "bilious," linked to a liver secretion. Even the details of the home "look exactly as if they were made out of gingerbread," a homey dessert. In short, in her mild disgust with her new living arrangement, Virginia turns her house inside out in this description, linking its most heinous features to familiar objects associated with hidden interiors. It is as if she wishes to efface the exterior of the unattractive house by casting it as a more intimate, although perhaps still repellant, interior space. This type of retreat from an exterior world brings to mind Glasgow's own frustrations with her disability and her attempts to remain at home, to keep a family member with her in case someone should speak to her, and to focus on her writing when social engagements became cumbersome. Like Glasgow, Virginia implies in her letter that only the *insides* of things truly signify, and she takes this attitude to heart when she isolates herself in the duties of housekeeping.

Once pregnant, Virginia continues her focus on interiors until she slips into near agoraphobia. In a letter, she tells her mother that the doctor believes she will become ill if she does not get some exercise outdoors. Yet Virginia uses her domestic heritage to defy the doctor's recommendation in the same letter to her mother: "But you stay in the house all the time and so did grandmother, so I don't believe there's a word of truth in what he says" (173). Interestingly, this is one of the only instances when Virginia is able to defy masculine authority successfully, if only momentarily. This defiance suggests that the forces of claustrophobic domesticity are powerful enough to override even the voice of a medical authority, and it suggests a distinct prioritization of the home over the body.

Virginia finally concedes to a nightly walk with Oliver, if only in the darkest reaches of the town. To her mother, she reports: "I go out for a little walk with Oliver every night. I am so afraid that somebody will see me that I really hate to go out at all, and always choose the darkest streets I can find. Last night I had a bad stumble, and Oliver says he doesn't care if the whole town discovers us, he's not going to take me down any more unlighted alleys" (167). Oliver's comments reflect his fear of what has already turned out to be an "unlighted alley" — Virginia's body. Although he placates Virginia in his attempts to help her conceal her pregnant body from public view, Glasgow makes Oliver's own confusion about Virginia's very biology clear. When Virginia announces her pregnancy, Oliver "looked amazed — as if he had never thought of its happening" and was not "the least bit glad about it" (166). Oliver continues, in the wisdom of his time, to view Virginia's condition as "a diseaselike or 'disabling' condition" (Rothman 468). As in Kornasky's paradigm of Glasgow's mix of identifiers, Virginia takes on the pregnancy as a "master status," a permission to stay indoors far more and to focus, once again, on an unseen presence, though now the baby's rather than Oliver's. She undertakes this task in the form of making every stitch of the baby's clothing with her own hands long before the birth. Oliver, now permanently forced into the domestic background, remarks that the baby girl "caused more trouble than she is worth" (170). The epistolary chapter concludes with a catalog of

Virginia's worries about the baby and Oliver's resistance to those worries. The final letter announces a second pregnancy, soon after the first, and again, Oliver's surprise. Because Oliver is at this time still quite focused on both the new home and Virginia herself, he seems to have joined her in a domestic deafness that extends to the workings of sex and pregnancy. It is as if he believes his wife so thoroughly "domesticated" (and "pure" in the manner of the Victorian "angel in the house") as to remain beyond the reach of reproductive sex.

With Glasgow's return to third-person omniscient narration after the epistolary chapter, the reader is able to note Virginia's sharp focus on the interior even in her descriptions of family relationships. Glasgow has used the epistolary mode to establish Virginia's own obsession with domestic details for several reasons. On the practical side, Virginia needs her mother's help and advice to make the transition from belle to housekeeper. But more importantly, only a full catalog of domestic details can create for the reader Virginia's own voluntary entrapment. The letters, after all, are not vital in terms of plot. They are not "literary" letters in the traditional sense — those structurally designed by an author to nuance the plot, create suspense, or reveal a secret to the audience at an opportune moment. Nor do the letters establish the mother-daughter bond. Since the chapter does not include Mrs. Pendleton's replies, we can only guess at her emotional response, and Virginia indicates sorrow several times that her mother will not be able to visit — at Christmas and at the birth of her first child. Over and over again in this chapter, Virginia seals herself within the envelope of her home, then mails it to her mother.

Home Ties That Bind: Virginia's "Sacred Inner Circle"

For Virginia, when a family member is physically within the home, he or she becomes as much a part of the home's static contents as any piece of furniture. She cannot distinguish between being *in* the home and being *of* the home — and therefore she cannot allow herself thoughts, feelings, and an intellect that exceed the physical boundaries of the home space. When she goes to a New York hotel room to nurse Oliver after his play fails, Virginia carries with her the "sacred inner circle" of an emotional home, and is able to feel the threats against this sacred circle only outside her own home[4]:

A new element, something for which neither her training nor her experience had prepared her, entered at that instant into her life. Not the external world, but the sacred inner circle in which they had loved and known each other was suddenly clouded. Everything outside of this was the same, but the fact confronted her there as grimly as a physical sore. The evil struck at the very heart of her love, since it was not life, but Oliver, that had changed [222].

Glasgow's narrative persona belies Virginia's own naiveté at this point. The comment on the lack of preparation in Virginia's "training and experience" for coping with an extramarital affair reads as highly ironic in light of her upbringing by a compulsively optimistic, idealistic rector's family and her schooling with Miss Priscilla. The second sentence of this passage abruptly switches from a singular to a plural pronoun, indicating Virginia's illusion that Oliver still stands within her own "sacred inner circle" of home and love, which are, to Virginia, one and the same. Also, the coupling of external and internal worlds — "not the external world but the sacred inner circle," "everything outside of this was the same," "not life, but Oliver, ... had changed" — privileges the internal over the external. For Virginia, a change in the external world, no matter how catastrophic, is preferable to any violation of "the sacred inner circle."

In contrast, for Oliver the sacred inner circle feels much like a noose around his neck. When Oliver thinks that he will fail at writing, he begins to look toward other outlets for his intellect and finds his home distinctly barren of such resources: "As a wife, Virginia was perfect, as a mental companion, she barely existed at all. She was, he had come to recognize, profoundly indifferent to the actual world. Her universe was a fiction except the part of it that concerned him or the children" (231). What appears to Virginia as a tight family bond and the predominance of home over other concerns appears to Oliver as nonexistence and indifference. Yet Glasgow crafts Oliver's thoughts to betray the contradictions implicit in housekeeping. While in practice housekeeping sustains numerous family members, Oliver refuses to see this work as part of the "actual world." Perhaps this division is due, in part, to Virginia's own silence about her household rituals — rituals that she reveals only to her mother in her letters. As the marriage dissolves, Glasgow explores the dangers of a mutual lack of communication: both Virginia's picture of Oliver's literary world and Oliver's picture of Virginia's domestic duties remain inaccurate and incomplete.

But Virginia's domestic details eventually become the only sustainable realities of her life when Oliver leaves her for an actress who appears in his plays. In many ways, the actress appears as Virginia's double in an artistic rather than a domestic role. While Margaret Oldcastle can hold Oliver's interest in a conversation, she is still ultimately under his control. Like Virginia's, hers is an identity mainly of Oliver's creation; she is an actress who has built her career on the roles Oliver has written.

Virginia, however, cannot retain Oliver's interest even as an object of his control. In his absence, she turns to her domestic life as a dual source of comfort and bedevilment. Deciding to occupy herself by going to market, Virginia remarks, "I cannot live if I stay in this room any longer. I cannot live if I look at these things" (379). The narration continues, "As she turned away to put on her hat, she was seized by a superstitious feeling that she might escape her suffering by fleeing from these inanimate reminders of her marriage. It was as though the chair and the rug and the clock had become possessed with some demoniacal spirit" (379). Virginia's thoughts reveal Glasgow's ultimate pronouncement on the dangers of domestic isolation. The objects that a housewife spends a lifetime tending will not sustain her in a moment of crisis; instead they turn on her with a "demoniacal" presence.

Glasgow represents the tension between the inside and the outside of the home as Virginia experiences a panic attack on the literal border of her home: she "stopped, with a sensation of panic, beside the bed of crimson dahlias at the foot of the steps" (379). Finally, the memory of the "hated objects" flashes up, and Virginia forces herself to continue on what remains, unfortunately, a circular trip back into the "inner circle" of her home. The "demoniacal spirit" of the chair, the rug, and the clock represents the domestic ideal that has trapped Virginia within her home and made her all but unfit for the larger world.

Short Fiction in the "Slough of Despond": Revising the Domestic Ideal

In her correspondence, Glasgow notes that "Virginia was the passive and helpless victim of the ideal of feminine self-sacrifice" (Meeker 5). The enclosed, cyclical spatial patterns of domesticity (such as Virginia's trip to the market that will only lead her back to the home with more objects) combine with the reader's imprisonment in the depths of Virginia's superficial, detail-oriented thoughts to create an intensely claustrophobic reading experience. Yet this induced claustrophobia is not without a political goal: it supports the idea that for Virginia the domestic ideal strangles, and even kills, its staunch supporters.

Glasgow's portrayal of Virginia as "passive and helpless" in the face of a psychologically and physically threatening domesticity aligns the "ideal of feminine self-sacrifice" with disease and illness. In this scenario, the domestic ideal "strikes" women in their prime, just as Glasgow's own deafness began to strike while she was still in her twenties. Yet the terms "passive" and "helpless" suggest variable levels of complicity in one's own disease. "Passive" would seem to indicate that Virginia *chooses* not to fight the domestic ideal, while "helpless" indicates that she was *unable* to resist, or that perhaps she was beyond the reach of all aid once she had fallen "ill."

In *Illness as Metaphor* (1977), and later in *AIDS and Its Metaphors* (1997), Susan Sontag explores the socially constructed nature of disease through an examination of the metaphorical discourse surrounding different diseases, as well as the cultural perception of those with disease. Sontag notes,

> Illness is interpreted as, basically, a psychological event, and people are encouraged to believe that they get sick because they (unconsciously) want to, and that they can cure themselves by the mobilization of will; that they can choose not to die of the disease. These two hypotheses are complementary. As the first seems to relieve guilt, the second reinstates it [57].

In much the same way, Glasgow paints the domestic ideal as rendering one both passive (weak, unwilling to resist, deserving of blame) and helpless (unable to resist, beyond all aid). Sontag dates these concepts of disease to the nineteenth century, and Glasgow seems to have suffered under these misconceptions as well, especially when she complains that "morbid sensitiveness was tracking me down" (*The Woman Within* 118). Glasgow's doctors, prescribing cumbersome ear trumpets, seemed to believe that hers was a problem she could cure by herself, with the help of minor technologies, even if the cure destroyed her ability to function socially. As a result, Glasgow viewed herself, like the women disabled by an exacting domestic ideal, as both complicit in and resistant to her illness.

It is interesting, too, that Glasgow tends to depict her own physical deafness as feeling "quite ill" rather than as a disability (Rouse 77). Illness may have appeared as a socially acceptable condition, while deafness might have been deemed unattractive or unfeminine. Sontag recognizes this phenomenon in the romance, frailty, and sensitivity associated with nineteenth-century depictions of tuberculosis (13). Tuberculosis was a socially acceptable (and even glorified) disease for women, or for "creative" or "sensitive" men. But because she calls herself ill rather than partially or wholly deaf, it would seem that Glasgow cannot bring herself to expose the full extent of her own pain. Like Virginia, she is unwilling to name and confront her own burden. Even while recognizing herself as unwell, and aligning herself sympathetically with those who faced the ills of domesticity, Glasgow still took pains to maintain a sense of femininity, and to disguise the true nature of her own (often invisible) disability.

In the ways that Glasgow chose to hide her disability, her physical torment bore the mark of "the feminine ideal of self-sacrifice" (Meeker 5). It was necessary even for an unconventional female writer to maintain a certain sense of feminine decorum, one that held little place for disease or illness. This strain, however, seems to have sensitized Glasgow to the plight of domestic women around her, even though she herself largely eschewed the domestic role. For Glasgow, domesticity, like disability, acted as a form of imposed bodily control. The extent of this control, including the restraint required to maintain silence in the face of discomfort and isolation, had to be hidden from society in order to gain social approval.

But if traditional domesticity's bodily control, like the bodily control enforced by disease, often began invisibly and even with the seeming complicity of its victim, then how was it to be accurately represented outside the long genre of the novel? In the novel, the domestic ideal as a physical presence appears in heavy draperies; close, unaired rooms; darkness; and the relentless narration of Virginia's (sometimes compulsive) thoughts. But the problem of how to portray an ideal becomes much more complex when we turn to Glasgow's short stories. Without the long structure of a novel and the space to cast subtly recurring patterns of narration and patterns of describing physical space in suffocating terms, Glasgow must come up with a kind of shorthand figure to stand in for the domestic ideal. In her short fiction, she comes up with a kind of bullying, disease-like figure that forces women to submit to its powers, then leaves them without intellectual, emotional, or financial resources.

Glasgow often wrote short stories for magazines because she needed the money in her early career to finance large medical bills, frequent travel, and the upkeep of the family residence after her father's death in 1916 (Meeker 5). Yet in what Meeker calls the "first hint" of Glasgow's "real" reasons for turning back to the short story, Glasgow engages in a process of meditating on the specific nature of the feminine struggles she wished to chronicle, struggles that often centered on domesticity. Glasgow notes that while "Virginia was the passive and helpless victim of the ideal of feminine self-sacrifice ... Gabriella was the product of the same school, but instead of being used by circumstances, she used them to create her own destiny." Glasgow adds, "The third book may never be written. If it should be, it will deal with a woman who faces her world with weapons of indirect influence of subtlety" (5). Meeker goes on to characterize this trilogy as unfinished and to attribute what he calls a "faltering" between *Life and Gabriella* (1916) and *Barren Ground* (1925) solely to "a world gone mad" during World War I when Glasgow "lost her ability to compose large canvases, that is, lost her sense of evolution" (6).

On the surface, Meeker's reasoning seems solid. A writer in the midst of a successful career falters, or loses her ability to look at the big picture because the world's own big picture of the moment has turned to wartime chaos. Yet Meeker bases this biographical critique of Glasgow's writing pattern on a portion of a 1923 letter to Hugh Walpole:

> Ah, I've been through the Slough of Despond about my work. After I wrote *Life and Gabriella* about 8 or 10 years ago, I let go and gave up. I was passing through an experience that seemed to drain everything out of me — vitality, imagination, interest, everything. In that time I lost a great deal, and I slipped somehow, naturally, I suppose, away from what I had won. Now, I have boiled up, I hope, out of those depths, and I am trying to win back what I have lost [6].

While Meeker does note that Glasgow's disillusion was both "public and private" during the period she describes, he focuses on World War I as the reason that Glasgow briefly "lost her ability to compose large canvases" (6). I want to argue that this type of criticism falls along the lines of Fred Hobson's interest in the "grand historical narratives" that, in his view, male authors tend to write. In other words, to blame Glasgow's movement away from the novel and towards the short story as based on the events of war is to force her into a masculinized historical narrative. The actual words of her letter do not emphasize or even mention war itself, but instead, refer to a trying personal time that corresponded with several family tragedies for Glasgow. She traces her own "Slough of Despond" to 1913 or 1915. In 1910, Glasgow's brother, Frank, committed suicide and in August of 1911 her sister passed away as well. In 1911, she left Richmond for New York to escape the painful reminders of her loss. After her father's death in 1916, Glasgow returned home to face what was "one of the most difficult periods of her life." Her own health, both physical and mental, was weakened. Perhaps because of the stress she was under, Glasgow believed that she had begun to see the ghosts of her own dead family members within her house, and these ghostly figures began to make their way into her fiction (Carpenter, *Haunting* 118).

While war may have been a factor in all of her upheaval, it was hardly the reason for her return to the short story. Rather, Glasgow seems to have been involved in an even deeper struggle with her own ideology of masculine and feminine domestic roles. In her new position as head of household, Glasgow was forced to make choices about her own domestic habitat, without the stern controlling hand of her father (one of the "ghosts" she saw). Further, Glasgow was engaged in her own form of a very physical domestic renewal during the period of short story writing: with funding from Arthur Glasgow, her brother, she was redecorating the family home. A letter from the summer of 1916 shows a hope to "paper over" the old, and bring in the new:

> The men have not begun work yet on the house. Will you let me know, by the way, if any rooms are to be repapered? I do not want to make any additional expense, but the paper is so old in some places that I think it would be better to make less expensive improvements elsewhere, and put on fresh paper and paint. After this, bathrooms [and] electricity are the essential things — for the gas here is perfectly dreadful. It is lovely for you to do all this for me — and I hope it won't cost a great deal [Rouse 64].

Despite Meeker's claims, Glasgow's letters indicate a home-based focus, split between feeling the effects of her own bodily torment, mourning for her family "ghosts," and remodeling her home in a project of domestic renewal.

Instead of using the short story form as an escape from an inability to write novels, I argue that Glasgow was using the truncated form to work out her own ideology of domesticity and its effect on women. Before she could find the "woman who faces her world with weapons of indirect influence or subtlety" (her idea for balanced, competent female protagonist of the third novel in her original trilogy), she must truly understand the nature of that woman's world, including the forces that required the use of indirect influence or subtlety, rather than frank confrontation. In short, she must find out what made the domestic ideal similar to disability — one that forces submission, then refuses to be cured or even discussed.

The fact that Glasgow claims to be "excruciatingly" bored by the short story form also lends credit to the fact that she felt compelled to work out ideological material for her novels through the stories. Her comments on the nature of the form do the same: "All the best of the short stories must be painfully condensed with slight regard for the evolutionary causes bringing about this or that effect" (qtd. in Meeker 6). I read this statement as a rationale for the "painful" condensation the short stories required. the condensation forced a very nearly symbolic representation of cause and effect. The long-term cause of feminine displeasure — years of education into domesticity, followed by submission to an impossible domestic ideal (as seen vividly in *Virginia*)—cannot be explored fully in the short form. Instead, many of these forces became condensed into ghosts or ghostly presences.

In her essay "'Experience Illuminated': Veristic Representation in Glasgow's Short Stories," Stephanie Branson combines a Todorovian notion of the fantastic with what she depicts as Glasgow's own notion of verism—a "fluctuation from the material to the numinous" using various distancing devices (76). Exploring Glasgow's navigation of this brand of verism (as opposed to the more formal verist school that more closely approximated documentary realism), Branson adds the critically accepted notion of ghost stories as feminist.[5] She writes,

> Glasgow's interior world included a belief in the invisible, and the external world was metaphysical as well as physical. As feminist fantastic fictions, Glasgow's short stories deserve to be moved from the critical category of *Trivialliteratur* to the category of "literature of vision"—Kathryn Humes' term for fantastic stories that "make us feel the limitations of our notions of reality, often by presenting one that seems more rich, more intense, more coherent (or incoherent), or somehow more significant" (82). These fantastic fictions provide a rich, intense, coherent, and feminist view of reality that does more (and less) than offer an avenue of escape from quotidian difficulties. Glasgow's stories illuminate female experience through veristic distancing and unity, as a blueprint for the processing of human experience at large [85].

Branson valorizes the "ghosts" of the ghost stories as feminist constructions of the fantastic genre that permit a large view of feminine experience—including the experience of a kind of feminine sixth sense. She also points to Glasgow's depictions of sisterhood—often between a member of the realistic and ghost worlds of the fiction. Though Branson is correct to identify Glasgow's ghost stories as representative of a large view of feminine experience, several questions remain. First, what is the point of a feminist fantastic genre, other than the glorification of women's lives and friendships? Why is the figure of a ghost needed? Must the feminism of the stories be aligned with a more traditional vision of the fantastic (in the form of Todorov) before it is worthy of examination? And most importantly, might the ghost represent something negative, as an obstacle to the feminism Branson uncovers?

I am most interested in Branson's concluding remark on the "feminist view of reality that does more (and less) than offer an avenue of escape from quotidian difficulties"(85). Branson does not offer any insights to what she might mean by "more" and "less" than quotidian difficulties. She does, however, imply that the project of escaping from these quotidian difficulties (both physically and mentally) is not quite "enough" to be the actual subject of the stories.

Branson is not alone in casting the ghost stories as feminist works.[6] Lynette Carpenter depicts the stories as "Glasgow's exploration of the alternatives of conventional heterosexual romance and female community" ("Visions of Female Community" in *Haunting the House of Fiction* 118) and praises "Dare's Gift" in particular for Glasgow's "skill in condensation" ("The Daring Gift" 102). Yet Wagner, Branson, and Carpenter all emphasize the female voice and female communities, implying that these women must struggle to find voices and be heard, as well as to find one another, if only in the form of ghosts. The feminist critiques of the short stories often sublimate the obstacles the women are fighting, namely, the overpowering, debilitating domestic ideal of the early twentieth century. Similarly, it becomes easier to cast the ghosts as specters of "feminine community" rather than to analyze them as complex symbols of a past—a past that included women who enforced the domestic ideal, including its burden of guilt, when younger women wanted to break free from the nineteenth-century role of the angel in the house.

I argue that during this period of concentrated short story writing (1916–1923), Glasgow was regrouping from the writing of *Virginia* (1913) and *Life and Gabriella* (1916) and asking herself critical questions about her female protagonists. What were the forces holding them back from self-actualization, from complete lives? What were the "dis-eases" other women faced, the bodily constrictions that could not be discussed in polite company? The answer she found became the spirit of these ghosts and what Branson calls "living houses" (83). The undying domestic ideal, in which women became responsible for the material and emotional welfare of every being in the house, haunted every Glasgow household, but was made manifest as the "ghosts" in "Dare's Gift," "The Past," "The Shadowy Third," and "Whispering Leaves."

While Glasgow turned to short stories because of the crises in her own family and in order to work out the new domestic ideologies of her later novels, her works also fell within the "ghostly" tradition of homes haunted by specters both seen and unseen. Two of Glasgow's most important predecessors in this area include Charlotte Perkins Gilman and Edgar Allan Poe. Similar to Gilman's "The Yellow Wallpaper," Glasgow's ghost stories expressed a deep concern over the problem of "the imprisoned female imagination" (Goodman 167)—a problem that was often translated by male doctors, husbands, or family members into a diagnosis of "nervousness," depression, or outright insanity. Poe, on the other hand, brought the tradition closer to home through his Richmond roots, and Glasgow admired what she called his "shabby splendor" (Goodman 248). Poe's short story "Ligea" (1845) contains the element of a second wife haunted by the first that Glasgow would incorporate into her story "The Past." Further, this tradition of a ghostly presence that persuades the woman of the house to believe herself mad continued in works such as Du Maurier's *Rebecca* (1938) and Patrick Hamilton's play *Gaslight* (1939), titled *Angel Street* in its 1942 publication, both of which became popular American films during the 1940s.

What distinguishes Glasgow's stories from the others in this tradition, however, is her intense focus on domestic details. Both Poe and Gilman describe the interiors of homes in great detail, then animate the details (the wallpaper, the draperies) of the home through an unseen or possibly imagined ghostly presence. Much of the dramatic tension of the works of Poe and Gilman (and later, Du Maurier and Hamilton) lies in the reader's ability to determine what is "real"—who is sane and who is insane, who may be deemed reliable as a narrator, who will be able to use social power to gain control of the narrative. In contrast, Glasgow often paints her haunted women far more sympathetically—the practiced homemaker or caretaker figure is often the only figure whose account can be believed, as she is confident of what she has seen, and so capable of her duties, that we, as readers, do not doubt her at all. A further distinguishing trait of Glasgow's ghost stories is their emphasis on work. The female protagonists often work, and even if they do not, they tend to recognize lovely homes as products of hard labor. Both of these traits of Glasgow's stories—the emphasis on belief in women's narratives and on work—highlight Glasgow's use of the ghostly tradition as a vehicle for counteracting the harmful effects of the domestic ideal on women. In short, in a far less subtle fashion than Gilman, Glasgow uses the ghost as rallying cry, a piece of tangible evidence that all was not right in the world of the home.

In "Dare's Gift," Harold takes his wife, Mildred, to a home on Virginia's James River, where she is to rest and recover from a nervous breakdown. The story is narrated from Harold's first-person perspective, but Glasgow takes great pains to portray Harold as entirely self-absorbed, mocking the patronizing "concern" he occasionally remembers to express for his wife. Harold must leave Mildred alone to manage a home that is, in fact, in ill repair, when he takes on an important legal case. As she spends more time alone, presumably managing the care of the home by herself, Mildred begins to withdraw from her husband emotionally. We first learn of Mildred's betrayal of her husband, a corporate lawyer, when she reveals information he has uncovered about his current case. When the information reaches the papers, Mildred's husband, Harold, the narrator, knows that it is his wife who is responsible for the betrayal because of the language of the newspaper article: "It was all there, every ugly detail — every secret proof of the illegal transactions on which I had stumbled. It was all there, phrase for phrase, as I alone could have told it — as I alone, in my folly, had told it to Mildred" (101). At this point in the narrative, we are not aware of the spirit of Lucy Dare, a woman who betrayed her lover during the Civil War because he fought on the side of the North, the spirit that has infected Mildred and led to her choice of justice over family. While Branson points to the feminist "kindred spirit" relationship between Lucy and Mildred, I would argue that Mildred's actions are inspired by the precise *lack* of such a kindred spirit. Mildred becomes subject to the influence of Lucy's ghost because she is so isolated.

Unlike the other ghost stories, "Dare's Gift" never produces a visible ghost of any sort. Rather, we have the narration of Lucy's legend by an old local, Harrison, who stresses the absence of a ghost and the presence of the long-term memory of the house itself. When Harold asks, "The house, then, is haunted?" Harrison carefully replies, "The house is saturated with a thought. It is haunted by treachery" (104). During the narration of Lucy's tale, as the narrator begins to understand the mechanism of the transference of "treachery," he asks a more informed question: "What she did, then, was so terrible that it has haunted the house ever since?" Reiterating the notion, Harrison replies, "What she did was so terrible that the house has never forgotten" (106).

As the men work through the synthesis of the two tales, they begin to describe the house as a presence with an agency all its own, the ability to hold a thought, not to forget. The house is not, then, the passive victim of a ghost's meanderings and evil deeds, but a force that has the capacity to take offense at the actions of women, to "never forget" their treachery.

Yet just what makes these women guilty? Harold takes pains to make clear that he has stumbled onto material that is severely damaging to his client, that it has, in his words "come to a question of personal honesty" (99). Further, he never assures the reader that he will reveal this information to the proper authorities, that he will take the moral high ground in this case. In fact, even after "confessing" his problems to Mildred, Harold "was still worrying over that case — wondering if [he] could find a way to draw out of it," not wondering if he should reveal what he has found.

Similarly, Harrison indicts Lucy for "treachery," calling her "diabolical" and "a strange soul" who may have taken her stand due to the effects of "improper nourishment." Yet just as Harold never convinces the reader that he will do the right thing, then races to blame his wife, so does Harrison take pains to convince us that Lucy's moral standards were in keeping with those of the times, even though he is all too ready to blame her for her actions, and even for Mildred's. He remarks that Lucy "was, of course, intoxicated, obsessed, with the idea of the Confederacy; but, then, so were all of us. There wasn't anything unusual or abnormal in that exalted illusion. It was the common property of our generation" (108). While his narration expresses ambiguity, his conclusions do not: both Mildred and Lucy became "diabolically" possessed by ideals, ideals that made them turn away from love, marriage, and peaceful households and toward classic "masculine" realms of justice: the legal system and war.

Both women also use masculine language to express their causes. Mildred repeats, nearly word for word, her husband's words about his moral dilemma, which end up in the newspaper. Lucy cries, "My first duty is to my country," in the parlance of a soldier, forsaking both a feminine supporting role in war and a feminine domestic role in the home. I want to suggest that what offends the two men about the women is not the impulsive and uncharacteristic nature of the acts (as they claim) but the women's ability to deploy their own personal understandings of public justice and to sacrifice home for it, quickly and decisively, a feat that the men in their lives never achieve.

Both Harrison and Harold want to characterize the women as temporarily crazed or momentarily possessed by evil; they cannot indict the women for taking the stands they know that they should or would have taken. Instead of dealing directly with their own guilt, the men take comfortable refuge in the idea of the home as a depository of strange impulses that affect the sensitive natures of women. Yet in terms of the physical house, it is cast as "never forgetting the treachery," perhaps also never forgetting that its cause — the domestic ideal — was forsaken by each woman in a pursuit of justice. In this way, the men are able to align themselves with the safety and sanity of the house. Taking this stand, they are forced neither to despise the women, nor to blame themselves for not pursuing and supporting particulars causes in war and law. The house "bullies" Mildred into action because it "remembers" and is haunted by Lucy's treachery. The lesson that the men learn is that the domestic ideal, once violated by a woman, will continue to wreak havoc for generations to come.

Glasgow, however, seems to cast doubt on this notion by introducing both men as unreliable narrators, as those who refuse to make a stand, then over-analyze the situation in retrospect, introducing plenty of conflicting information into their own narratives. The glaring repetition of the personification of the house, rather than a visible ghost, implies a certain satire on Glasgow's part. Additionally, the choice of the women to enter into the masculine realms of war and law signals that women are only able to resist the strong pull of domesticity when the house is already somehow disfigured — in Lucy's case, by the infiltration of a Northern soldier (her lover), and in Mildred's case by the "haunting" of Lucy's deed.

Glasgow also figures the house as the marker of domestic well-being in the short story "The Past," although this time, in conjunction with a visible ghost, that of the first Mrs. Vanderbridge. Yet long before the ghost is made manifest, a new entrant into the house — Miss Wrenn, the new social secretary — senses the palpable psychic disorder of the home:

> I had no sooner entered the house than I knew something was wrong. Though I had never been in so splendid a place before — it was one of those big houses just off Fifth Avenue — I had a suspicion from the first that the magnificence covered a secret disturbance. I was always quick to receive impressions, and when the black iron doors swung together behind me, I felt as if I were shut inside a prison [119].

The language that casts the home as prison echoes the long buildup in tone and descriptive detail that signals the protagonist's homebound entrapment in *Virginia*. But here, in the truncated form of a short story, Glasgow must "imprison" her reader immediately within the unhappy home, through the eyes of an outsider. Similarly, she must present the disfiguring domestic ideal quickly and definitively: as the ghost of the first Mrs. Vanderbridge. Interestingly, the ghost makes her first appearance at Miss Wrenn's first family dinner. Glasgow carefully juxtaposes physical domestic perfection with the home's emotional turmoil. Miss Wrenn remarks: "I had never seen so beautiful a dinner table, and I was gazing with pleasure at the damask and glass and silver — there was a silver basket of chrysanthemums, I remember, in the center of the table — when I noticed a nervous movement of Mrs. Vanderbridge's head" (125). This turn of the head, of course, signals the entrance of the ghost of the first Mrs. Vanderbridge, who appears "so much frailer, so much more elusive, as if she would vanish if you touched her" (126). Miss Wrenn goes on to remark, "I can't describe, even months afterward, the singular way in which she attracted and repelled me" (126).

Like the domestic ideal itself, the ghost appears in the form of a woman, yet she is elusive, untouchable, simultaneously attractive and repellant. Similarly, after her appearance on the scene in a visible form, the dinner is all but ruined, and "dragged on heavily" despite the previously described splendor and cheerfulness of the table. That is, once the domestic ideal, the required slavery to beauty and order in the household, appears from behind the façade of a lovely table, the product of domesticity — the dinner itself — can no longer be enjoyed.

While Miss Wrenn has become uncomfortable during dinner, she becomes even more uncomfortable when she discovers that only she and the current Mrs. Vanderbridge can see the ghost. "Not even the servants appeared to notice her," because the servants, unlike the mistress of the house, are not emotionally invested in the full scope of the domestic ideal — its compulsion toward physical and spiritual perfection of the home (*The Collected Stories* 126). They are paid for their domestic services, then released from the house and its hauntings. While most of the servants cannot see the ghost, Mrs. Vanderbridge's own personal maid, Hopkins, senses her presence, calling her "the Other One" and remarking that while she doesn't *seem* to be doing any tangible harm, she is "killing" the lady of the house (*The Collected Stories* 129). Later, Hopkins plainly reveals her ignorance of the ghost's presence by walking *through* her as she puts another log on the fire. She evades the frightening presence of the domestic ideal personified by simply going about her work, without putting her own self worth on trial if the house appears to fail in some intangible way. Significantly, the Other One is standing motionless on the hearth rug, at the feet of Mr. Vanderbridge.

Miss Wrenn learns, not surprisingly, that Mr. Vanderbridge cannot see the ghost either, but that he does feel fits of depression in her presence. When Miss Wrenn asks Hopkins why Mrs. Vanderbridge doesn't tell her husband about the ghost, Hopkins replies, "She is the sort that would die first — just the opposite from the Other One — for she leaves him free, she never clutches and strangles. It isn't her way" (131). Untouched by the pressures of maintaining a perfect family and home, Mr. Vanderbridge remains ignorant of the source of his wife's — and his own — domestic troubles. Mrs. Vanderbridge is complicit in the status quo because she refuses to "clutch and strangle" her husband with her own burdens of domesticity. As she draws Miss Wrenn into her confidences, she repeats Hopkins' words — "it is killing me" and Miss Wrenn narrates, "It *was* killing her" (133).

But which tenet of the domestic ideal "kills" Mrs. Vanderbridge? Branson accurately describes the situation as "the fatal static condition of the Vanderbridge marriage." While Branson would argue that female friendship facilitates a happy marriage in this story, I would stress, instead, the tragic nature of Mrs. Vanderbridge's sense that her marriage "which appears perfect from the outside" is, in fact, flawed (80). In the midst of a wealthy and tastefully furnished home, she has failed to restore her husband to domestic bliss after the tragic death of his first wife in childbirth. She even attributes the presence of the ghost to her husband's mind, calling her "his thought of her" (132).

Yet much like Lucy, the ghost, too, has her reasons for continuing to haunt the house. The first Mrs. Vanderbridge is revealed to have had an extramarital affair. Miss Wrenn finds a set of love letters in a secret drawer of a desk she is cleaning. In her own attempts to heal the family, Miss Wrenn first decides to dispose of the letters, then changes her mind, counseling Mrs. Vanderbridge to show them to her husband, in hopes that the letters will change his "thought" of his first wife, and hence, rid the house of the ghost that only the women can see. Mrs. Vanderbridge, however, realizes that to reveal the letters is to damage not only Mr. Vanderbridge's memory of his first wife, but also the domestic memory of the house. By choosing to burn the letters without showing them to her husband, Mrs. Vanderbridge frees the home from its own violation of domestic order (the invasive presence of the record of an extra-marital affair). She psychically "cleans house" for her ghostly counterpart, and the ghost is able to disappear. The ghost represents the "old" domestic ideal of a house forever infused with the presence of its original mistress, so much so that the presence of a new wife represents a kind of sacrilege.

As the dominant emotional drive behind the domestic ideal, guilt makes perhaps its most impressive display in the story that became the centerpiece and title story for Glasgow's collection, "The Shadowy Third." While the title of the story seems to refer solely to the ghost of Mrs. Maradick's dead child, I am interested in the ways in which Glasgow deals with more than one "shadowy third" figure in the story, and especially with the way that she confronts the anathema of the domestic realm — the New Woman.

A sense of homelessness pervades the story long before the young, inexperienced nurse, Margaret, reaches the home where she will reside as a live-in nurse. While we read details of the hospital, its halls, and its grounds in the opening of the story, Margaret's quick trip to her own home is summarized in the following lines: "My preparations took only a few minutes. In those days I always kept a suitcase packed and ready for sudden calls" (55). Glasgow presents the modern working woman as quite literally a homeless figure, one whose most intimate spaces are likely to be the more feminine refuges of her profession (such as the hospital office) or the homes of her employers.

Home comforts, such as the nurturance of family, are equally difficult to find in the workplace. Even though Miss Hemphill, the superintendent of nurses, is a "distant Canadian relative" of Margaret's mother (52), Miss Hemphill takes every opportunity to send a jab or a back-handed compliment in Margaret's direction. When Margaret surmises that her new patient must have a mental disorder, she wonders how she was chosen for the case — "And that makes it all the stranger that he should select me, for I have had so few mental cases," to which Miss Hemphill replies, "So few cases of any kind" (53).

Similarly, when Margaret tries to guess the details of her new arrangement, Miss Hemphill warns, "Only try not to get too emotional, Margaret" (54). When Miss Hemphill finally takes pity on Margaret and divulges what she does know about the case, she remarks on Mrs. Maradick's passion for the doctor early in their courtship: "We never tired of watching her," but is quick to follow up with a remark on her professional status: "I wasn't superintendent then, so I had more time to look out of the window while I was on day duty" (*The Collected Stories* 53). The remark serves as a thinly veiled criticism of Margaret's "dreamy" nature and a concern with her suitability for professional life.

While the opening paragraphs have received little critical attention, they become essential to the story as the background of a stark dichotomy: Glasgow pits the harsh world of the hospital (where one's own relatives are likely to chastise and a sentimental nature is scorned) to the Maradick home: a place of emotional intensities where Margaret's main duties will be those of listener and companion. The sharp contrast signifies the working woman's constant status as a "shadowy third": she is not a true professional (we know that she has just finished training school and is plagued by her "excess" of imagination) nor is she a true part of any family, even the Maradicks'. Interestingly, Glasgow cannot help but link herself directly to the position of the "shadowy third." Miss Hemphill pointedly asks Margaret, "I wonder how long you will keep your sympathy and your imagination? After all, wouldn't you be a better novelist than a nurse?" (53). Here Glasgow comments on the problem of an "excess" of imagination: it makes a woman unfit for home and unfit for professional life, leaving only the position of the female novelist, a position deemed socially suitable and one that allowed imaginative work within a home setting.

The suggestion that Margaret is somehow suited for the role of female novelist is supported by Mrs. Maradick's own conclusions about the nurse. Upon entry into the home, Margaret notes the presence of a small girl and attempts to give the girl her ball when it rolls under a piece of furniture. These actions receive strange looks from the household help; only Mrs. Maradick will respond to Margaret's inquiries about the child by saying, "Then I know you're good.... If you weren't good you couldn't have seen her" (59). As readers, we know that the little girl is the "hallucination" that forms the evidence for Mrs. Maradick's mental illness. Mrs. Maradick's comment on Margaret's goodness hints at something special in the nurse's character; the opening pages of the story lead the reader to associate a degree of innocence, imagination, and non-professionalization as related to the vague goodness of Margaret. Unlike the day nurse, she is not "depressing," perhaps because she is not used to the emotional distance required for her profession (*The Collected Stories* 57).

The remainder of the story falls into a half-familiar pattern of the mystery story: we learn that Dr. Maradick was once engaged to a woman who ultimately rejected him because he was poor. He puts Mrs. Maradick in a home with the hope that she will die there, so that he might add her fortune to his own and marry the former fiancée. The story suggests that the child was killed by Dr. Maradick so that he could be sure of inheriting his wife's fortune. The child/ghost repays him in kind, though, when she leaves her ghostly jump rope on the stairs, and the newly single Dr. Maradick falls to his death.

The ghost of this story serves as a double warning on the subject of the domestic ideal. Most obviously, she suggests that excessive wealth in the home is dangerous, to both wives and children alike. She also calls for an active mother, one who is able to protect the children at all times and who cannot be incapacitated by medical care foisted upon her. Last, and most subtly, the ghost hints at the dangers of over-professionalization for young women. If a young woman's only contact with a home of any kind is through a sterile, distanced profession, the young woman runs the risk of losing her own womanly intuition or "goodness" — the ability to see beyond the tangible household/medical details. So far, Margaret has avoided this danger, but Mr. Maradick's death by jump rope serves as a warning against any type of masculinized professional life that would force out feminine intuition and imagination.

This type of intuition/imagination operates in the female protagonist of each of these ghost stories, often isolating the protagonist and allowing her to see the ghost of the story when others do not. Glasgow implies that only a sensitive nature will question and see clearly the ghostly and often harmful over-influence of the domestic ideal within each of these houses.

As in "The Shadowy Third," in "Whispering Leaves," the over-influence of the domestic ideal appears in a man given over to worldly comforts. Early in the story, Mr. Blanton becomes almost synonymous with gluttony:

> Evidently, I decided, the second Mrs. Blanton was the right wife for him. Vain, spoiled, selfish, amiable as long as he was given everything that he wanted, and still good-looking in an obvious and somewhat flashing style, he had long ago passed into that tranquil state of mind which follows a complete surrender to the habits of life. I wondered how his first wife, Clarissa of the romantic name and flaming hair, had endured existence in this lonely neighborhood with the companionship of a man who thought of nothing but food and drink [152–53].

Effie is isolated by her own northern upbringing, her ignorance of this side of her family, and most of all, her sensitive nature; it seems likely that she, even as a visitor to Whispering Leaves, might compare herself to Mr. Blanton's former wife, Clarissa. This pattern of isolation and relation to an earlier feminine figure is established in "Dare's Gift" as well, as is the notion of seeing the ghost as a test of character in "The Shadowy Third." By the time Glasgow was writing the fourth of her short stories, several patterns of isolation had been established.

Another commonality is the use of the first-person narrator. The first-person, female narrator calls to mind the epistolary chapter of *Virginia* when Glasgow must shift perspectives to detail the inner workings of the house, to show how those details consumed Virginia, and to call attention to Virginia's isolation in Matoaca City. The truncated story form requires an instant recognition of domestic isolation by the reader in order to portray the disease-like ghostly domestic ideal in a fashion that is "believable" in the context of the fantastic. In other words, the reader's sensation of needing to cling to the first-person narrator in an unfamiliar, possibly dangerous territory incites the level of sympathy necessary to trust the narrator's description of a ghost. Only "Dare's Gift" violates this pattern by allowing Harold to narrate. Yet I would argue that here Glasgow uses a male narrator for manipulative reasons; only Harold can gain access to the masculine version of the legend of Lucy Dare, one that stresses feminine weakness/hypersensitivity in such a manner as to allow for Glasgow's infamous irony. The story told by Harrison only throws into relief the story the reader *hears*: Mildred is so isolated that a ghost's ideal held more sway with her than her husband. To add insult to injury, her story became isolated and lost, chalked up to "feminine sensitivity" rather than depicted as a moral act.

The first-person feminine narrative of the short stories also allows Glasgow to create voices that emphasize their own isolation, rather than slowly building atmospheres that reinforce the notion of growing isolation over years and years. The convention of an outsider visiting or working in the home, too, allows for sweeping, at times almost melodramatic descriptions. Upon her arrival, Effie remarks, "Dusk, dusk, dusk. As we drove on rapidly beneath the high, closely woven arch of the cedars, I was conscious again of a deep intuitive feeling that the world in which I moved was as unreal as the surroundings in a dream" (147). Glasgow implies that only the outsider to the home can afford the sensation of conscious recognition, of intuition, and even of verbal repetition (It is difficult to imagine Virginia Pendleton saying to herself "Dusk, dusk, dusk," as these would be three words "wasted" on her own private thoughts rather than her family).

Yet the ghost of this story is perhaps the most frightening of all, because she threatens the independence of a young, single woman accustomed to an active life in the North. During her visit, she becomes attached to the family pariah and stepchild, a small boy named Pell. Unlike other members of the family, Pell sees and speaks to his dead mammy,[7] a woman who had promised his mother to watch over him always. Apparently Mammy has taken the burden of this promise beyond even her own grave. Yet one night, Pell begins to repeat the phrase "Mammy says you must take me with her when you go away" (161). On the surface, Effie seems to provide the perfect solution to Pell's upbringing: the young boy will no longer be alternately ignored and mistreated by his family. Yet Effie herself voices quite a few reservations: "How could I take the child away with me? I asked at last, as if I were disputing with some invisible presence at my side. What room was there for a child in my active life? I loved Pell; I hated to leave him, but how could I possibly take him with me when I went away in the morning?" (161). Here, Effie voices the idea that loving a child is not a sufficient reason for giving one's life over to that child.

The plot, as well as the ghost/domestic ideal of the story, ends in chaos. A fire breaks out and Effie cannot find Pell. Watching the house burn, she sees Mammy rescue him, then place Pell in her own arms:

> Her eyes found me at last, and I knew, in that moment of vision, what the message was that she had for me. Without a word I stepped forward, and held out my arms. As I did so I saw a glory break in the dim features. Then, even while I gave

my voiceless answer, the face melted from me into spirals of smoke. Was it a dream, after all? Was the only reality the fact that I held the child safe and unharmed in my arms? [163].

The ending remains ambiguous for a number of reasons. Was Mammy's message simply for Effie to "take Pell with her" when she left the burning house, not when she left the house for good? Or, having almost lost Pell, is Effie now committed to raising him herself? Though she gives Mammy a "voiceless answer" (to an unheard question), Effie seems to question her own commitment to the child by asking "Was it a dream?" and asking whether or not the child in her arms (at that *moment*) is the "only reality."

Thus, Glasgow gives Effie an out. If her love for the child is the "only reality," then she is not obligated to take him home with her. If, however, she is intended to take Mammy's message literally, she must now devote her once "active" life to rearing a child. While ambiguous, the ending also gives the reader an out. A sentimental magazine reader could easily read the "happy ending" of Effie and Pell together as mother and child. Yet Glasgow subtly valorizes Effie's entire character, including her resistance to sudden motherhood. First, Effie is able to see the ghost of Mammy. From her other short stories, we know that within Glasgow's set of conventions, being able to see the ghost implies morality and a positive type of intuition. Second, Effie is depicted as one who knows more about childrearing, by responding to children intuitively and kindly, than the far more domestic Mrs. Blanton, and Effie's resistance to motherhood is not portrayed as simple unpreparedness. Last, Effie is not punished for her doubts about taking Pell. In fact, Mammy seems to reward her for even considering raising Pell, implying that simply to care for him and worry for him during the house fire is, somehow, enough. In this way, Glasgow makes it possible to satisfy a magazine readership's sentimental tastes without sacrificing a young woman's independence.

In these four short stories, all of the women obey the ghosts — the spirits of the house — but not blindly. Each woman must craft her own version of domesticity by revising the ghost's "old" domestic ideal. She takes on this task by appeasing the ghost in some ways, while asserting her own will in others. This type of compromise suggests that Glasgow did not intend for all intelligent young women to follow in her own footsteps by resisting the domestic ideal in a headstrong pursuit of a career. The important factor for Glasgow is that women, learning from Virginia's cautionary tale, do not blindly serve and serve, scarcely noticing when there is no one left to serve. Yet Glasgow resists the temptation to write nothing but the cautionary tale. Looking for a middle ground between Virginia, who is sucked into the mire of her eponymous home state, and Gabriella, who must leave home, class, and family behind in order to fight the destiny of domestic servitude, Glasgow began to write short stories in the years between 1916 and 1925.

Not only did the stories help her to more closely define her ideas about the nature of the domestic ideal that suffocated women, the stories presented new types of characters absent from the early novels, characters who could both work and hold influence in a family. Influence, even command of a family was possible, even if that family was not one's own. With this idea of "surrogate" families, Glasgow valorizes women who worked in another home, such as social secretaries or nurses. Yet a profession is not required to escape the ghost of the domestic ideal; a commitment to an ideal (other than the domestic) works just as well. Headstrong women like Miss Wrenn, Mildred, Margaret and Effie do not loudly revolt, nor do they cave (or fall "helpless") at the power of the domestic ideal of their time. Glasgow informs women that compromising oneself is not an option; compromising the domestic ideal is. Creative, intuitive solutions for household peace are Glasgow's order of the day.

In *Virginia* and in *Life and Gabriella*, Glasgow renders sympathy for the domestic woman, using her own insights about disability to point to the nature of the domestic ideal's strict bodily control. In the novels, the overachieving homemaker, once her children and husband have no more need for her, is left with a mental condition bordering on agoraphobia. With so many years of household and family care behind her, including long years of an education to make her a "fit" wife, the outside world becomes a conundrum. The homemaker has made others so able to enter the outside world easily and readily that she has deprived herself of a job. Thus, the walls begin to close in, but the outside world has never been her place and remains unfamiliar in old age as well. In these homemakers, Glasgow saw herself— a victim of an imposed bodily control. While Glasgow's bodily control was imposed by outside forces (family recommending "rest," doctors, and the hearing devices that were supposed to aid her), the homemaker's bodily control was imposed by the needs and demands of children and family, as well as the isolation (disguised as aid) offered by a battery of new household gadgets and amenities. Yet Glasgow was able to escape her disability, like the modern proponents of Deaf culture, linguistically, through writing about it. Glasgow seems to have recognized her own escape from disability as such. While the short stories began as a mode of working out the ideology of a novel heroine who might be able to overcome the restrictions of domesticity, as well as an entry point into the popular ghost story tradition, Glasgow was able to accomplish far more. In the stories, she allows her female protagonists their own escapes, just as she herself had found an escape, by allowing them to do battle with the household ghosts. Often the battle with the ghost ties the domestic woman to a larger history or to the "public" culture around her. The notion of domestic women as possessing (and deploying) the potential to become "public" is reminiscent of Romero's observation that the notion of separate spheres (both within domestic novels and within the criticism of those novels) is highly constructed in nature. Rather than leaving readers with the tragic fate of domestic women such as Virginia, Glasgow proposes that, as the twentieth century progressed, the domestic ideal, with its haunted charm, was not invincible.

Chapter Three

SEXING THE DOMESTIC
Eudora Welty's Delta Wedding
and the Sexology Movement

At the end of Ellen Glasgow's *Virginia*, the title character eagerly awaits the arrival of her son, an arrival proposed by his one-line message: "Dearest mother, I am coming home to you, Harry" (526). Harry presumably writes this note in response to the publicity surrounding his father's adulterous affair with an actress. In the language of Harry's note, Glasgow signals the change in Virginia's position within her family, a belabored change that is the subtext of the entire novel. The words Harry chooses — "mother, I am coming home to you" — rather than "I am coming to you" or "I am coming home" align Virginia with her home in a complete fashion. For her children, her identity is solely a domestic one; Virginia *is* home. Further, Harry's own words strike a chord with reader and protagonist alike because they are the very words that Virginia wishes to hear from her husband, who has been producing plays in New York for several years and conducting an affair with an actress. In this way, the son replaces the father, coming home to rescue his mother from the embarrassing publicity and from her domestic isolation.

Yet Harry's note does not constitute an entirely felicitous conclusion to the novel, especially since he is one of the factors in her state of isolation. Virginia has willingly chosen domestic absorption; Glasgow painstakingly catalogues the demise of Virginia's beauty as a consequence of childbearing, overwork, and anxiety. Oliver's affair is, in many ways, depicted as an inevitable consequence for a woman who succumbs to a kind of domestic obsession, an unhealthy passion for childrearing and housework that obliterates any other interests in her life, including sexual desire. Virginia is willing to forgo completely a non-maternal sexual identity in the name of ideal domesticity. Glasgow makes clear the deep division between the two identities, portraying sexuality and domesticity as contradicting forces requiring many women to make a choice between the two during the late nineteenth and early twentieth centuries.

In contrast, Eudora Welty portrays a growing sense of sexual freedom for women during the 1920s through the 1940s within the southern United States domestic tradition. When read in conjunction with the historical artifacts and texts of the early twentieth-century sexology movement, Welty's work reconfigures the stereotype of the isolated 1920s southern woman who remains uninfluenced by her northern sisters and the popular culture depictions of their increasing sexual freedoms. Critics of Welty's work, like those of many other southern women writers, sometimes overlook her references to historical events and ideological shifts. Yet Welty catalogues a distinct shift in domestic thinking — one that integrates domestic and sexual roles for the southern woman even in her supposed isolation from such innovation. This shift was due in large part to the new availability of sexual information and to the general cultural influence of the sexology movement. As Welty's characters navigate conventional images of the southern belle, plantation culture, and social groups such as the garden club, they are indeed *navigating*, rather than making binary choices between "appropriate" and "inappropriate" roles.

Welty makes this sense of navigational possibilities explicit at times, particularly through her younger characters in *Delta Wedding*. Immediately before Dabney Fairchild's wedding to the family's overseer, Troy Flavin (a marriage choice that might not have been as readily available to Dabney a decade earlier and is still controversial within her family), Dabney partakes of her own form of overseeing. She tours the family land, including Marmion, the home that is to be hers. As Dabney looks into the river that bounds the family property, her horse "turned with Dabney, willfully, and took the path back toward Shellmound" (159). With her horse seeming to express its own agency, one that would encourage Dabney to stay within the safe confines of the family, Dabney realizes her own will as it pertains to her marriage:

> "I will never give up anything!" Dabney thought, bending forward and laying her head against the soft neck. "Never! Never! For I am happy, and to give up nothing will prove it. I will never give up anything, never give up Troy — or *to* Troy!" She thought smilingly of Troy, coming slowly, this was the last day, slowly plodding and figuring, sprung all over with red-gold hairs [159].

Here, Welty allows Dabney not only to defy the options presented in domestic and sexual identities, but also to defy even the convention of *making* such a choice. Dabney's wish to prove her own happiness by "giving up nothing" signals a sharp change from a character such as Virginia who not only gives up everything, but cannot even concede that she has made a choice to do so. Dabney, in contrast, realizes that an over-adherence to a certain type of domestic role, or even the role of dominant wife, might force her to "give up" Troy, at least in the romantic-sexual light in which she now sees him. Welty makes clear Dabney's sexualized notion of Troy through constant references to his differences from the Fairchilds (his slowness)[1] and through references to his body — "all sprung over with red-gold hairs" — an image that indicates both an immediacy and an animalistic edge to Troy's own sexual nature. Troy's slowness, too, seems appealing to Dabney because he is not sexually threatening. Yet this same slowness often makes him unfit for the social world of the quick-witted Fairchilds. In this sense, Troy's difference offers Dabney an ability to lead, to guide Troy socially, and if not to lead sexually, to avoid, at least, complete sexual submission. The reference of giving up "*to* Troy" seems to indicate a resistance to both a submissive domestic role and a submissive sexual role. Dabney does not acknowledge a binary choice between sexual and domestic roles for herself. That Dabney does not structure her choice of a marriage role as domestic versus sexual, nor as dominant versus submissive, indicates that she is able to envision these roles as at least somewhat integrated, in contrast to the either or mentality of Glasgow's Virginia.

Dabney's assertion that she will forge her own neither submissive nor dominant feminine role represents only a part of the continuum of sexual and domestic choices that Welty presents for her female characters. A decision that might be seen as the reverse of the one that Glasgow's Virginia makes — the choice to favor a sexual role over a domestic role — also exists for Welty's women. This choice, too, does not have to be an absolute. In Welty's South, unlike Glasgow's, everyone enters the kitchen and everyone eats; even the most sexual and sensuous women are depicted as serving more basic human needs. A comparison of Glasgow's Abby Goode, the town flirt who is described as "awfully good fun" (142) and Welty's sexualized characters such as Virgie Rainey ("The Wanderers") or Fay McKelva (*The Optimist's Daughter*) reveals this difference. While Fay and Virgie may not live up to the town "belle" standards, both are featured in their own homes, performing (although sometimes under-performing) domestic activities. In contrast, Abby Goode typically appears on horseback, hair in the wind, laughing, or flitting from group to group at a garden party — not in a kitchen, and not even in her own home.

In the concluding story of *The Golden Apples*, "The Wanderers," Welty retrieves the sexual-domestic binary from the sub-text of the story and places it at the heart of her plot. Throughout the story, characters express varying degrees of surprise and wonder at finding themselves within the Rainey household. They have come out of duty, to attend the viewing and wake of Katie Rainey, each one pausing just before reaching the door: "Each one who came seemed stopped by the enormous dead boxwood, like a yellow sponge, that stood by the steps; it had to be gone around" (*The Collected Stories of Eudora Welty* 432). Like the dead boxwood, the fact that many of the people at the wake would not have paid an ordinary social call at the Rainey home must also "be gone around" in polite conversation. Clearly, part of the reason for the Raineys' social isolation is the "wild" reputation of Virgie Rainey as well as what had been Katie Rainey's increasing dementia. Yet the women in the kitchen at the wake take the social isolation a step further. It is as if they suppose that because they have never thought of Virgie in a domestic role that she must not be able to perform even the simplest domestic tasks:

> Virgie went back once more to the kitchen, but again the women stopped what they were doing and looked at her as though something — not only today — should prevent her from knowing at all how to cook — the thing they knew. She went to the stove, took a fork, and turned over a piece or two of the chicken, to see Missie Spights look at her with eyes wide in a kind of wonder and belligerence [*Collected Stories* 434].

The women express more than surprise at Virgie's interest in food preparation; they also express a territorial domestic nature — Missie Spights feels not just wonder, but also belligerence at Virgie's "invasion" of the kitchen, even in Virgie's own home. The phrase "the thing they all knew" operates on two levels. Homemaking is clearly "the thing they all knew" but there is also the inference of a "thing they all knew" about Virgie that should prevent her from cooking: her open sexuality. Here, Welty presents the binary of sexuality versus domesticity even as she offers up an alternative force in the form of Virgie Rainey. Virgie resists social convention by performing a complete version of domesticity — she is even sewing at the moment of her mother's death — despite being unmarried and "publicly" sexual since her teens.

Virgie Rainey is no Abby Goode — she not only has a kitchen, she uses it. Further, she represents a fully developed character, rather than Abby's laugh and flash of shiny hair that hint at Oliver Treadwell's infidelities. In this way, Welty allows the sexualized woman to achieve a complete identity: she must deal with hardships such as death and commonplaces such as domestic chores. However, this type of complete realization of sexualized feminine characters is only possible within a different type of narrative structure. As readers, we cannot know Abby Goode's domestic habits because we are enveloped in the claustrophobic third-person narration of Virginia's every thought and move. Welty, in contrast, moves among feminine voices, offering numerous accounts of domestic practice along the way. The result of this type of narration is an expanded sense of what a home looks like, beyond the ideal of domestic perfection.

"...Never give up anything!": The Fusion of Sexual and Domestic Identities

In her analysis of sexuality in *Delta Wedding* (1946) and *The Optimist's Daughter* (1972), Danielle Fuller remarks that "the multi-voiced narrative of *Delta Wedding* makes it impossible to ignore the parallels and echoes between the journeys toward selfhood of Laura, Shelley, Robbie, and Dabney" (297). In her comparisons of these characters' changing roles as women, Fuller clearly equates selfhood with at least some degree of realization of a sexual role. She is right to note that Welty's narratological structure of multiple fused points of view exposes women's sexual identities in relation to one another, not as purely heterosexual dyads nor as individual journeys. Fuller does not address the role of domesticity on the formation of these identities; however, Welty's characters frequently evaluate each other in terms of more than sexuality. In *Delta Wedding*, for instance, several Fairchild women regard Robbie Reid with suspicion not only because of her overt sexuality, but also because of her domestic ineptitude. Welty crafts a narrative structure that allows the reader to eavesdrop on the women's judgments of each other. Frequently, these judgments do not focus entirely on the performance of one role or the other. Instead, the female characters examine how well another woman has *integrated* her sexual and domestic identities.

Rather than using domestic skills as the sole measurement of a woman's worth, Welty creates characters who struggle to integrate new attitudes about sexuality into lives rich with family traditions and legends. Instead of placing her characters in an isolated southern cultural bubble, Welty places them squarely within their era: an era saturated with many new ideas, including new ideas about sexuality, sexual practices, and women's sexual roles. This is not to say, however, that Welty crafts polemical novels that do for sexology what Fielding Burke did for unionization. Welty's incorporation of cultural materials, such as her use of advertisements, songs, and fashions, is typically subtle, as are her references to a new sexual culture. But if we overlook these references, however subtle, we risk the marginalization of Welty as just another southern woman writer, isolated from her larger environment.

It comes as no surprise that the women in Welty's 1920s–1940s Mississippi might turn to one another for guidance on establishing and maintaining domestic norms. Ann Romines comments on the conditioning of southern women to "read" the "texts" of domestic products, such as cakes and recipes, for their commentary on social life: "In the United States, especially in the South, most cakes have been baked by women, and domestic female culture has often been oriented to texts such as the cake, while male culture has been devoted to objects and destinations of fixity and permanence" ("Reading the Cakes" 602). Romines claims for cakes — specifically, the cakes of *Delta Wedding* — the status of land ownership or job titles for men; she remarks that one "might say that culture consists in — recipes" (602). At first glance, a recipe might appear to be wholly asexual, even in its cultural associations. Yet as Romines notes, the cakes of *Delta Wedding* tend to take on narrative lives of their own. In an examination of Ellen's cake-baking narrative, Romines remarks on the contiguous nature of text and recipe as "a single rich text," one that is even capable of producing an actual cake (609). But is the "single rich text" simply made up of narration and recipe? I would argue that Ellen's thoughts — of how "Robbie had tantalizingly let herself be chased and had jumped in the river with George in after her, everybody screaming from where they lay" (30) — form a sexual subtext to the recipe-narrative, a far stronger element than what Romines describes as Ellen's meditations on George's "troubled" marriage (608). What we have instead is a metaphorical rape-within-a-recipe-within-a-narrative. Welty seamlessly weaves together Ellen's action of beating eggs with her mental re-telling of the "rape and rescue" scene.

Critics acknowledge the significance of both the sexual and the domestic in *Delta Wedding*, but the two realms of experience have not been fully explored in relationship to one another and as interdependent forces.[2] The two elements often appear directly linked, and even intertwined, as either a scene of domestic action infused with a meditation on a sexual topic or a primarily sexual scene infused with domesticity; during the aforementioned rape and rescue, Jim Allen and Primrose are seen "trembling for their sweet peas" (31). Critics' dissections of the scenes, on the other hand, often privilege one element or the other.[3] I would attribute this critical tendency, at least in part, to Welty's image as a writer, an image Rebecca Mark describes as that of a "nice southern lady." In *The Dragon's Blood*, Mark notes a critical ellipsis in terms of Welty's "implicit and explicit critique of a Western heroic tradition." Mark claims that this ellipsis occurs "not only because no one could imagine a nice southern lady doing such a thing, but primarily because no one has consistently applied a close feminist textual and intertextual analysis to this collection of stories [*The Golden Apples*]" (4). Challenging the notion that Welty's allusions are solely mythological, Mark forges new feminist connections[4] among Welty's stories in *The Golden Apples* as well as noting Welty's implicit cultural criticism of masculinist American modernism.

Mark's work is clearly a valuable addition to feminist studies of Welty, especially in its contextualization of Welty as a writer aware of, and consciously responding to, her cultural and literary milieux, including her own "nice southern lady" image. I agree with Mark that this very image can inhibit the critics of southern literature from noting the sexual and the sensual in Welty's writings, particularly when the allusions to desirous bodies are framed in secrecy.

Interestingly, Welty's autobiography reveals self-consciousness about the desire to know the sexualized unknowable from the time she was a small child. Critics often cite the first section of *One Writer's Beginnings*, "Listening," as early evidence of Welty's concern with both narrative and drama, forces that would later make her a "scenic" writer.[5] Yet Welty is often more explicit: not only did she want to hear stories, she wanted to hear the stories that remained untold, at least to her ears, specifically because of their content:

> This was Fannie. This old black sewing woman, along with her speed and dexterity, brought along a great provision of up-to-the-minute news. She spent her life going from family to family in town and worked right in its bosom, and nothing could stop her. My mother would try, while I stood being pinned up. "Fannie, I'd rather Eudora didn't hear that." "That" would be just what I was longing to hear, whatever it was. "I don't want her exposed to gossip"—as if gossip were measles and I could catch it. I did catch some of it but not enough. "Mrs. O'Neil's oldest daughter she had her wedding dress tried on, and all her fine underclothes feather-stitched and ribbon run in and then—" "I think that will do, Fannie," said my mother. It was tantalizing never to be exposed long enough to hear the end [15].

Fannie's liminal position—neither household domestic worker nor professional seamstress, but instead sewing woman—offers a unique glimpse of the lives of other domestic situations and the ability to hear those stories. The lack of loyalty to one family, as well as Fannie's status as racial and class Other to the families she works for, allows her the freedom to exchange the stories she hears as well. Welty's choice of words — the positioning of Fannie in the "bosom" of town as well as the sense of "exposure" to gossip as exposure to disease — casts a distinctly physical focus on the discourse within the domestic scene of females being fitted for clothes. Welty marks her complicity in the fascination with bodies by remarking that what she "caught" was "not enough." Finally, Welty tantalizes her reader just as she remembers being tantalized — within this vignette she only gives the reader a small portion of the story, surely not a full "exposure." Fannie begins a figurative "undressing" of the bride, noting first her wedding dress, then her underthings. Yet just at the moment that we might see the naked, virgin (or not so virgin) bride, Mrs. Welty interrupts the narrative to stop the force of "gossip." In this way, the reader receives a piece of information almost as shocking as the vision of the bride undressed. Through Welty's vignette, we learn of the existence of an untold narrative which complicates a normative, heterosexual marriage plot. We learn, just as the young Eudora Welty did, that there are other sexual options for women — including premarital sex, out-of-wedlock pregnancy, and homosocial if not homosexual relationships — even if those options cannot be told in full detail. In recounting her childhood memories, Welty forges an important link between the home, the domestic activities of women, and the exchange of sexual information.

This pattern of the exchange of sexual information in the midst of women's domestic routines prevails throughout Welty's novels and short stories. For instance, in *Delta Wedding*, the aunts chide India for her mention of Dabney's honeymoon, although the marriage and the honeymoon itineraries are well known within the larger family circle (59). Later, the same aunts refer to Dabney's remark about having children right away as "something a little ugly, a little unbecoming for Battle's daughter" (63). The implication is less that these remarks are inappropriate in themselves than that they are not polite conversation for afternoon tea with one's maiden aunts. Within their peer group, Dabney, India, and the other girls at Shellmound feel free to exchange this type of sexual information. India casually asks Dabney whether she will bring the nightlight on her honeymoon (59), Dabney jokes that her bridesmaids are "those fast girls I run with.... The ones that dance all night barefooted" (55), and Lady Clare tells Laura to "ask Shelley can Troy French-kiss" (94). The girls are comfortable with this type of exchange even in the midst of a "purely" domestic situation such as the ritual of tea or the custom of "bringing something" when one pays a visit. But to the characters of the aunts' generation in Welty's novels, the something one brings to a neighbor or family member's home should not be a piece of sexual gossip nor a sexualized confessional narrative, as indicated by their protests in response to the remarks they find inappropriate (55, 59).

Welty clearly portrays a difference between the generations, in both their stringent domestic standards and their opinions on which personal information can and cannot be shared socially. But why might Welty want to showcase the shift in attitudes about sharing one's sexuality or sexual information? What were the cultural influences of the 1920s through the 1940s that might have led her to replay the need for "exposure" that she expresses in *One Writer's Beginnings*? For one possible answer, we may turn to the growing field of early twentieth-century sexology.

Sex, War, and Havelock Ellis

Delta Wedding (1946) is set in 1923. Welty chose this year by looking in the almanac "to find a year that was uneventful" (Bunting 50, in *Conversations with Eudora Welty*), a year "without wars or other natural or economic disasters to disrupt the domestic sphere" (Romines 605). Critic Ann Romines also notes that Welty chose

> a year during the period of her own adolescence, when she would have been fourteen, deep in puberty and engrossed in the issues of gender, family and self-possession that the novel explores. *Delta Wedding* inscribes the ambivalence of the 1920s toward two of the most traditional forms female power has taken: childbearing and housekeeping. It is the story of a plantation daughter's wedding, in the course of which a whole household of girls and women must puzzle out what those traditions may mean for them ["Reading the Cakes" 605].

Despite the choice of setting the novel in a year in which nothing supposedly happened, and Welty's focus on feminine domestic practices and relationships, *Delta Wedding* (like Welty's other novels and stories) does contain references to its historical setting. Though many critics allude only briefly to race and class as the historical markers of a primarily insular, domestic, family-oriented text, Welty draws on a wide variety of cultural materials, even beyond the well-covered areas of music and mythology. As Rebecca Mark notes, "Welty uses every kind of cultural artifact from folktales, literary texts, fairy tales, and oral narratives to musical scores, popular songs, advertisements, children's rhymes, and newspaper articles to challenge dominant literary conventions" (3). For example, in the opening of *Delta Wedding*, Welty sets the scene of the Fairchild household, depicting the older girls dressed in the fashionable colors of "jade and flamingo" and dancing to songs such as "I Wish I Could Shimmy Like My Sister Kate" and "Stop Yer Ticklin', Jock" (9). With these references, Welty depicts a household in touch with its cultural milieu, with the subtle indications of a modern sensuality. Given Welty's concern with this wide variety of cultural materials as well as her concern with gender and family, it follows that she would have been well aware of changing attitudes in the 1920s. Also, because of her concern with the "untold" stories, as highlighted in *One Writer's Beginnings*, she was likely aware of the specific alterations in thinking about sexuality (including a new openness in the discourse) that occurred during the early twentieth century, largely due to the growing influence of a new discipline: sexology.

Sexology can be thought of as, quite simply, "the scientific study of sex" (Irvine 531). Yet its origins also speak to its wide range of influence. Sexology is not a single type of study, but instead "an umbrella term denoting the activity of a multidisciplinary group of researchers, clinicians, and educators concerned with sexuality" (531). In his groundbreaking work, *Psychology of Sex* (1933), Havelock Ellis notes the importance of what he calls "Sex Psychology" (prior to the rise of the term "sexology"), or "the subject of sex in its psychic and social bearings." Further, Ellis proclaims that, for medical practitioners, a knowledge of sex "confined to general anatomy, physiology, and pathology, is now altogether inadequate" (v).

Studies began in Europe, as a strategy for coping with the public problems of prostitution and venereal disease. Sexology also received support as a movement from eugenicists and racist groups seeking to limit reproduction in "supposedly inferior groups such as immigrants, Blacks and Jews" (Irvine 531). Unlike Freud himself and Freudian psychologists, sexologists were concerned primarily with practical applications of sexual surveys and studies, including sex therapy. As early as the late nineteenth century, in a climate of rising industrialism and urbanization, sexual ideologies began to shift away from a reproductive model of sexuality and toward a model that held as its ideal the sexual pleasure and fulfillment of both partners. The first sexological institute was founded in 1919 in Berlin, but much of the German research was destroyed by Nazis in raids during World War II. Leaders in this movement included the British Ellis and the American sexologists Clelia Mosher and Robert Latou Dickinson (Irvine 531–32). The work of Ellis, Mosher and Dickinson paved the way for later and more widely acclaimed studies by

Alfred Kinsey in the 1930s and 1940s, as well as by William Masters and Virginia Johnson in the 1950s and 1960s.

Although sexology had become an important and established field by the advent of World War II, it is important to note the ways in which the earliest sexologists and their purported views differ from both later twentieth century sexual liberalism and from nineteenth-century home-centered sexual ideology. On one hand, Ellis explicitly claims a feminist identity for himself, yet throughout his *Essays in War-Time* (1917) he refers to his belief in biological determinism. Like the men and women of Welty's Shellmound, he has no qualms about women as leaders, but he clings to the notion that "a woman is a woman throughout, and that difference is manifest in all the energies of body and soul" (95).

Ellis was also strongly influenced by World War I and wartime culture. In *Essays in War-Time*, he counters the procreation propaganda of the day, claiming that war's effect of "pouring out the blood of the young manhood of the race" is positive because it avoids the "menace" of overpopulation (29, 74). Further, Ellis casts himself as a pacifist, resisting German and other European propaganda that claimed that war made for strong, healthy (and presumably white, Anglo-Saxon) populations. He writes that, in 1917, "we are not called upon to choose between the manly virtues of war and the effeminate degeneracy of peace" (40). He calls, instead, for the "virtues of daring and endurance" that "will never fail in any progressive community of men, alike in the causes of war and peace" (40).

In essence, Ellis resists the glorification of war as a necessary or "natural" event. Further, he resists the masculinization of war and the feminization of peace, as well as the call to support one's country through sexual reproduction within marriage. In the light of Ellis' politics (which were some of the most influential in the sexology movement), Welty's choice of setting her novel in 1923 can be seen as more than a simple desire to avoid the larger, "masculine" trope of war and to concentrate on a smaller, domestic, and intrinsically "peaceful" sphere. Welty's notion that "a sheltered life can be a daring life" (*One Writer's Beginnings* 114) clearly resonates with Ellis' idea of "daring and endurance" within peacetime. Welty furthers this questioning of wartime sexual and gender politics by her portrayal of Denis's "fineness" and of his death in the war as a wasteful tragedy: "the fineness could look so delicate — nobody could get tireder, fall sicker and more quickly so, than her men. She thought yet of the other brother Denis who was dead in France holding this look; from the grave he gave her that look, partly of hurt: 'How could I have been brought like this?'" (28). Like Ellis, Welty questions the hyper-masculinity of war, as well as the notion that war breeds fertility and strength — both moral and physical. For Denis, war castrates rather than bolsters; war fells a sensitive man (one who might have flourished as a "refined" Delta character) and marks him —"brought like this"— as infertile, unable to carry on the family line, despite his heroism.

Beyond his scope as a popular wartime essayist, Ellis made his greatest inroad in the field of sexology with his publication of *Studies in the Psychology of Sex*, a massive seven-volume work collected and published in installments between 1897 and 1928. The work marked two major changes from the field's former conception under the heading of gynecology. First, in his treatise on sexology, Ellis claims that gynecology goes beyond the purely physical; there is a psychological aspect of the physiological that has been largely ignored. Second, he disdains the current medical training that offers only "an unqualified warning against what would now be called contraception" (v). Here, Ellis notes the newness of even the term "contraception." The remaining content of Ellis' work, including basic notions of anatomy and biology, Freudian "erotic symbols," homosexuality, and "the sexual impulse in youth" was considered revolutionary in his day, particularly because it was intended to be used in the training of future physicians.

Despite the progressive nature of his work, Ellis did not intend to offer purely amoral, psychological and biological information and advice, nor did he feel that such was the proper role for the general practitioner. He writes,

> Certainly the sexual impulse may, within limits, be guided and controlled at will to a much greater extent than some are willing to admit. But the sexual impulse is, to an incomparably greater degree than the nutritive impulse, held in certain paths and shut out of other paths, by traditional influences of religion, morality, and social convention. There are a few physicians who hold that these influences should be ignored. The physician has nothing to do with morals or with conventions, they argue; he must consider what is for his patient's good and advise him accordingly, without any regard to moral and conventional dictates. That, however, is a short-sighted course of action which leads to many awkward positions, to all kinds of inconsistencies, not seldom to a greater evil than the evil it is sought to cure. For it is the special characteristic of the sexual impulse, as distinct from the nutritive impulsive, that its normal gratification involves another person [5].

Ellis notes the presence of "evil," revealing his continuing reliance on, and advocacy of, morality in sexology. Yet Ellis' closest site of comparison for the "sexual impulse" lies within "the nutritive impulse." While he notes that sexual practice contains even more religious, moral, and social constraints than eating, he cannot escape the linkage of sex and food practices. Welty also cel-

ebrates this link throughout *Delta Wedding*. Yet Ellis writes from a masculinized viewpoint. It seems likely that Welty would disagree with Ellis that the
"sexual impulse" is a moral one because it involves another person, while
"the nutritive impulse" is less moral because it does not. For Welty, the
larger realm of familial domestic practice always circumscribes both sexuality and foodways. Or, to put it another way, sex and food are always family
affairs.

Throughout *Delta Wedding*, Welty critiques the stereotypical sexual roles
of women — the type of "pure" sexuality that can only be expressed through
maternity and domesticity. She treats her characters who support the solely
maternal sexuality of women with more than a little facetiousness. For
instance, Welty treats Dr. Murdoch, who appears in the graveyard when Shelley, India, and Laura visit Laura's mother's grave, as almost a mirage, a cari-
cature of the type of "moral" doctor Ellis recommends. Dr. Murdoch gears
his advice toward reproduction, asking, "How many more of you are there?"
after only tipping his hat (176). After pointing out where the Fairchild dead
will be placed within the graveyard and how many children each is likely to
bear, he asks Shelley, "You — what are you going to do, let your little sisters
get ahead of you? You ought to get married and stop that God-forsaken mooning. Who is it, Dickie Boy Featherstone? I don't like the white of your
eye." The doctor then "all at once" pulls down Shelley's eyelid with his thumb
for a closer look. He continues his unsolicited proscription, saying, "You're
mooning. All of you stay up too late, dancing and what not, you all eat enough
rich food to kill a regiment, but I won't try to stop the inevitable" (177).

The doctor's disapproval of Shelley's "mooning" reflects a more generalized anxiety about the sexuality of single women during the 1920s. Marriage
is presented as a cure for "mooning," a label that might have been attached
to any type of mental or intellectual pursuit of a young girl, including not
only daydreaming but also "excessive" writing, bookishness, talking, unguided
walks or journeys, and unsanctioned fantasy. Any activity beyond either the
domestic realm or the "proper" pursuit of marriage was seen as suspect because
it might lead to either "unsuitable" marriage or spinsterhood. Dr. Murdoch
continues to expound on the unhealthy nature of Shelley's environment by
critiquing the family's habits: staying up late, combined with dancing and
rich food, are likely to cause disease, discomfort, death, or even worse, a type
of non-normative domestic life. Yet Welty shows her depiction of the doctor by presenting him as a buffoon, unable to make polite conversation, and
certainly unable to understand the ways of Shellmound, thus critiquing the

"moral" sex-oriented doctor. As they leave the doctor, all three girls vow that they will never marry, subverting medical (and social) authority.

The Family Romance

It is important to note that while Ellis and other sexologists were not ready to forsake the moral stance of doctors, they were able to understand the purpose of, and even approve to an extent, the sexual activity of unmarried young girls. In his chapter on "The Biology of Sex," Ellis notes the importance of the early tactile stimulation of young girls as leading to a type of normative sexuality, remarking that "the sexual awakening of girls at puberty shows itself in a desire for kisses and caresses rather than intercourse" (42). While Ellis overlooks the possibility that a young girl, even under a doctor's questioning, might admit only to this type of desire, he displays a progressive attitude in espousing any type of sexuality at all for girls of this age, an age when they were expected to be at the height of their "purity," both sexually and socially.

Welty, too, reflects the changing sexual mores of the period in respect to young girls, again, largely through Shelley, who is constantly made to defend her lack of marriage prospects. Within the southern belle ideal, the type of coquetry that leads to multiple dance partners and "harmless" flirtations is tantamount to social success; one who does not have these social skills is viewed as seriously defective. Shelley, as the oldest Fairchild daughter, is quite literally "out of order": she is not marrying on time (as noted by Dr. Murdoch and many others) and her sister has surpassed her. The discomfort with a younger daughter marrying before an older daughter extends beyond Shelley's emotions and the family's questions. Dabney seems to compensate for her unease with the disorder in another way. With her breathlessness and flushes, combined with her choice of a less than socially suitable groom, it is as if Dabney must over-act to perform the role of the bride. Dabney chooses her groom (and we can assume this choice is Dabney's, based on her active social life with other young men), then sexualizes her performance of the bride role[6]: "How beautiful she was — all flushed and knowing" (19). The combination of these actions hints at a certain urgency of the marriage, a need to prove the "wild" Fairchild women as marriageable and therefore completely socially viable.

Shelley's reaction to the events around her is not what the reader might expect. But what Shelley lacks in outward displays of jealousy, she makes up for in her reaction to Dabney's performative, normative sexuality. When Mr. Rondo, the preacher, comes to lunch, the Fairchilds begin the train trestle narrative. For the Fairchilds, this narrative serves as a quick character sketch and family history all rolled into one. It is as if the Fairchilds use this scenario to explain to themselves and to others their quirky brand of loyalty and bravery, as well as their "natural" tendency to become hapless survivors of near-tragedies. They use the story as a kind of boundary marker: Laura wasn't there, therefore she cannot fully participate in the telling or in Shellmound; she will always experience their world as a visitor. Robbie Reid was there but cannot understand. She will always be marked as "family by marriage" and she will never comprehend the Fairchild creed of loyalty to family and to family type. George must always play the role of romanticized defender because that is how his family sees him, just as Battle will always be the harried father because to be a Fairchild means a complete willingness to succumb to the quirk that has been assigned by the family.

Though Shelley is tapped by Battle to do the honors of storytelling, she cries, "Oh, Papa, not me!" and allows India to narrate (75). Shelley's cry serves as both an answer to his request that she tell the tale and as an answer to the novel's unasked question, "Why doesn't Shelley marry before Dabney?" As well as answering her father on the question of marriage and narration ("not me!"), Shelley also performs what we can assume will be her next step, should she continue to shun marriage: she hands the situation off to India. In this way, the telling of the tale acts as the feminine birthright to first marriage among sisters, a birthright still actively championed among some contemporary American families who feel that it is somehow "not right" to marry off a younger sister first. Within this schema, the narration of the family tale is distinctly feminized. While it might seem that George's bravery is at the center of the narrative, the sub-text and context of *the scene of the narration* indicate that much of the family history is based on the choices of its women, both about and within their marriages.

Shelley, however, has internalized the family rhetoric on conformity to type: she has become the sensitive, artistic daughter her family expects, but she has learned to play this role so well that she cannot conceive of integrating her current role with the role of bride. In essence, the Fairchild clan has begun to valorize familial role-playing and loyalty to family above all else, even the expansion of the clan through its progeny. Again, this shift in thinking remains consistent with the sexology of the time, particularly in light of

Ellis's claim that a declining birth rate would lead to a prosperous, resourceful nation (*Essays in War-Time* 29, 74). Despite the new acceptance of declining birth rates, Shelley herself is not insensitive to the events surrounding her. She expresses herself in a manner true to her family type, especially during the trestle narrative, just at the point when India relates Robbie Reid's outrage:

> Dabney cried, "You should have heard her!"
> Shelley went white.
> "Robbie said, 'George Fairchild, you didn't do this for me!'" India repeated.
> "Look, Shelley's upset."
> "Shelley can't stand anything, it looks like, with all this Dabney excitement," said Battle. "Now don't let me see you cry."
> "Leave me alone," Shelley said.
> "She's crying," India said, with finality. "Look, Mr. Rondo: she's the oldest" [79].

Dabney's cry of derision at the recollection of Robbie's behavior places Dabney herself at the center of the family narrative for a moment. More importantly, it also establishes Dabney as one of the arbiters of protocol, a position she has only begun to occupy as a bride, even if through a less-than-ideal (according to social standards) marriage. Shelley turns white not because of some unspoken sympathy with Robbie, but because she realizes that the familial acceptance of Dabney's judgment on Robbie signals that Dabney is no longer a child within the family. In short, Shelley has not been able to create a bulwark against her greatest fear — the disruption of the family — through her decision not to marry. India's exclamation for Mr. Rondo to "look" because "she's the oldest" emphasizes Shelley's relinquishment of the marriage order birthright. While she might have been in Dabney's position of marking family insiders and outsiders, she has now been reduced to the position of a child admonished not to cry, figuratively changing places even with India, who has successfully documented the family history for the minister.

Shelley realizes the exact nature of her familial displacement, making it all the more emotionally painful for her. She is, however, able to reconfigure her new position within the bounds of her sense of agency. Obviously, Shelley's reinterpretation of this transition cannot take place until her own narrative section of *Delta Wedding*; the reader needs Shelley's voice to know how she will re-position herself in the family. Yet Shelley's narrative voice alone is not quite forceful enough for such a task; instead, Welty allows her free reign for her "revenge" in the novel's only explicitly embedded text — Shelley's journal. Shelley writes:

> I heard Papa talking about me to Uncle G. without knowing I was running by the library door not to meet T. when he came in (but waiting, I did) and Papa said I was the next one to worry about, I was prissy — priggish. Uncle G. said nobody could be born that way, they had to be humiliated. Can you be humiliated without knowing it? I would know it. He said I was not priggish, I only liked to resist. So does Dabney like it — I know. So does anybody but India, and young children [111].

Shelley uses her journal not only as a creative outlet, but also as a form of emotional defense. She claims her agency as she writes, denying a past humiliation while asserting a preference for resistance to sexual advances, for the choice to resist. Further, she normalizes her sexuality by aligning herself with Dabney. This alignment is made possible through Shelley's view of Dabney's entire marriage not as an act of submission, but as an act of resistance. Shelley casts the marriage as Dabney's resistance to family norms, a kind of acting out against the social conventions that dictate that Dabney should marry from her own class. Shelley sees the marriage as a resistance to the family romance already in play, alluded to throughout the novel even in the descriptions of the family (their "lips caught, then parted, as if in constant expectation") and their postures ("now the two sisters stretched on the settee, each with her head elevated and her stocking feet in her sister's hair") (26, 22).

In his groundbreaking work on female sexuality, Robert Latou Dickinson, an American follower of Ellis, writes that the family frequently serves as "the love affair of youth" (299). Dickinson and the other sexologists draw on the Freudian concept of the family romance, but for them the family romance is even more literal than the Freudian construct. Throughout his chapter entitled "Family," Dickinson relates cases of incest in his patients' own words with no medical or psychological commentary other than a brief introduction that places family experiences as developmentally important in terms of sexuality. Interestingly, the term "incest" is never used, and the long line of case histories strung together without medical commentary serves to normalize the cases of incest that are reported within the text. One woman even notes her fiancée's regret "that I did not have intercourse with my brother. When he was twelve, a ten-year-old cousin who had not menstruated lived with his family and they had intercourse daily in the attic for three years" (313).

This pattern of case histories melded to present a unified whole serves to normalize a variety of sexual behaviors that might be considered deviant by conservative twenty-first century standards, as well as criminal in some cases. Dickinson further naturalizes a wide variety of sexual behavior — including pre-marital sex, "auto-erotism," child-to-child incest, homosexual sex, and celibacy — through his reliance on the sexual history's ability to speak for itself. When the history does not speak for itself, rather than offering medical commentary Dickinson takes the unusual step of supplementing his research with quotations from literary sources. These quotations do not serve as epigraphs or chapter subtitles; rather, they are fully integrated into the text of the case histories, often with little or no introduction and no explanation. In a section of his introduction to *The Single Woman* entitled "Unity," Dickinson comments on his methodology:

> The exposition quotes from poetry, letters, autobiographies and other studies by the single [person]. This is because literary material is from the raw stuff of case histories; literature only projects case material clarified and arranged in design. The violent and casual remarks of the sick about sexual life and desire often differ from poetry only as the latter has superior thought and form.
>
> The juxtaposition of poetry with the most extreme sexual statements and with detailed descriptions of the sexual organs is a way of saying that expression is from one origin; words and muscular movement are from the same impulse; poetry is heart-beat and music is the nervous system. The loose verbiage, cruder sexual manifestations, possible local inflammation and general illness of the patient are best understood if related in source with all human expression [xvii].

This methodology typifies the interdisciplinary aspects of sexology. In an ideology akin to late twentieth-century postmodernism, Dickinson valorizes the case history, Freudian psychology, a personal letter, and passages of poetry equally in terms of their commentary on human sexuality. Dickinson also remarks, "'Fact' and fiction each properly labeled may even be used in combination.... Witnesses of the ideals and standards of behavior of the past are ephemeral and in time fiction about them is the only fact that remains" (xvii). Like Welty (who uses songs, poems, slogans, newspaper articles, advertisements and other cultural materials in her writings), Dickinson draws on a wide range of cultural artifacts to craft a full picture of feminine sexuality. A further similarity in the methodology of Welty and Dickinson lies in their tendency to meld and fuse narratives together. If the reader is confused about the identity of a given narrator, the border between one narrative and the next, or the boundary between narrative and cultural artifact, then all the better. Because of the necessity of documenting changing conceptions of sexuality, both in medicine and in fiction, new narrative forms are born, and the new types of narratives are made to correspond to the nature of the sexuality they document. The enclosed narrative of earlier twentieth-century southern domestic novels cannot encapsulate a freely formed, fluid sexuality. The new narrative patterns reflect a sense of changing American mores: specifically, the notion that perhaps one type of sexuality, and even one type of specific sexual practice, is just as valid as another. Yet Dickinson pushes the point even further in his speculation that the literary artifact *is* a case study; it tells a sexual history that can be said to represent its cultural milieux.

Robert Latou Dickinson and the National Committee on Maternal Health

Dickinson was not alone in his groundbreaking sexology studies and methodologies. The support he garnered from a portion of the medical community may have been part of the reason he felt free to publish previously unavailable information in an innovative format. His support came from a committee that was formed in 1923, the same year as the setting of *Delta Wedding*. In that year, the National Committee on Maternal Health was formed, with the goal of following dual "lines of inquiry: first the actual sex life and endowment of socially normal persons as revealed in medical case histories; and second, the control of fertility by such measures as contraception, sterilization, therapeutic abortion and the prevention and relief of involuntary sterility" (Preface to *The Single Woman* v). Given these "lines of inquiry," the committee's name (The Committee on *Maternal* Health) seems ironic, especially since many of the above items under "inquiry" were controversial to say the least, and were procedures specifically designed to *prevent* motherhood. Dickinson's books within the series "Medical Aspects of Human Fertility," issued by the National Committee on Maternal Health, include titles such as *The Single Woman*, *A Thousand Marriages*, and *Control of Conception*. The rubric of "maternal health" seems designed, at least in part, to disguise the radical intent of the committee to distribute accurate information about sexual practices and effective birth control to the general public by way of like-minded practitioners. *Control of Conception*, for instance, credits Margaret Sanger, at the time an extremely controversial figure known for her birth control clinics, for aiding the committee to have "samples of nearly all contraceptive devices ... in hand" and "for the privilege of making records of their remarkably complete collection gathered in Europe" (vii).

Though the term "maternal" was gaining new, sexualized import with its medical and psychological association with birth control methods, it is important to note that this change did not happen overnight. Similarly, despite the progress that had been made on the contraception front, reliable methods of birth control were not universally available. Although the Committee for Maternal Health, along with other organizations at the time, worked to distribute information about birth control, this information was often inaccurate in the late 1920s and 1930s. For instance, douching was still touted "as a contraceptive measure" used "among the better conditioned classes in Europe and this country" (69). Further, Dickinson realized the social strictures that might prevent one from buying contraception, though it was available in many drugstores. To alleviate the problem of purchasing contraception, he makes mention of a class of "household remedies" that blend domestic work and sexology. Suggested "remedies" included douches and pre-coitus foams, mixed up at home from the "recipes" Dickinson provides, using soap, vinegar, alum, shaving creams, toothpaste, or even a Lysol solution (43). It is not difficult to imagine that these "remedies" might have caused a variety of gynecological problems, not to mention the physical discomfort and the probability of failure as birth control methods.

Though condoms were available, Dickinson remarks that they might be used with some reluctance by married couples, owing to the popular wisdom that "the condom is the great engine of debauchery and promiscuity" (62). Further, just how "available" condoms may have been, especially to women hoping to procure them on their own, remains debatable. Dickinson notes that condoms "are not uncommonly put up for sale and concealment in cigarette papers and in cigarette cases" (65). Even if a woman should ask her doctor or clinician for condoms, Dickinson recommends that "the husband be sent for, to be sure he treats his sheath properly; and, if each condom is used several times, that he knows how to clean and dry and keep it rightly" (66). Despite the supposed attitude of "openness" about female sexuality and health among the sexologists, it is clear that many felt that some tasks were better left to men. Even if the couple was able to procure this preferred method of birth control, the quality of the condoms that were available left much to be desired. Patients at one clinic reported a 50% failure rate for the condom as contraceptive measure. Condoms made of animal skins were very common, even though they had no elasticity. The advice that condoms should be washed and re-used repeatedly, and the notation that a single condom might last from three months to three years, made them far less effective than the condoms of the twenty-first century. Near the end of his section on the condom, Dickinson even offers up a recipe for the proper type of rubber for making condoms, complete with gram weight measurements and heating instructions. Presumably this recipe was intended for other medical experts, yet with ingredients such as glue, water, glycerin, and castor oil, the recipe appears less complex than the cake Ellen bakes at the beginning of *Delta Wedding*. Throughout *Control of Conception*, Dickinson, along with his assistant, Louise Bryant, treats the subject of sex not as an abstract medical field but as a real-life practice involving trips to the doctor, the drugstore, and even the kitchen. In short, rather than a mystery or a medical "problem," sex is integrated into the overall practices of lives, both feminine and masculine. Hence, Dickinson and Welty seem to construct their texts from the same principle of integration: Dickinson concerns himself primarily with incorporating the details of one's everyday life and circumstances into a full picture of sexuality, while Welty shows how one's sexuality functions in conjunction with the overwhelming details of domesticity.

In this same vein of integration, "maternal health" is used as a tool for the committee to gain recognition and financial support; The Committee for Maternal Health was incorporated nationally in 1931. It was also a buzzword (along with "fertility") for the investigation of sexual health, practice, and education — but most importantly, to research and educate on the topic of birth control. In this manner, the committee and its publication also worked to change the concept of the very term "maternity." If medical maternal research now included birth control, then maternity was no longer an "accident," a "natural consequence" or a simple mystery. Instead, the very word "maternal" might now carry the connotations of sexual choice and sexual agency, a marked change from Victorian American gynecology.

With the figure of Ellen, Welty also plays with the concept of what it means to be maternal. One of Ellen's primary characteristics, and one that separates her from the Fairchild brood, is a sense of frankness untainted by "feminine" whimsy. This frankness, in part, makes her one of Welty's more reliable narrators, as well as a somewhat reputable source for outside information on the Fairchild clan and their characteristics. We gather hints of Ellen's honesty as she narrates a dream, one that turns out to be heavy with sexual import, to her youngest child as a bedtime story. Within this act, Ellen draws on her frank nature to seamlessly blend the notions of the maternal and the sexual. In the paragraph preceding Ellen's telling of her dream, Bluet is described as "like a busy housewife" as she fills her days with the play that is the child's work. Directly before the narration of the dream, Ellen holds down Bluet's leg "which wanted to kick like a dancer's" (83). These two images, of Bluet as both housewife and dancer, serve as a miniature portrait of Ellen's struggle between the orderly world of the stereotypical southern maternal role and the "dark woods" realm of sexuality and the creativity of formulating one's own sensual life and persona. Though Ellen must literally hold Bluet down (or raise her within the confines of social norms), at the same time she has no qualms about privately telling Bluet her own sexual history (disguised as a dream), one that might have easily been incorporated into the 1920s and 1930s sexology studies of Ellis or Dickinson:

> "Mama dreamed about a thing she lost long time ago before you were born. It was a little red breastpin, and she wanted to find it. Mama put on her beautiful gown and she went to see. She went to the woods by James's Bayou, and on and on. She came to a great big tree."
>
> "Great big tree," breathed the child.
>
> "Hundreds of years old, never chopped down, that great big tree. And under the tree was sure enough that little breastpin. It was shining in the leaves like fire. She went and knelt down and took her pin back, pinned it to her breast and wore it. Yes, she took her pin back — she pinned it to her breast — to her breast and wore it — away — away" [83–84].

Because Ellen is describing something "lost" long before Bluet's birth, the facile interpretation of the pin becomes Ellen's lost sexual innocence. Yet I would argue that, because of Ellen's agency within the dream, as well as her agency in choosing to tell the sexual tale to her youngest female offspring, something else has been "lost." First, Ellen does not appear melancholy about this loss. Instead, she dresses up to meet it, putting on a beautiful gown, as though she would need to woo the thing lost. Also, she knows to look for the breast pin under a tree, where she finds it "shining ... like fire." As a symbol of Ellen's sexual agency and sensuality, the breastpin is not an object of remorse or pity, but something that still burns in Ellen's mind, something that she is capable of reclaiming, unlike sexual innocence. The halting, repetitive nature of Ellen's narrated act of reclamation — "Yes, she took her pin back — she pinned it to her breast — to her breast and wore it — away — away" — reveals Ellen's desire to see this dream come to fruition and to know herself as a sexual being, not only as a mother. Interestingly, after Ellen tells the dream, Bluet's leg is quiet, as though her mother has calmed the non-domestic "dancer" in her. The narrator remarks, "The dream Ellen told Bluet was an actual one, for it would never have occurred to her to tell anything untrue to a child, even an untrue version of a dream" (84). This story, however, does more than calm a restless child. Through the dream, Ellen offers a subtle pattern for sexual agency; she suggests that women have choices in terms of their sexual destiny, and that a sensual side awaits, to be pinned back to one's breast, whenever one wishes.

While Ellen reclaims her sensuality primarily within a dream, and not within her waking life, several parallel scenes within the novel suggest that the reclamation of a sexual self that is both maternal and sensual is not "only a dream." When Ellen does set off into the woods, she finds not the breast-pin, but a wayward traveling girl. At first Ellen cannot conceive of the girl's existence. She is white, alone in the woods, clearly running away, and unknown to Ellen and the Fairchild clan. Ellen notes her own surprise: "for a moment the girl was not a trespasser, but someone who lived in the woods, a dark creature not hiding, but waiting to be seen, careless on the pottery bank" (90). Like the breastpin, she is not so much lost as not yet found, or waiting to be found again. Yet the surprise almost proves too much for Ellen to comprehend, as she notes, "So she was white. A whole mystery of life opened up" (90). The mystery is not the girl's identity nor the fact that she could exist in the woods, but instead, the existence of unprotected female "virtue," or more accurately, unaccompanied and unbounded white feminine sensuality. Ellen expresses surprise that the girl is white; for her, white fem-ininity needs protection because of its very desirability. In contrast, Ellen views African American femininity and sexuality as invisible because her rela-tionship to African Americans is one of employer to employee. When the African American women she knows are not working for her (as in the case of illness), she infantilizes them, once again erasing any kind of sexuality. So, for Ellen, a black woman or girl alone in the forest might have been safe, because in Ellen's mind, her sexuality was invisible. A white woman or girl, in con-trast, represents other possibilities that Ellen has not yet accounted for, such as a white woman expressing sexual agency, or roaming through a forest.

Reading this scene as a parallel to the dream of the pin places the girl in the same position as the pin. She acts as Ellen's reminder that there is another way; white feminine sexuality is within easy reach, but it offers both pleas-ures and risks. Ellen seems to feel something like relief when George later tells her that he slept with the girl in the old gin: "She [Ellen] seemed to let go in her whole body, and stood languidly still under her star a moment, then pulled her apron where it still shone white in the dogwood tree and tried to tie it back on" (90). If George slept with or raped the girl, then Ellen was right: the unbridled sexuality of a young, single, white woman is dangerous, and Ellen is not obligated to go into the woods and pursue her lost sexuality again, whether in her dreams or in her reality. The "mystery" of a woman acting on her own is no longer mysterious. The girl cannot escape the social threat of sexual danger to young women who do what they please. Ellen may now tie on her apron, the talisman of her domestic role, without guilt. She has not "lost" an opportunity to craft her sexual life so much as she has narrowly escaped danger herself, a notion supported when the girl from the woods is eventually killed by the train. Ironically, the danger the girl encountered came from within Ellen's familial circle. Yet George's confession does not rattle Ellen; rather, it makes her correct on two counts: danger did come to the girl, and sexuality does, ultimately for Ellen, belong within the rubric of familial roles, not as an "outside" opportunity for women. Much like Laura, later in the novel (233), Ellen has seen the breastpin up close only to lose it once again.

Like Ellen, Laura adopts a sense of peacefulness on the subject of her loss, in her case, of the literal breastpin: "It was in the Yazoo River now. How fleetingly she had held to her treasure. It seemed to her that the flight of the ducks going over had lasted longer than the time she kept the pin" (236). Unlike Ellen, however, Laura does not have to console herself with a substitute for sexual agency within the chimera of domesticity or familial devotion — at least not yet. The new sexual possibilities opened to Laura by way of Shelley's refusal to marry, combined with her creative endeavors, and Dabney's marriage to a man outside the Shellmound social realm, suggest that Laura may have even more options for sexual agency because of the rapidly changing sexual climate of her time period. Laura McRaven is still a prepubescent — nine years old — in 1923, the year of the formation of the National Committee for Maternal Health, the largest federation of American sexologists up to that time. In 1942, four years before the publication of *Delta Wedding*, and in the year that would have been Laura's twenty-eighth, Planned Parenthood was formed from the American Birth Control League, with Margaret Sanger as its honorary chairperson. The event met with the following brief announcement in the *New York Times* on March 6, 1942:

> The Planned Parenthood Federation of America, Inc. is the new corporate name of the Birth Control Federation of America, Inc., according to the organization's board of directors. Dr. Richard N. Pierson, the president said the organization would continue to emphasize the proper spacing of children or limitation of births as dictated by medical or sociological conditions ["Parenthood Group Renamed" 23:7].

Given the increasing coverage of the birth control movement during the 1940s, and given Welty's annual trips to New York, as well as her position at the *New York Times Book Review* copy desk in the summer of 1944 (McHaney xiii), it seems likely that she would have been aware of these developments. In this context, Welty creates a character whose sexual awakening and transformation into adulthood parallels the rise of the sexology movement, which began with concerns over wartime birth rates and would later become, in effect, the birth control movement. Because of her young age in a rapidly changing sexual climate, Laura will not face the stifling binary choice of a large family or spinsterhood. Her choices for sexual identity and sexual agency will likely extend even beyond Dabney's groundbreaking choice of a husband who lies outside Shellmound's social norms.

The multiplicity of the voices that Welty uses to craft her narrative seems to stand, in a way, outside time. Because Laura McRaven hears the voices as a blend, as a force akin to the steady hum of the cotton gin, propelling her onward, the voices are inseparable. Each voice gives a message, either a command or request about what the "poor motherless girl" should or might do. Even the stories that the Fairchilds "tell on themselves" come to represent a demarcation of boundary lines, of who does and does not belong within the inner circle of Shellmound and why. Often these boundary lines are explicitly sexual. While class, race, and gender configurations might seem to place a character at a certain excluded or included position in terms of what "is" and "isn't" Fairchildian, it is ultimately a character's sexual behavior that cements that status. The most obvious example of this use of sexual or sexualized behavior as a family boundary can be found in the character of Robbie Reid. Much of the novel's surface-level confrontation — and, in fact, the novel's most explicit arguments — center on Robbie Reid's violations of the rules for sexual behavior. It is acceptable, for instance, to express a brand of sexual rebellion by marrying outside one's class (as in the case of both Dabney and Robbie Reid), but it is less acceptable to exhibit one's sexual desire and sexual need once the cross-class marriage has been made.[7] In short, just as the women will eventually inherit the control of land that does not belong to them,[8] they are also expected to inherit the family standard of sexual self-control for women. Even the most private searches for the "uncontrolled" sexual self (as with Ellen's) are likely to be, at best, futile. At worst, they may reveal "ugly" truths about sexual double standards both for men and women and between "blood" and "non-blood" Fairchilds. Any indiscretion on Dabney's part might be overlooked, while Ellen must be far more careful.

Without a mother, Laura has little guidance to sort through the cacophony of voices she hears and the various remarks she will make herself. She is the perfect fulcrum for the novel because she promises her reader early on, through her flighty yet detailed descriptions of her journey to the Delta by train, to absorb everything equally. This opening, in which the death of Laura's mother and the flight of a yellow butterfly seem to take on equal narrative weight, serves as a precursor to Laura's function. She is not a narrative filter, but a narrative sieve, letting everything through, merely stopping on certain events longer than others. Just as the train pushes her onward to Shellmound, so will the group force of the voices she hears there propel her narrative journey through the novel. Welty also implies that what Laura hears at Shellmound — stories of domesticity, sexuality, and the creative forces that bind and navigate the two — will inform her persona as she ages, making the Delta not a mystical southern fairyland, but a microcosm of contemporary United States culture bombarded by new voices about the changing sexual and domestic roles for women. While the daily details of each woman's role might seem virtually unchanged, many women would embark on a radical change in perception: they would begin to see themselves as integrated selves, not as "bedroom" selves one moment and "kitchen" selves the next. This type of ideological change sets the course for new literary models of domesticity and new modes of writing women's experiences.

Sexuality would not be the only visible changing facet of life for American women if we were to extrapolate the life of Laura McRaven. Even the train she travels on, the Yazoo, would eventually change from a small line with a conductor known by name (Old Man Doolittle) to part of a larger, national railway service bringing a constant supply of new goods to the Delta. Just as the ideal of individual, unfailing sexual "purity" for women would begin to falter and morph into new and multiple patterns of sexuality, so would the mythical nature of small, rambling railroad lines disappear in favor of national expansion of the webs of corporate railroads. Women, aided by various forms of technology, would become part of their own network. In the latter half of the twentieth century, we see a domestic ideological shift that allows women to see themselves as united because they are able to communicate with each other on daily matters through improved mail service and they are able to procure nationally known domestic products, making regional differences less common, and in many cases less desirable. The unification of north-south railway lines, which began in the 1880s, as well as other technological expansions throughout the late nineteenth and early twentieth centuries, brought about the mechanics of these changes. The resulting domestic changes would proceed slowly, culminating in the popular cultural ideal of domestic conformity in the 1950s. In short, once women could conceptualize their primary role as that of an integrated being (a goal advanced, in part, by changes in medical thinking about sexuality), not simply extensions of a kitchen or a child, then could they begin to see themselves as part of a larger domestic culture. Integrated sexual and domestic personae would pave the way for networked domestic communities. Domesticity existed not outside, nor tangential to, the developing medical and technological systems of the United States, but as an integral part of those systems.

Chapter Four

TRAINS, LETTERS, AND PICKLED PEPPERS
Lee Smith and the Effect of Railway Unification on Appalachian Domesticity

Path to Destruction, Path to Freedom: Railroads in Early Twentieth-Century Southern Literature

No one would deny the widespread influence of the railway train on the practices of segregation in the Reconstruction-era American South. Edward Ayers, in *The Promise of the New South: Life After Reconstruction*, depicts trains as the major site of racial conflict, noting that "most of the debates about race relations focused on the railroads of the New South" (137). Yet in the realm of southern literature, as in the realm of southern culture, rather than simply acting as a site of segregation, the train became intimately and symbolically linked with the divisions it enforced. In many ways, the train came to stand for segregation itself, as in the landmark 1896 Supreme Court case of *Plessy v. Ferguson*. Further, the train's rapid movement across regions, especially when this movement was from the North to the South, made clear the regional differences on the topic of race. North-South movement of the train engendered a color line where none had been; it forced the movement of passengers from car to car based on race alone. In the opening of *The Marrow of Tradition* (1901), Charles Chesnutt depicts a train from Philadelphia moving through Virginia. When the train crosses the Virginia border, the division of train cars, and the signage at the ends of the cars, becomes a literal rendering of the color line:

> The car was conspicuously labeled at either end with large cards, similar to those in the other car, except that they bore the word "Colored" in black letters upon a

white background. The author of this piece of legislation had contrived, with an ingenuity worthy of a better cause, that not merely should the passengers be separated by the color line, but that the reason for this division should be kept constantly in mind [513].

The train and its labeled cards, rather than the law, become the signs and the sites of segregation. Critics note the ways in which Chesnutt's train scene points to the primacy of race, drawing on the perspective of Dr. Miller (the black doctor who is forced to move to the "colored" car despite his purchase of a first-class fare and his companionship with a white doctor in that car) and his feeling that the division of race is far more "arbitrary" than the division based on class.[1] The train functions as the ultimate symbol of Jim Crow era racism in action, negating bonds of class, occupation, gender, and friendship, as well as the agency to choose one's surroundings.

The image of the train illuminates Reconstruction culture; it makes visible the racial inequity of the South as nothing else can. Yet the trains transported more than racist segregation policies. The newly unified North-South railway lines also brought new goods, services, and ways of viewing the world to previously isolated areas. These functions, however, are often hidden within the southern literary train's powerful associations with race and segregation law. The southern trains have been historicized as floating racial barriers, dividing the races, but also dividing the trains themselves from their additional cultural function as harbingers of economic and social change to those who did *not* travel on them. Further, in addition to constructing segregationist ideas and policies, railroads also played a part in constructing a new vision of white, southern femininity, one that offered new liberties as it took away others. *In Home on the Rails: Women, the Railroad, and the Rise of Public Domesticity*, Amy Richter claims that

> the railroad takes on significance because of its modern qualities — as a commercial space subject to the demands of the market, as a mobile space carrying people beyond local controls and knowledge, as a small and intimate space challenging notions of what constituted respectable contact among strangers, as a socially diverse and fluid space capable of blurring the lines of class and caste [5].

Richter portrays the train as a nexus of social issues, and as her title indicates, trains changed the very nature of domesticity. Although Richter focuses on the public domesticity within train cars and stations, trains affected the home as well. The specific ways in which southern literary trains have been politicized would seem to separate the train from individual southern homes altogether, but white southern women writers, like African American southern male writers before them, have also used trains symbolically in their writings. Because of the privileged racial and class status of many of these writers, the train symbolism they use is often both positive and negative: trains represent a new found freedom from a suffocating and isolating form of domesticity as well as varying degrees of destruction of regional domesticity and landscapes.

White southern women writers also draw on the narratives of black southerners such as Chesnutt when they cast trains as symbols of contrasting ideas. For just as a southbound train would (often cruelly and brutally) enforce and come to represent the color line, so could a northbound train bring about and come to represent freedom in the less racist North. Southern white women writers replicate this paradigm of railroad as both freedom and destruction in their early twentieth-century writings, even though their characters might never leave the house. The train becomes a symbol of freedom not because of the exodus it offers (though some southern women did leave home by train), but because of the material products it brings into homes and because of the new domestic ideologies that would come with those products. To a lesser degree, the train functions as a symbol of destruction in Appalachian domestic novels, as families leave the "hill country" for towns that have already been ravaged by industry. The same industrial forces (primarily mining and textiles) would later encroach upon their old mountain homeplaces, making the dream of a return to the hills an impossibility. Richard Gray describes this phenomenon in terms of the roads, rather than the railroads, that were built in the Appalachian region: "Roads were not the roads to freedom; on the contrary, they are conceived of as freedom's enemy, because they puncture the vacuum in which the aboriginal, pioneer liberty of the hill people was supposedly preserved" (305).

Because the railroads brought far more material goods to the rural areas than the roads, and at a faster rate, trains, especially in writings of the late twentieth century, appear in a more positive light than the roads that came before them. Later twentieth-century southern white women writers, in turn, would replicate the "train as freedom/train as destruction" paradigm, but with a twist. Because of their historical position, these writers, Lee Smith among them, would view trains more critically and with a greater degree of awareness about how trains would change lives, especially in the previously isolated Appalachian mountain region of the South. That is to say, Smith's historical distance from her subject allows her to blend the possibilities of freedom and destruction that the train offers, and to add to this mix the longstanding changes in domestic habits and ideologies the train would bring about, changes not yet obvious in, for example, the 1930s novels of Fielding Burke (pseudonym of Olive Dargan), another Appalachian writer. Rather than casting those who welcome the train and all it transports to the Appalachian region as either naïve or greedy, and rather than casting mountaineers as isolationists, Smith shows us characters who are flexible and creative, both in their dealings with harsh economic circumstances, and with their incorporation of new domestic ideologies into traditional foodways.

The Things They Carried: Railway Unification Day, Rural Free Delivery, and the Great Southern Mail Route

The changes in the kinds of goods and services available in rural southern areas, and the corresponding changes in domesticity in those areas, could not have happened without the introduction of standard gauge rails and the unification of local railway lines, particularly those that ran from the North to the South. The introduction of standard gauge rails ended an era of trains that served only the needs of intra-state commerce and transportation (Taylor 46). The movement toward the standard railroad gauge began in the 1870s, and was not complete until a massive southern switch-over that took place on Monday, May 31 and Tuesday, June 1, 1886. These dates were agreed upon by numerous southern officials from ten separate railway lines, and they became a two-day holiday for many families, who came from great distances to watch the crews perform the physical shifting of railway lines (Taylor 80–81).

The image of groups of southern families picnicking along the railroad lines as they watch laborers re-lay the rails works against much of what we know as the cultural history of trains in the South. Beyond the associations with racial conflict, other common late nineteenth- and early twentieth-century associations between the South and the railroad industry include Civil War evacuations of entire towns, Bull Run (a battle fought over a railroad junction), as well as post-war images of carpetbaggers and Depression-era mining towns and their early gravity-powered coal trains. Yet the families that watched the railway change-over day in 1886 represent a pivotal moment in a cultural change that would take place on what might be considered multiple, smaller scales of individual homes. Once the railway lines were unified to form efficient commercial and transportation routes to the North, southern domesticity, in both practice and ideology, would be radically and permanently altered.

Perhaps because of the "large-scale" images of southern trains as literal embodiments of the color line, as well as images of post-war industrialization, the changes in southern domesticity brought about by the train have not been closely examined within literary history. Yet there is evidence that access to a more efficient postal service as well as personal and business transportation changed the domestic practice of many southerners while also changing their ideas about what constituted a home and one's loyalty to the homeland.

In *Passage to Union: How the Railroads Transformed American Life, 1829–1929* (1996), Sarah Gordon notes that the fight for control of the railroads during the Civil War crystallized many of the war's ideological issues as they related to family and home:

> They (Northern businessmen) also saw in the railroad the ability to expand civilization beyond its historical boundaries, for the railroad seemed to promise that towns, cities, and industries could be put down anywhere as long as they were tied to the rest of the Union by rail.... The South saw land in a more traditional light, as home and heritage, not just as a natural resource to benefit capital and state. Southerners saw Northern advances as a kind of imperialism. The willingness of the North to put down roots anywhere in order to find profit demonstrated a lack of loyalty to place, an opportunism. Thus the definition of the Union as a commercial venture, controlled by private enterprise based in Northern cities, troubled the Southerners as much as the slavery issue [136].

While Gordon's North-South conceptualization veers toward dualism at times, she identifies the important difference that trains made in the regional, ideological vision of the home. That is, if every home could now be connected to every other home through a system of railways, then what was to make one home preferable to or different from another? This idea of the interchangeability of homes, and even towns and states, was undoubtedly problematic for many southerners, given southern cultural associations of family, land, and home. If many southerners considered one's ancestry to be almost *physically within* the land that one owns, then railway unification would have amounted to large-scale trespassing and grave robbing.

Yet Gordon also points out the changes in this mentality in the postwar years and after the unification of the rail system. Acquiring household and farm goods became top priorities within many homes, and the new unified railway system was able to provide them at a time when such provisions were scarce in the South. Gordon notes that although the mail-order business had been around since the 1830s, "it grew rapidly after the war with the introduction of mail-order businesses, such as Montgomery Ward, and farm tool companies, headquartered in Chicago, which sent catalogs and delivered goods throughout the country by way of the railroad" (169). While southerners' fears that whole towns would become interchangeable and rootless did not immediately materialize with railroad unification, the fear that homes could become more and more interchangeable, at least in terms of their household goods, did hold some truth. Ayers notes, "Parcels contained fashions from New York or patterns from Butterick, shoes from Massachusetts or suits from Philadelphia. No matter its contents, each box carried more than an inert product. It brought an implicit message: this is the new way of the world" (81).

The desire for these kinds of new household goods, as well as the depiction of trains rumbling through tiny Appalachian towns, figures prominently in the novels of Lee Smith. Two of Smith's novels in particular, *Oral History* (1983) and *Fair and Tender Ladies* (1988), chronicle the domestic changes in Appalachian homes throughout the early twentieth century. Smith weaves trains in and out of her plots as they bring new characters, family members, goods, and even new ideas into mountain homes. The changes wrought directly or indirectly by the introduction of train lines might be divided into several categories, including postal service (with sub-categories of mail-order goods, news media, and private letters), people (including exposure to new professions as well as new habits and foodways), new types of homes and family structures (such as the boardinghouse), and last, new home aesthetics and domestic ideologies brought about as a combination of the aforementioned additions to the home.

1864 marked the invention of the first railway post office, coinciding with a rapid increase in U.S. mail delivery efficiency due to the use of the steamship and the railroad, which replaced many routes that had been traversed by foot, horse, or boat ("Railroad Maps," Library of Congress web site). Yet even with these advances in mail service, many rural farmers went without mail for weeks at a time because there were no standardized mail routes: "[T]he farmer's main links to the outside world were the mail and the newspapers that came by mail to the nearest post office. Since the mail had to be picked up, this meant a trip to the post office, often involving a day's travel, round trip." Farmers would wait, often for a month or a time, to combine the post office trip with a trip to town for supplies, a practice also chronicled throughout *Fair and Tender Ladies* as Ivy wonders who will carry her letter to town for her, often including this question within the body of the letter itself ("History of the U.S. Postal Service," United States Postal Service).

In 1896, the Postmaster General began a rural free delivery program (RFD), including the first experimental routes in West Virginia, with a rather hostile response on many fronts. Critics cited the impractical and expensive nature of the program, but rural farmers "were delighted with the service and the new world open to them." One farmer remarked that "it would take away part of life to give it up" ("History," USPS).

Once only able to receive late mail, rural customers now had access to current publications, as chronicled by the fashion and food trends mentioned in both *Oral History* and *Fair and Tender Ladies*. New home goods became widely available by train transport, especially by mid–century, including home appliances, which Ivy links to changes in domestic intimacy when she remarks, "The divorce like the T.V. is the wave of the future it seems to me!" (277).

A more subtle change that occurred through the rapid delivery of mail was an increased sense of immediacy through letters. Just as a phone call, an email, or a text message today might take a different tone than a letter, a letter that would be received within days or weeks at most might have an altered tone from one that would take many months to arrive. The changed time table for mail delivery meant more conversational letters, rather than long epistles chronicling the important events of an extended time period. We see this type of change in Ivy's letters as they span from 1912 to the mid–1970s in *Fair and Tender Ladies*. During one of Ivy's last letters to her daughter, Joli, Ivy adopts such a sense of immediacy as to place herself within Joli's kitchen, telling Joli to "put down everything you are doing right now and listen to me. I mean it. Make yourself a cup of coffee and sit down and put your feet up" (279). In this instance, Ivy is able to place herself in Joli's kitchen through the epistolary form, an act that would have required much more imagination in 1900, the year of Ivy's birth and the beginning of widespread changes in the standardization of rural mail delivery.

Better mail routes utilizing the railroads brought with them better passenger routes, sometimes quite literally. An early 1900s advertisement for the "Great Southern Mail Route" encourages passengers to take this train because of reliable, regular service that would allow them to "go through as fast as the mail" (Gordon 171). With new routes, new visitors to rural areas became common, particularly in the Appalachian region in the early 1900s, when profitable gravity-driven coal lines had encouraged investors to build and then re-sell steam powered lines that paralleled the old mining lines (Hubbard 299). In Smith's novels, the new passenger lines lead directly to education (in both an academic and a worldly sense) for women, as seen in the train arrival of both Richard Burlage in *Oral History* and Gertrude Torrington in *Fair and Tender Ladies*. Neither Ivy nor Dory, however, is able to leave the pull of domestic duty and family loyalty. Because of the arrival of these "outsider" characters by train, both Dory and Ivy (Smith's native Appalachian characters) are haunted by images of unlived lives in the big city, and are forced to examine the domestic role as a career choice rather than as part of a "natural" or inevitable system.

With the new travelers, new types of homes emerge as well, as in Majestic's boardinghouse (which becomes Ivy's workplace) and Richard's spells of boarding with Appalachian families, followed by the residence he makes in a corner of the schoolhouse. Just as women must consider domesticity as something other than natural after exposure to educational and vocational opportunities, so must they realize that there is no one type of family dwelling after witnessing new family organizations and semi-public dwelling spaces. Further, the visitors bring with them an outsider perspective, one that encourages the native Appalachian characters to adopt outsider status for a moment and to re-examine their communities with new eyes. As Ivy remarks, "Miss Torrington is a missionary. This means that she has come from the Presbyterian Church in Boston to visit the school here, and describe the conditions. I cannot imagine what she will say. It seems to me that conditions are very good" (95). While Ivy does not disparage local conditions, Miss Torrington's presence forces her to re-examine, to try to "imagine what she will say" about both school and home life from an outsider position. Ivy's imaginings of another life do not conclude with Miss Torrington's visit, however. Smith includes decades of Ivy's letters to Miss Torrington within the text of the epistolary novel, and Ivy imagines both Miss Torrington's outsider perspective as well as her own alternate path had she moved to Boston.

While postal service, new family structures, and visitors changed the domestic aspect of rural communities, these categories of change also combined to effect subtler ideological changes within domestic culture. These changes in domestic ideologies came about as direct products of the new train lines and their new locations in rural neighborhoods. In a chapter entitled "Why Bigger Towns Get Better Service," Gordon comments on the legal right, legislated by individual states, of towns and cities to petition for increased service, multiple stops within one city, cheap fares, and even comfortable depots and waiting areas. Yet these provisions often required two hundred to three hundred petitioners, a number easily obtainable in a centralized town, but far less attainable in rural areas (208–09). In the most basic terms, the states' laws that required train companies to act as utilities (rather than as private corporations) benefited cities and towns while ultimately punishing rural areas. Petitions legislated where railroads would build lines and when the trains would run. Thus, in a rural area, one might find a train running through one's residential backyard several times a day and have little or no recourse against the service provider.

Besides creating an even greater class and regional difference between town and rural areas, the new routes changed domestic ideologies, even if the train's nearest stop was dozens of miles away. The habit of watching a train pass through town on a daily basis facilitated a change in the outlook of many rural southerners. The visible railroad line positioned the home, quite literally, as one link in a long chain of family homes. Even without direct access to the train, each home in the railroad link was likely to be supplied with the same kinds of goods from centralized points near the depots, such as town general stores. In this way, the kitchen (and particularly the kitchen with a direct view of a train line, common in many Appalachian mining towns by the 1920s and 1930s) could no longer be considered as the supply center for an isolated hub of domestic activity. The view of the train forced homemakers to think of themselves as sub-depots on the rail, with *the train and its provisions*, rather than the home and *provisions made or manufactured within the home*, as central to daily life and survival.[2] The thrust of this shift in thinking was that the train, not the home itself and its domestic practice, served as the primary domestic provider.

This change in domestic ideology is reflected in Ivy's description of Diamond in her first letter to Silvaney from her new home. The centrality of the train figures in the narrative construction of the letter; through Ivy's persona, Smith positions the train in the heart of the letter, both in terms of content and structure. Through Ivy's meditation on the train, Smith conveys multiple aspects of coal town life, including its financial, political, and social structures. She also positions the train as a common element, weaving in and out of Ivy's description of her new life. Further, Smith allows the train center stage, giving it a longer portion of the letter than Ivy's description of her own home or her pregnancy. Smith positions the train contiguous to descriptions of Ivy's own new home with Beulah (including its positioning in the social/physical hierarchy of homes) and her physical/sexual experience of pregnancy ("The caboose is full of boys that tip their hats and yell and wave to little John

Arthur and me, but they do not look at me <u>like a girl</u> since I am so big now. I can not get use to it" [135, emphasis Smith's]). By using the train as a connector not only literally, between mining town and city, but narratively, between home and family, Smith acknowledges, and even insists upon, the train's place within the domestic realm. Ivy turns and returns to the train again, marveling at its presence in her own daily life:

> But I see I have forgotten the main thing probably, which is the railroad that cuts through this bottom like a knife following Diamond Creek and then the Big Sandy — next stop, Hazard, Kentucky. The train comes along every morning and every evening just about suppertime, and I reckon I will *never* get used to it! I still drop whatever I am doing and fly to the door just to see it pass through the town, the locomotive puffing out great clouds of white smoke and shooting up columns of red sparks. It gives you a real excited feeling to watch the train. And sometimes when I take little John Arthur downtown to get him out of Beulah's hair — for she has been short with him lately, ever since Curtis Junior has come — why then sometimes we will put our hands on the track and see can we feel it vibrate, or put our ears down there and see can we hear it hum [134].

Here, Ivy uses the same language — "I will never get used to it" — to describe the physical presence of the train as well as her new sexual status as a pregnant woman — "I can not get use to it" — uniting the changes in her body and her family life with the technological change that has altered the community. Further, Ivy marks domestic time — the daily event of supper and the interruptions in her chores — by the passing of the train, further mapping the image and sound of a passing train onto her domestic realm. Her "real excited feeling" does not pull her out of the domestic realm; instead, Ivy incorporates the rhythm of the train into her domestic routine, creating a new kind of rural domesticity that is tied to a larger cultural and technological force. The train — not her new home, nor her pregnancy — becomes the "main thing," in Ivy's words, that shapes the new variety of mining town domesticity that she reports to Silvaney in her letter.

In contrast to Smith's reflective and self-conscious positioning of the train as central to Ivy's life, earlier authors of Appalachian fiction depict the train as a means to an end, a symbol of the ever-present option of flight and escape. In *Call Home the Heart*, Olive Dargan (pen name Fielding Burke) explores the changes wrought on mountain life by the exodus of young people for work in mill towns. Dargan's narrative also documents a fictional version of the 1929 cotton mill strike in Gastonia, North Carolina. Interestingly, however, the emphasis of the novel is on "the experience of mountain *women*, as they struggle to reconcile their traditional status as matriarchal keepers of the house with the new demands made on them by an oppressive system of wage labor and the poverty and deprivation attendant upon it" (313, emphasis Gray's). In accordance with Dargan's historical proximity to her subject matter (*Call Home the Heart* was published in 1932, just three years after the strike), the train of her novel shows a marked contrast to the ideological centrality and progressive nature of Smith's trains. Rather than acting as a "main thing," for Dargan, the train is simply the escape route that Ishma Waycaster, the union organizer and protagonist of the novel, uses when she fails personally and professionally and wants to return to the hills: "Half a block away she saw the lights of the station, and pushed toward it, coming up just as the train pulled in. It was a coach train, the 2 A.M. for Spartanburg. At Spartanburg one took the 6 A.M. for Asheville. From Asheville one could go — well, anywhere" (384). Here, the train appears as a timetable; it can take one "anywhere" at any time. Hence, its phenomenal nature lies, not in the fact that it changes the ideas and outlooks of even those who do not board it, but wholly within the still-new, practical possibilities for escape that it holds out, even for a woman in the middle of the night.

Smith, in contrast, writing from an era of air travel and computer technology, emphasizes the train's ideological effect on a town, not only the changes it brings to the town's material culture, but also its status, unlike the mine (which only produces raw materials), as the "main thing." The train, in this case, is central not only because of what it transports, but because it forces each unit of the town — down to even the smallest home — to see itself as integrated into a national technological network. Dargan's train *is* escape, while Smith's train represents a town's reaction to the process of being networked to a nation — physically, materially, and ideologically.

Further, the concept of networking is reiterated by Smith's own narrative technologies.[3] Smith represents this climate of change not only through the plot machinations of both novels, but also through networked narrative structures, that is, narratives that emphasize both the individual home as a single point (or "depot") in a larger regional, and even national, community. Smith also produces networked narrative structures by combining the large-scale technology of the train with domestic life and daily routine, with no boundary between public and private realms. The ideology of the network appears in Smith's work on a structural level when she utilizes the traditions of the epistolary novel as well as those of the oral history. Further, she "networks" *Oral History* structurally by creating a series of narratives, one after another, separated by each narrator's name as a title of his or her account.

This type of group oral history, in which each narrator re-tells a portion of the previous events from a different vantage point, contains within it the idea that each of these narratives and each of the homes described within each narrative, is, on a fundamental level, equal, if not interchangeable.

We see the effects of this type of diffusion of region-specific domesticity across the twentieth century when we compare Smith's work to Glasgow's early twentieth century novels. For instance, in *Virginia* when the title character moves to Matoaca City, West Virginia, she begins an obsessive project of precisely recreating the household traditions of Dinwiddie, Virginia, only to meet with little success and open hostility from her neighbors. It does not occur to Virginia that she might adopt the bourgeois habits of her neighbors. These neighbors serve little purpose other than as a foil to Virginia's unfailing domestic "perfection." In *Fair and Tender Ladies*, however, Ivy, more accustomed to the idea of her home and even her community as a nodal point on the railway chain, quite literally takes whatever the train will bring into her new domestic realm in Diamond as she embraces new habits and new goods. Of course, social class undoubtedly plays a role in this difference. Ivy is poor and ready to grasp new goods as she can afford them, while Virginia has been schooled in a strict middle-class domesticity that looks askance at most things new and different. However, I would argue that the logic of multiple domestic narratives with no "master narrative" (as seen in Smith's novel) is reaffirmed and underscored by the rapid exchanges of domestic information and goods facilitated by the trains.

Smith chooses the shapes of oral history and the epistolary form to convey a multiplicity of domestic narratives and a diffused domesticity. But while Smith adopts the traditions of the oral history and the epistolary novel, she also adapts and manipulates these traditions to suit her depictions of rugged mountaineers who follow a strict code of simultaneous independence and communal activity. These communities respect the Appalachian ideal of independence (as in the Rowe family refrain of "we will not be beholden") at the same time that they promote certain features of communal living, particularly in the areas of husbandry, food preparation, and child care. The "commune of independents" version of domestic life experienced by Smith's characters, like the incorporation of train technology into the home, also manifests itself in the narrative structure of short, interlaced narratives (either as letters or as individual oral histories). Each individual Appalachian family operates in the manner of an individual narrative piece: as a functional piece of an integrated whole. Smith's narrative technologies embody the notion of domestic life as a group product and a shared experience made up of, for instance, Rose Hibbits' housekeeping, Granny Younger's homemade medicine, and Ora Mae's pickled peppers. These entities might be found in a number of homes other than their points of origin, but each product becomes necessary to reasonably comfortable survival. Thus, narratives come to function as domestic products. The reader often follows a literal domestic product (including the quilts and letters in *Fair and Tender Ladies*) from home to home throughout the overall narrative. The return of a remedy or a jar of pickles in a new narrator's tale often reminds the reader that she is hearing the same tale again, from another perspective. The physical products of domesticity mark domestic time while signaling the presence of multiple domestic viewpoints within a single community. In this schema of fragmentation within unification, Smith depicts a unified regional domestic culture in which each kitchen along the fragmented mountain landscape belongs to a single family, but holds the tradition and the products of the community as a whole.

Storms Brewing: The Appalachian Kitchen as Indicator of Social Change in Lee Smith's Oral History

When the Appalachian home of the early twentieth century became a unit connected to other similar units across a long stretch of landscape connected only by trains, the transmission rate of images and tales of the "perfect home" increased dramatically through newspapers, magazines, and their advertising. Yet, as we might expect, the Appalachian home itself would not change as rapidly as this new onslaught of images and information could now reach it, and in some cases, would not change much at all for decades. In Lee Smith's novel *Oral History* (1983), the home of the first half of the twentieth century is a site of social and cultural tension, a liminal space bridging death and survival as well as old and new ways of living in the Appalachian region of Virginia, particularly in the period of the 1920s to the 1940s. This portrayal serves as a marked contrast to the type of home that appeared in the popular cultural imagination during this time: a place of warmth, safety, and above all, stability.

Yet Smith resists more than the paradigm of kitchen as warm, safe, happy enclave; she continues to subvert traditional domestic ideology (such as the nineteenth- and early twentieth-century notion of the angel in the house) with female characters who find domestic life problematic for a variety of reasons. However, these "problematic" homemakers are not isolated misfits. Each woman's struggle reflects the spirit of her decade. In other words, Smith's characters can be seen as responding to, and ultimately resisting, the domestic advice of their time, specifically, the onslaught of hygienic, practical, and moral advice for the establishment and maintenance of the home found in women's magazines in the early twentieth century, and instead, creating their own varied and individual domestic ideals.

The crafting of personalized domestic rituals did not mean, however, that Appalachians were entirely immune to the mass media. Even while depicting "problematic" homemakers (those who undertake the role begrudgingly or only with the help of magic), Smith clearly places her characters within the reach of mass media influences (Pearl, a child of the 1930s, not only reads *Life* magazine, but collects its photographs for her scrapbook, cataloguing images of plains, deserts and violent storms rather than images of her family or the surrounding mountains). Here, Smith shatters another myth about Appalachian culture as well: that Appalachians lived, during the twenties, thirties, and forties, in a subsistence economy, free from the desire for store-bought dresses, canned goods, and kitchen appliances, and tied to the coal mines through the company store and its own closed-circuit economy. Coal miners and their families were often dependent on the mining companies to the extent that they were paid in scrip (an alternate form of money, redeemable for goods only at the company store) (Bernstein 365). Yet despite their dependence on the company, according to some cultural critics, Appalachian miners may have put an even *greater* value than their urban counterparts on modern kitchen conveniences now available to miners by train transport, such as canned and pre-prepared foods.

In *Paradox of Plenty: A Social History of Eating in Modern America*, Harvey Levenstein notes that "poor Appalachian farmers shunned tasty country hams in favor of water-logged canned ones; they sold home-grown vegetables to buy the brand-name canned variety" (27). A sociological study conducted in the early 1940s by Margaret Cussler and Mary L. de Give on the eating habits of rural southerners indicates that store-bought foods were used when entertaining either out-of-town guests or local guests on special occasions. Cussler and de Give note one respondent's remark, "We like country ham for ourselves, but when we have company we feel like we ought to have something else" (113). Another respondent takes offense at the visiting preacher's question "Who ever heard of having ice cream and cake out here?"

She cheekily replies, "Why we have ice cream and cake twice a week, sometimes more" (113). Cussler and de Give add that "canned asparagus or boiled ham or bananas may be served, and special efforts are made to serve the meal in accordance with the urban standards expounded in a magazine like *Woman's Home Companion*" (113). Therefore, when Smith depicts Pearl, an avid magazine reader, as a young woman bent on putting up the canned peppers in red and green layers to make them "pretty," she is not only fashioning an artistic misfit character but also documenting the influence of women's magazines and other forms of popular media on Appalachian culture during the 1930s. Smith allows her female characters to create travel fantasies, artistic outlets, and even new and more urbane personalities through the work that they perform in the home.

We can read Lee Smith as resisting the popular notions about American and Appalachian domestic life in three distinct ways. She resists the notions 1) that every Appalachian home was the essence of physical and emotional warmth and safety prescribed by the American cultural imagination, 2) that every Appalachian homemaker was concerned with the basic needs of her family to the exclusion of the thought of herself as a "professional" with an occupation outside the home, and 3) that Appalachian homes and Appalachian homemakers were beyond the physical and cultural reach of the mass media during the 1920s through the 1940s (a myth refuted also by the history of the railroad in the region).

Smith cuts through the domestic mythology of Appalachia by depicting turbulent homes as well as misfit and even "witchy" homemakers in *Oral History*. Yet she aligns these "misfit" homemakers with their more traditional sisters, women who valiantly use the kitchen as a means of escape, a place to dream about the ways that life might be different if only one ate different foods, or prepared or ate them in different ways. Smith's characters react in one of two ways to the kitchen: either they fight its confines with their own magical powers and spells (as witches and healers) or they try to alter the food itself (as traditional homemakers). The wish to alter the food acts as a kind of incorporation fantasy: if I eat the food that belongs to a different life, then I will have that different life. By placing the "witches" and those affected by the incorporation fantasy in direct comparison, Smith seems to make their actions interchangeable. In other words, the power to change what the family consumes is itself magical. Thus, Smith reevaluates kitchen work, casting it as a collection of powerful, transformative actions rather than a series of mundane tasks.

In addition to writing characters that subvert the popular notions of kitchen culture, Smith creates a subversive type of narrative structure within *Oral History*. The novel is structured not only by chapter divisions, but also by subdivisions of multiple narrators. Each new narrator is introduced by his or her name as the title of the chapter section. This type of structure not only reflects the "feel" of an oral history, it also focuses on the individuality and individual struggles of each Appalachian. Yet because it functions as a collection of highly individualized narrators, the narrative highlights the ideological comparisons Smith makes in a way that a more traditional narrative would not. For instance, a witch and an "artistic" homemaker coexisting within a sustained third-person narrative might seem to be rather fantastic creations, highlighting the narrator's own thoughts and fears of the kitchen. But when allowed to "speak" under the subtitle of their own names, Smith uses her characters to craft the comparisons of witches, healers, and traditional homemakers in more subtle ways, largely by placing these characters and their narratives in close proximity to each other within the text. Smith blurs the boundaries between homes not through her characters' actions but through her own careful narrative structure. Thus, when Granny Younger walks down to Pricey Jane's home to help her give birth, and the narrative voice then switches to Pricey Jane (with only the dividing line of her name between the two narratives), we see that the folk healer and the traditional homemaker are one and the same. Both contain transformative powers overly contained and constrained by the space of the home. As Pricey Jane says,

> There's not any reason to leave, and no place to go if she went. None of the women-folks do much traveling. Oh, she's been to Granny Younger's, and over to Rhoda's cabin on Hurricane, and down to Joe Johnson's store in Tug, and to meeting when Brother Lucius comes and holds it beneath the big sycamore down at the mouth of Grassy, and other places. But mostly Pricey Jane stays home, and Almarine brings it all back. Wild roses from along the creekbed, storebought shoes from Roseann, a cardinal feather, an ironstone platter with a yellow house painted on it he got from a woman in Black Rock [70].

Pricey Jane contradicts herself when she says that the women do not travel. Rather, they are always traveling, making the transformative journey into the homes of other women, affecting the health and happiness of each other's families each time that they bring over something to eat or a new healing spell or witchcraft trick. In Smith's narrative, it is their comparatively short journeys, not the journeys of the men, that are well documented in deed, detail, and result. When the men walk away from the hollow, however, it is as though they walk off the face of the earth. Smith rarely follows them, except, as in the case of Almarine, when they go in search of a wife. And, while Almarine may bring back the goods from the "outside" world, it is Pricey Jane who arranges, wears, and decides how to use these goods. Almarine may "bring it all back," but Pricey Jane, like the other mountain women, decides how, when, and where the goods will be displayed and consumed. She has the ultimate power to decide how much influence the outside world will have on her family. She also has control over the ratio of store-bought goods to those found or made in her home. Pricey Jane subtly displays her own sense of control as she lists the objects Almarine has brought back, alternating natural objects with bought goods. The platter with a house painted on it functions as the last object in this lineup in a particularly telling way. Pricey Jane is well aware that Almarine will continue to offer her the goods she desires, along with the power to consume them, when she notes that he has offered her, quite literally, a house on a platter.

The very structure of Smith's writing re-configures Appalachia as a culture of individuals, relating their struggles not only to the hardships of Appalachian life but to the larger forces at work on American women in particular, in the form of the pervasive current domestic ideals. I want to resist the reading of Smith's work as (in the words of one critic) "books for people who want to read what they think of as 'Southern' fiction" (Reed 23) because, particularly in her Appalachian fiction and in *Oral History* especially, Smith writes against the grain of what we think of as Appalachian fiction and what many think of as Appalachian culture. Smith's characters are individuals, not stereotypes, and their struggles with domesticity and the domestic role reflect those of the early twentieth-century domestic woman and include personal interest or talent versus care of the family, emotional duty versus material duty, and creativity versus utility in the home arts. A secondary struggle for each character includes responding to the popular culture wisdom of the day about how to perform the domestic role to perfection.

Yet not all of Smith's characters act on their own beliefs about the importance of the domestic role. Granny Younger, like the contradiction in her name, resists a domestic role for herself, while encouraging Almarine, upon his return to the mountains, to find a wife because he needs the traditional, but undefined "woman's touch in the house" (36). Granny Younger makes this recommendation even though she has achieved what is, in the terms of the Appalachian community, a professional role as a healer, one that brings her a good deal of fame. Time seems not to touch Granny Younger; her usefulness is not circumscribed by her family's needs. Her own sense of what is domestic extends to the acts of premonition and spiritual/medical care for others.

The wife Almarine chooses is, much like Granny Younger herself, untrained in domestic skills but talented in areas outside her own home. Cast as a witch, Red Emmy has trouble becoming a homemaker. As Granny Younger notes (about a scene she did not witness), "She looked like all the sadness in the world was in her heart. She knowed it [the successful management of home and family] couldn't happen, that is why" (49).

Red Emmy's role extends beyond that of an antagonist "witch"; she is domesticity gone sour, exposing the worst-case consequence of a confining domestic role. Smith details Emmy's domestic difficulties — not with farm chores, but with smiling and being nice (53). Further, she must struggle to find a sexual role that can be reconciled with "pleasant" domesticity, a struggle represented by Emmy's vampiristic "riding" of Almarine (or using his body as a vehicle for travel) during the night (53). Instead of Granny's recommendation that a woman service him, Almarine finds himself in service to a woman who cannot be contained by the physical or psychological bounds of her home.

Granny Younger and Red Emmy do not fit the community's standards for domestic women; their talents fall so far from traditional roles that each is depicted as a woman with supernatural powers. Unlike Emmy, Granny Younger does not pretend to be domestic. At a picnic, she clearly defines her own role: "Womenfolks and the gals carries the cookpots around. Now you won't catch me a-carrying no cookpots. But I have borned my share of these folks, and I am an old, old woman, and I aim to do as I please" (38). Granny's short statement performs several functions: first, she separates herself verbally from "womenfolks": she does not perform their tasks, therefore she can not join in their community. Second, she defines her duty as already completed: she has "borned" these people, therefore she is exempt from feeding them. Last, she calls on her age as an excuse, though her age has not stopped her from performing as a healer. Therefore, her last statement seems the most accurate, and one that most women of the early 1900s were unable to make: "I aim to do as I please."

Smith links Granny Younger and Red Emmy the witch as the positive and negative forces acting on Almarine as he sets up house. After seeing Red Emmy, Almarine approaches Granny for a love charm. She refuses him although she was able to help, and her butter refuses to form in the churn that day, because, as Granny says, "butter won't come on a lie" (46). Here, Smith depicts the incompatibility of magical powers, or talents in areas outside the home, and domesticity. Later, Red Emmy puts a curse on Granny for spying on her with Almarine (52). While Granny uses her powers for good (to heal and to deliver babies), Red Emmy has "fucked with the devil" (in the words of Granny Younger). Yet Smith binds them together through their struggle for Almarine's soul as each woman tries to establish him within her version of ideal domesticity. In this way, each woman works toward the same goal of caring for Almarine (though by very different means) and establishing his family line. Granny Younger urges Almarine to take another, non-witch woman for a wife, while Red Emmy attempts to defy the curse of being an isolated mountain witch by playing house. That these two very different women (one old, one young, one a witch, one a folk healer) could even temporarily value traditional domesticity over the use of their own powers forms a commentary on the strength of a twentieth-century domestic ideal. This new ideal was not one of effortless work (like the earlier nineteenth-century ideal), but one of woman as the feminine bedrock of order, thrift, and physical well-being. Smith's characters are only partially able to escape the traditional role of mountain domestic farm wife, which, in 1900, required ten hours of labor in winter and thirteen in the summer (Mintz and Kellogg 104). Each woman possesses talent and magical power in abundance, yet, when it comes to the care and feeding of a handsome, respected man, the domestic ideal becomes far stronger than even magic.

Smith's comparison of magical power and domesticity draws on the domestic ideology of the period, that of equating good housekeeping with morality, and investing the kitchen itself with a kind of mystical, magical, even foreboding aura, an attitude that would lead to magazine articles with titles like "Reading Your Character in Your Kitchen" (*Ladies' Home Journal* March 1933). This article asks women, "Did you ever consult *your* kitchen? If you really want to find out something about your inner self that one room will give you a truer character reading than the stars, your palm, the tea leaves or a crystal ball. Try it some day after luncheon" (Bane 34). If the kitchen itself held the magical key to one's character, then woe to the woman who was absent from her kitchen in order to perform spells or healings of her own. Smith's women get what the magazine's editors might have thought that they deserved: Granny Younger is isolated in her old age, and Red Emmy is thrown out of Almarine's home while pregnant because he claims that he "won't have no witch-children in my holler" (55). Through the public condemnation of these two characters, Smith critiques the hegemony of traditional domestic roles and shows the unfortunate alternatives to these roles through characters who learn that the "magic" of domesticity dominates their own talents.

As *Oral History* moves from the early 1900s to the Depression-era 1930s, witches and folk healers give way to women who are simply different from the pervasive domestic ideal. In this period, the ideal shifted from an expert in organizational and hygienic skills to a thrifty homemaker able to manage her family on pennies a day. One school of thought in the creation of this new ideal offered women's self-sufficiency as the cure to the Depression, and "in 1931 sales of glass jars reached an eleven-year high even though demand for store-bought bottled and canned foods declined ... (as) many Americans tried to return to an earlier state of self-sufficiency" (Mintz and Kellogg 138).

Though the Wade family of Smith's novel arduously undertakes the task of canning during the 1930s, the women themselves are torn between the period's grand ideal of material self-sufficiency and the necessity of taking emotional care of one's family. As Sally Wade helps her mother can tomatoes during a thunderstorm, her mother undergoes one of her "spells," periods of incoherence and aimless wandering through the mountains. But Sally stands fixed in the kitchen, unable to run after her mother, unable, as it turns out, to save her mother from an impending suicide:

> That was the first thing I had to deal with, whether or not she had put in the sugar yet or whether I ought to put it in. So I had to get me a spoonful of tomatoes, and blow on it to cool it off, and taste it, and then add the sugar and some salt and cook it down before I could put it in the jars. All the time the wind was rising, and the storm was coming on, and I had an awful empty space in my stomach because I knew that something was wrong [246].

The force of domestic habit, the idea that the law of the kitchen is order, is too strong for Sally Wade. In this scene, one that will haunt her, the kitchen loses its power of order and comes to represent a space of emotional confusion. She finds that she must choose between emotional intelligence (which tells her to save her mother) and a powerful need to turn the fruits of the land into practical goods in an organized, ritualized manner. From this scene she learns that, despite what she has been taught as her mother's helper, an emotional crisis may be more important than several pounds of lost food. In her mind, the kitchen becomes a place where she learns to mature in habit (to help her mother with chores) and as a young woman who must now grieve for her loss.

The loss of Dory, the girls' mother, carries added symbolic weight because of the manner of her death. Although Sally tries to conceal her mother's behavior, Dory habitually walks along the railway, presumably thinking about her former lover, Richard Burlage, the schoolteacher who promised to take her away on the train to a new life in the city. Even before Richard's departure, Dory seems to fetishize the train itself, asking Richard to describe the train journey rather than the life they would have together (159). When Richard departs without her, Dory begins her walks by the railroad tracks, continuing them even after she forms a new family, until she "fell — or laid down — on the spur line, and the train cut off her head" (245). Here, Smith reveals the danger of the train's promise of new domestic lives, particularly when those promises are made in great detail and then abandoned.

Even with their mother gone, the girls know that the kitchen tradition of canning must continue. A year after her mother's death, as Pearl (Sally's sister) helps her ever-practical aunt Ora Mae make ready red and green peppers for pickling, Pearl has a new idea about the presentation of the pickles. She wants to layer the rings in red and green rows of stripes, asking, "Wouldn't that be pretty?" Yet Ora Mae resists the combination of what she sees as sustenance with an artistic endeavor, calling it a "waste of time." Pearl then claims, in the style of popular magazines of the time, that the colorful jars would make nice Christmas presents to give to friends, and Ora Mae responds in a way that marks the family's isolation: "Give them to *who*?" (252). In this moment (during the late 1930s), we encounter another change in kitchen ideology, a change fostered by an onslaught of women's magazines of the time and a resistance to the lean times of the Depression. Although this change was slow to arrive in rural Appalachia, women were learning that it was not enough to provide for their families; their food should be decorative as well as nourishing. In short, the kitchen was a place of artistic creation as well as a place of food preparation.

Holidays were essential to the "homemaker as artist" ideal; the October 1933 edition of *Ladies' Home Journal* recommends making candle holders out of apples and making an entrée of "Halloween surprises" by placing small cubes of fruit inside hamburger patties (King 31). A 1936 edition of the same magazine, in an article entitled "What a Difference Color Makes," suggests crafting false artichoke "leaves" out of a pureed pea mixture and piping the mixture onto artichoke bottoms to add "luster to both bottoms and peas" (Batchelder 38). In this sense, Pearl is true to the ideal of her time. She has learned to want to make her food pretty, but her elders, in this case, Ora Mae, are not ready for a change in the domestic ideal. This type of resistance to change might be linked to the fact that the Appalachian region was one of the hardest hit by the Depression due to fluctuations in the coal market. Pearl would like to "de-naturalize" the domestic, to make it an art form, or at the very least, a hobby, even in the harshest of circumstances. She does not view the work as "natural" to her role because she sees herself as more of an artist than a homemaker.

Interestingly, Sally, not Pearl, reacts strongly to this kitchen moment of Ora Mae's rejection of the creative idea, taking off her apron, running, falling, and crying along the mountain creek. Sally seems to recognize that she and her sister have shared a similar type of experience. Through the kitchen, a space usually associated with warmth and food, each has come to encounter an entirely new way of life: Sally bears the weight of letting her mother die while she continued to can surplus goods rather than let them go to waste. Thus, for Smith, the kitchen is not the bedrock of social and cultural stability, but instead, a site of loss, a place where the prevalent American domestic ideal is strong enough to silence emotional and creative needs.

Unlike authors who depict the commercialization of Appalachia as a solely destructive process, Smith points to the tension between this type of commercialization and domesticity itself, while offering some hope for Appalachian women. In the prologue to the novel, set in the 1970s, Debra and Almarine, Jr., make their joint living selling Amway products and spend their leisure time carpeting the interior of their van. While commercialization wreaks havoc on the mountain landscape, it also moves the domestic domain away from solitary housewives and positions domesticity as a material product, not a way of life. As a product, domesticity, like the carpeted van and Amway goods, becomes mobile and flexible: for instance, both men and women can participate in the domestic realm. A homemaker may clean the house or sell cleaning products to other families for a profit. Further, families are free to keep Appalachian traditions, such as folk songs and clogging, even while the television blares from the other room. Throughout *Oral History*, Smith depicts an early twentieth-century domestic ideal, one that requires feminine moral and material perfection, as a storm that must be met with both resistance and flexibility.

"What will last": The Domestication of the Public in Fair and Tender Ladies

Just as the improvement in southern railways would alter postal service, domestic life, and ultimately, the transmission and interpretation of the national domestic ideal, so would the historical event of the emergent railway network alter the ways in which an author would write about domesticity within the epistolary form. In *Fair and Tender Ladies*, Smith takes on what might be considered a new genre: a distinctly southern Appalachian epistolary novel. Smith infuses the letters of Ivy Rowe with traditions of southern orality, Appalachian landscape (including the physical presence of trains), and domesticity. The changing face of each of these areas adds up to an overwhelming sense of physical and psychological instability for Ivy. In response to this sense of instability, Ivy attempts to infuse each of her letters with the concrete aspects of her home as well as the life she experiences within it. It is as if Ivy believes that if she can package her domestic life within the confines of an envelope and send it away, then she will be able to stabilize and save it.

Ivy's sense of instability aligns with Smith's own biography: her mother was dying and her son was seriously ill at the time she was writing *Fair and Tender Ladies* (Herion-Sarafidis 7–8). Like Glasgow, who would return to the entrapment inherent in early twentieth-century domesticity when faced with her own sense of entrapment because of hearing loss, Smith transfers a sense of personal loss to more global issues of domestic women and loss. In this case, Smith's sense of personal instability expands to a more generalized anxiety about change in the South, where the spoken story gives way to telephone calls and the luxuries of electricity, and the landscape becomes ravished by development and mining. Ironically, Ivy struggles for permanence through her letters, stabilizing her own world by writing it down, then sending it across an irregular landscape on a speeding train. The physical vehicle of her letters (the train) is also the vehicle of the domestic change she initially resists.

This method of encapsulating domestic life in the letter form infuses the novel with a level of meta-discourse on the boundaries of public and private life. As we have seen, the trends in the criticism of nineteenth-century American literature reflect an urge to eradicate the public-private binary.[4] But, as I have argued, closer inspection of southern women's fiction indicates a need for a similar focus on the public-private binary and its increasing absence throughout twentieth-century literature.

As Patricia Yaeger notes in *Dirt and Desire: Reconstructing Southern Women's Writing, 1930–1990*, southern women's writing "challenges the public sphere" in ways not accounted for in what may be considered the traditional categories and elements of southern fiction: tragedy, pessimism, human

evil, and the sense of history and place (ix, 12).[5] Yaeger's comments point to
the tendency of critics of southern literature to categorize narrowly and in
ways that are ill suited for the criticism of southern women's novels. In her
own establishment of new categories, Yaeger acknowledges the participation
of women in public life, though this participation may occur beneath the radar
of traditional, masculinist conceptions of what constitutes "the public."

It is not my project to add my own set of categories to this discourse,
even for the purposes of discussing Smith's work, but instead, to uncover a
specific type of public-private melding that operates with the railroad as its
icon. If we return to the image of the families picnicking along the railway
lines on switch-over day in the spring of 1886 (when rail widths were standardized), a blending of public and private interests appears.[6] The picnickers have made the banks of the railway their transient dining rooms, with the
railway laborers as their spectacle, and the introduction of national train service as the celebratory event. Within this image, the picnickers seem to possess a certain degree of agency over the workings of this event; it is they who
have traveled and they who have packed the lunches. It is unlikely that a railway worker would have felt comfortable sitting down with them. In this sense,
the families along the track have privatized the event, placing it under the
already existent rubric of domesticity. They have taken a public event, one
that took place under the urging of businessmen, and without democratic
representation, and re-cast it as a domestic event, a holiday to be enjoyed by
families, even though this was not the intent of its sponsors. The spectators
of switch-over day domesticated an event that happened without their input,
and one that would have permanent effect on their daily lives. I want to pro-
pose that this urge to domesticate the public, to make radical technological
change comfortable and familiar, while undertheorized, may be more common in southern literature than its reverse: the phenomenon of the home and
its transition into a type of public space. Accordingly, I will examine how
Smith's characters conceptualize and incorporate public (technological) phenomena into their home lives.

In *Fair and Tender Ladies*, Smith goes further than simply transitioning
evenly between the public and private; instead, as in Ivy's description of the
train, she seems to sublimate those technologies considered public (mass transit, national mail delivery, the physical technology of the train itself) *into* the
domestic realm. The result is a kind of domesticity that cannot be described
as local or private — Ivy's domestic life, even in her own perception of it, now
reaches far beyond the mountains. Interestingly, Amy Richter makes a simi-

lar claim for American culture at large, but from the opposite angle, focusing on "the domestication of public life" on the trains themselves, within passenger cars, which changed "from a place of risk and social mixing to a setting in which both men and women sought to insulate themselves from social contact" (7). In both cases, the blending of the public-private divide, and the enormous impact of trains on this blending process, becomes evident.

Domesticity becomes a containment strategy (deployed by an individual) for the public realm, rather than acting as a containment strategy (deployed by a patriarchal society at large) for its female protagonist, as in Glasgow's *Virginia*. Smith allows her female characters the agency to do more than subvert domestic ideology and transgress public and private barriers by simply existing in both within and without the home. Instead, in the character of Ivy, Smith points to a type of outlook that uses the domestic knowledge of the home as a technology for grasping and coping with a rapidly changing region. Rather than becoming "domesticated" through working as a serving person, becoming a single mother, then marrying another man and bearing more children, Ivy "domesticates" her entire world. She accomplishes her own brand of "manifest domesticity" (to borrow Amy Kaplan's term) using domestic metaphor, imagery, and practical knowledge to make familiar the public and semi-public processes of storytelling, gaining a sexual persona, and coping with new physical technologies such as the railroad and electricity.

But this is not to say that Smith creates an infallible, rural "superwoman" protagonist able to deal with hardships innovatively while retaining a strict Protestant-based morality. Such characters can be found, particularly in 1930s southern rural settings, as in Dargan's *Call Home the Heart,* in the form of the inexhaustible Ishma Waycaster. The difference in characterization undoubtably lies in publication period. Dargan published her early feminist–Communist novel in 1932, to document the cotton mill strike of 1929 in Gastonia, North Carolina, for an audience eager to understand the politics of the Communist organizers of the National Textile Workers Union (Cook 101–107).

Despite the similarities in topic of the two novels, the focus and scope differ greatly. The dogmatic politics and sentimentality of Dargan's work would probably put off Smith's late twentieth-century audience, and Smith, accordingly, creates a novel that is far more subtle in its gender politics. Although Ivy mentions her support for the miner's union and is loosely affiliated with it through a friend, her concerns lie in the areas of reconciling herself to a rapidly changing Appalachian region and in recording every facet of the changing culture through what I would describe as a distinctly domestic lens.

Ivy's descriptions are not mitigated in their authenticity by her domestic outlook. She does not sugarcoat her environment. She often looks on it with both fear and astonishment, as in her description of the train stopping, "with its breaks screeching and white steam hissing all around, and the bell ringing like crazy.... It is all very loud and exciting and fast.... Then they are off again with a whistle and a grinding roaring noise, and the white numbers flash by on the passing cars" (138). Ivy cannot make such a sight "homey" or even comfortable; her method of domestication is a far subtler tactic. She domesticates the train through narrative containment (as does Emily Dickinson in "I like to see it lap the miles" with trains that "lick the Valleys up" and "feed ... at Tanks" [2–3]); Ivy positions the train between her more personal depictions of her new home and her new family life. Although she continues to refer to the train as "probably the main thing" of the town, she does not allow it dominance of her own narrative, nor does she describe it solely in the terms of its effect on her domestic sphere.

Maintaining this evenhanded refusal to depict Ivy as thinking or acting within a strictly public-private binary, Smith will not let Ivy ignore the effects of such changes on the town's overall domestic portrait. She recognizes that the train alters the shape of the town's domestic structure as a whole, remarking,

> Sometimes three or four trains will come through in one day, and they have put on a hoot owl shift at the mine now. The company has got too many people over here to put them all up so a bunch of men is living right out in the woods now, I don't know what will happen when it gets cold. It is getting rough around here, as Beulah says. It is a boom town [144].

Ivy realizes that the train and the mining company have caused a new phenomenon of public domesticity — men "living right out in the woods." Here, her portrayal of the train's direct effect on domestic standards places a new emphasis on the "boom town." To Ivy, the "boom" is not entirely positive at this juncture in the novel, and the explosion in standards of the home, represented by men living out of doors, indicates a serious decline in domesticity. In her actions — in taking on work outside the home or extra-marital lovers — Ivy draws few lines between the public and private spheres. The same holds true for her ideology: Ivy comes from the viewpoint of an integrated life, one where domesticity is both barometer of cultural change and a method of making sense of it, not a confining, constricting mentality for women.

Before Ivy can train her powers of domestication on the world at large, she must learn to use them on herself. In her description of the train, Ivy subtly casts the train in the language of orality — as a "screeching" and "hissing" beast. She uses these terms because she was brought up in an oral culture, in which the stories that one tells and even the noises that one makes (such as Silvaney's frequent screams and cries) make up a tangible part of the family's domestic life. Further, her use of animal imagery naturalizes the mechanical, making it as familiar as the tame and wild creatures that surrounded her childhood home.

In her letters, Ivy reproduces the plots of the stories she hears, but she also attempts to convey the sense that each story took on a physical presence in the household at the time of its telling and became a domestic product, the same as the livestock killed or the food prepared during the course of the day's work. In this vein, Smith casts Gaynelle and Virgie Cline, the sisters who arrive on the holiday of Old Christmas to tell stories, as a part of the evening's menu:

> Well, that was yesterday evening, and then we et us some sweet taters Momma had roasted in the fire and a pot of soup beans she had cooked with some fatback in them, and some cornbread Beulah made, her cornbread is bettern Mommas. So this was good. And Garnie and Ethel is getting some meat back on ther bones now Im proud to say, and Johnny he grows like a weed but Danny dont do no good, he carrys his head to the side and walks on a slant, it seems.
> And then all of a sudden, in comes Gaynelle and Virgie Cline! [32].

The listing of these foods, like the listing of the growth rates of siblings, is a point of pride for Ivy in her letter to her Dutch pen friend, Hanneke. Yet the entrance of Gaynelle and Virgie on Old Christmas becomes a similar point of pride, as well as a matter of sustenance: they will offer a kind of orality, in the form of their stories, as important as the food eaten on the holiday. Smith continues to link the sisters' entrance to a general, but tangible sense of orality through Ivy's cataloguing of the sounds made during their entrance. The sounds — "Beulah screamed bloody murder," "Law, law, Momma said," the sisters themselves "laghing like silver bells" and saying "Oh la" — resonate with Julia Kristeva's notion of the semiotic, the realm that "precedes the establishment of the symbolic and its subject" (41). According to Kristeva, these are the utterances one makes during a momentary breakthrough from the symbolic realm, the realm in which the subject is continually positing itself and the thetic (a kind of thesis of selfhood within the process of signification). The semiotic utterance then, becomes a "thing," an almost-object within discourse, one far less involved in the signification process than everyday grammatical utterances. The sounds that Ivy records also evoke Walter Ong's notion of the primacy of orality over literacy. Ivy's culture is not one of primary orality (a culture that depends strictly on orality for communication, with no use of writing), nor is her culture aligned with what Ong terms "secondary orality," that is, "the realm of present-day high-technology culture, in which a new orality is sustained by telephone, radio, television, and other electronic devices" (11). This liminal status (between primary and secondary orality) appears to grant Ivy a special understanding of the ways in which "writing makes 'words' appear similar to things" (Ong 11).

Here, I trace the linguistics of Smith's characters' utterances, first, because of their preponderance during the sisters' entrance. There are at least five utterances that might be classified as semiotic (or, in Ong's terminology, utterances displaying the primacy of orality within a culture) within the space of two paragraphs. Second, these utterances, particularly in combination with their phonetic spellings, mark the way in which Ivy views language as a "thing," and the narratives produced by language as household objects, as real as the cornbread or the pot that holds the beans. Third, Ivy's record of the semiotic "pre-story" aligns with her commentary on the literal exchange value of the stories. She writes that Gaynelle and Virgie "do not farm nor raise a thing but beans and flowers in the yard, nor have a cow, but folks takes them food just to hear ther storys." Ivy takes this system of exchange a step further, commenting, "I think myself they live on storys, they do not need much food" (33). In this moment, Ivy fuses the orality of storytelling and the orality of eating as she depicts words themselves as household goods.

Ivy's insistence on recording not just the events, nor even simply the text of the old folk tales that are told, represents her method of domesticating the "wild" tales. Yet this form of domestication does not make the stories any less powerful for Ivy. Rather, it makes them tangible and present in her kitchen. She valorizes the stories to the extent that they take on the tangibility of, and even become for her, the family's most valuable entity: its food.

Because Ivy realizes the physical power of words, as well as their sustaining qualities, she is forced to realize the power of her own letters, as the documentation of literal and cultural "feeding" processes. In this sense, she positions herself, even at the age of twelve, as a part of the family's economy. She traces the path of her letter in the following manner.

> But we raise what we need, we dont go to the store for nothing but coffee and
> shoes and nails and to get the mail, we do not get any mail much but sometimes a

letter from Daddys sister in Welch or Mommas friend Geneva Hunt from child-hood or a pattern Momma sent off for.... The post store is at Majestic it is the P.O. too. This is where Mrs. Brown will take my letter to you, then Bill Waldrop will put it in his saddlebag and carry it over the mountain, a ship will carry it over the sea. Does this seem magicle to you? It seems so to me [16].

Although the family has the ability to "raise what we need," Ivy has identified her own need for more than "coffee and shoes and nails" or sewing patterns. In Smith's historically accurate placement of the post office within the store, mail and its narrative content exist on an equal plane with store-bought neces-sities. Beyond the strictly domestic economy, however, Ivy has trouble envi-sioning her own role. Therefore, she resorts to casting the mail as "magical," after she has linked it to the domestic products of her own experience, and after it has passed through the hands of those she knows. In this way, Ivy uses her domestic knowledge as a key to unlock mysteries of technology and to serve as a bridge between human and mechanical technologies. But this sense of magic also aids Ivy in the containment her own epistolary project. She is unwilling, and perhaps unable, to consciously align herself with the impor-tant economic players in her life: her mother, the storekeeper, and the mail-man. She gestures toward, but cannot completely conceptualize, herself as a trader of words.

Although Ivy cannot claim the power of her own role in the economy of the family, she is able to practice productive domesticity through a type of performance found in the games she plays with her siblings. However, unlike her siblings, Ivy has meditated on and recorded domestic practice, both in its performative and "real" forms. Given the fates of her siblings, Smith suggests that Ivy's role as the recorder of performative and "real" domes-ticity allows her to discern between the two as she ages and to craft a more successful domestic role for herself than any of her brothers and sisters.

Performative domesticity takes place within the two favorite games of the Rowe children — "Party" and "Town." "Party" involves the use of made-up names, specific in their references to race, class, and euro-centricism. Beu-lah, who will imitate the culture of mining management families unsuccessfully as she ages, chooses the prophetic name "Miss Margaret White." While the family has little contact with other races at their original mountain home on Sugar Fork, Beulah and her husband Curtis will encounter blacks and whites Beulah considers "beneath" her at their mining camp home in Diamond, fam-ilies that live literally beneath them in Diamond Mountain's hierarchical struc-ture of homes. Ivy prefigures her own consternation with Beulah's racism and classism when she asks, as a twelve-year-old, "Who knows where she got that name?" (15). When Beulah leaves the games of the children to court Curtis Bostick, Ivy and Silvaney create a character to replace her—"Miss France" "who wears a big pink hat and sticks out her little finger and laghs la-la-la" (18). The class indicators of behavior and dress that the children choose are heightened in their impact because of the character's chosen name—a European country—as if to say that Beulah and her ways could not be more "foreign" to them.

Ivy's sense of the difference between herself and Beulah grows as they age, as Ivy witnesses Beulah's rise to the social status of mining management. Ivy remarks that even though Beulah "reads all the magazines and gets herself up just so," "it's like she is still playing party and doesn't believe it herself" (164). Coupled with these remarks, Ivy relates Beulah's invitation "to make an alter cloth for the church" with the mining town's important women, as well as Beulah's resulting migraine headache. Ivy's comments gesture toward the need to distance oneself from domestic practice to avoid adopting domesticity as a total identity. Ivy, unlike Beulah, remains conscious of her own domesticity as part creative act and part survival skill, containing its demands and keeping domestic practice from becoming overwhelming or unbalanced.

Ivy also notes the domestic tendencies of her brother Garnie when he agrees to play Town with the children. The structure of the game of Town is more rigorous in its performativity of domesticity, including an elaborate set of props:

> What you do is make you some little houses outen sticks and you can chink up your logs with mud iffen you wish too, and you can have some rocks for furniture, all covered over with moss that you find by the creek.... Now this will be your fancy furniture, that is your bed and chairs and all, and you will make corncob people, you can have pinecones for pigs, and a cow and the chicks in the yard [18].

Yet Ivy remarks that not every sibling will play in the same manner: "Iffen you want little old Garnie to play you have to let him preach a funeral and sing, been a long time travelling here below" (18). Here, too, Ivy captures what will be her brother's domestic future—"a long time travelling here below"—in the words of his own song. Unlike Beulah and her over-commitment to a "higher" domesticity for its classist and racist potential, Garnie will reject traditional domesticity outright, making his living as a morally corrupt travelling evangelist. But even here, Mr. Garnie's indicat performances are not without effect; Ivy remarks that when he preaches the funerals in the game of Town, "you will have to pour water on Silvaney's face, she crys so hard at a funeral" (18). Silvaney's overpowering response to Garnie's performance indicates her own domestic future as well; she will eventually enter the Elizabeth Masters Home for Girls in Roanoke, Virginia. Silvaney's earliest inability to perform domesticity prefigures her ultimate inability to sample a domestic life of her own as an adult in any context other than an institutional "home."

On one level, Ivy's perspective on her siblings' domestic performances operates as simple foreshadowing. As the letter writer, Ivy finds herself commenting on the behavior of her relatives throughout her life. Sometimes the choices they make as they set up and run households surprise her, and other times they do not. I would argue, however, that Smith offers more than a simple level of foreshadowing. First, Smith does not offer Ivy to the reader as a transparent lens or neutral third party. Ivy holds intimate ties to her family, but makes creative, out-of-the-ordinary domestic choices, such as the decision (in the 1910s) to become a single mother rather than to accept an offer of marriage from the baby's father. In this vein, Ivy does not function as the novel's "domestic heroine," a character who promotes the domestic ideal at all costs (as in *Virginia*). Therefore, while Smith allows Ivy to note the tendencies of her siblings to "fail" at domesticity or use it as a tool for promoting racist and classist ideologies, she does not place Ivy in a position to cast judgment. Instead, Smith creates a meta-commentary throughout the novel about the importance of meditation on one's daily tasks, especially for women. Through the invention of Ivy in the inside observer-recorder role, Smith notes the value of a lifetime habit of this type of meditation on what might seem to be the mundane. Because Ivy records her domestic experiences, she also gains a psychological distance from them, and she recognizes when the domestic patterns of her day will and will not be beneficial for her. Without reaching the extremes of slavish devotion to domestic ideal, or outright rejection of all things domestic, Ivy crafts her own version of domesticity, including many Appalachian rituals and practices and combining them with the outside influences she obtains through her work in the boarding-house. Through the counterexamples of Ivy's brothers and sisters, Smith points to the dangers of an unexamined domestic life.

In the chronicle of her own failing health and death, Ivy proves that her domestic life has been anything but unexamined. In one of her final letters to her daughter Joli, Ivy writes, "Oh Joli, you get so various as you get old! I have been so many people. And yet I think the most important thing is <u>Don't forget</u>" (265). Ivy has, indeed, proved to be "various." She has lived and worked in the rural community of Sugar Fork Mountain, the bustling town center of Majestic's boardinghouse, and in the company store of the mining town, Diamond. Through Ivy, Smith provides a window into three major areas of Appalachian life: rural wilderness, rural town, and coal mining company. Yet I would argue that Smith also documents Ivy's internal method for comparing her past and present selves: that of comparing her domestic modes. Throughout the epistolary novel, Ivy chronicles not her own internal emotional and intellectual changes, but the ways in which her own domestic role changed in each new location. For example, the reader knows that Ivy is exposed to new political, intellectual, and social ideas at Geneva Hunt's boardinghouse, but only because we gather Ivy's reaction to these characters as she waited on them at a meal. Similarly, we know that Ivy has access to a wide variety of new information and goods because of Diamond's prominent position on a coal line, but we know this only through her descriptions of Beulah's magazines and new dishes, or her trips to the train track for the entertainment of Beulah's children. Thus, Smith valorizes the domestic as a system for the historical comparison of changing rural cultures. Further, through the creation of an epistolary text, Smith makes a subtle argument for the historical and cultural importance of both recording and reading the domestic details of women's lives.

A reading of Smith's work is not complete without a historical understanding of the importance of the railroad in American domesticity, and particularly rural southern domesticity. Although the critics of domesticity have often studied the impact of advertising, magazines, kitchen appliances, and the television on the American kitchen, the mode of technology that made the wide distribution of those items possible is often given much less attention in such studies.[7] There is a need to study not only the material goods that influenced domesticity, but also the system that brought these goods to the sites of change. In short, American domesticity has not evolved in a vacuum, nor even in a cozy bubble of "women's" magazines and machines, but within an American industrial and corporate framework. My project throughout this work has been to document the influences of technology upon domesticity and of domesticity upon technology in southern women's literature. It is a mistake to confine the notion of "domestic technology" to the refrigerator and the stove. Instead, I am interested in the ways in which women writers have integrated the technologies around them, including medical procedures and industrial technologies such as the railroad, into their documentation of domestic culture, just as those technologies have integrated these writers and their works into newer cultures. Within these texts, the implication remains that twentieth-century American domesticity has never been a separate sphere, but always an integral part of the nation's technological power.

Here I have chosen to examine a role of the southern railway beyond the color line, which has received a great deal of attention in both southern history and literary criticism. This choice, however, is not meant to downplay the significance of segregation and racism on the changing face of American domesticity. In the next chapter, I will examine Toni Morrison's portrayals of African American urban, suburban, and rural domesticity, examining the strong ties to the history of slavery and to the hired domestic work of African American women, often in the homes of white women. This complex history of domesticity results in tensions between individuality and community, but it also results in transformative, healing domestic practices within private homes.

Chapter Five

"No Place Like and No Place but Home"

Domestic Resistance in Toni Morrison's
Jazz, Paradise, *and* Love

Much of this project has explored white domesticity in literature, and the ways in which fictional and actual southern white women experienced social, political, and economic structures through the home as a point of contact, with the kitchen frequently acting as a center of operations for this contact. This choice, however, does not reflect, and is not meant to reflect, the full picture of twentieth-century domesticity in the South, nor does this project attempt to compare various domesticities along racial lines. Even in a project that takes white southern domesticity as its focus, it would be remiss not to consider the complexity of a wider scope of domesticity and not to begin to push beyond the borders of this project into new territory. In this spirit, I offer this chapter not as a token nod to non-white domesticity, but as a springboard for new dialogues and as an indication of where I find some of the most radical, subversive, and fascinating domesticity in contemporary literature.

But why read Morrison as a domestic novelist at all? Does such a reading push an agenda of reforming the notion of literary domesticity, an agenda of viewing some domestic practices as radically subversive, onto a body of work better analyzed through different lenses? Although I asked myself these questions as I began to read Morrison in this way, her own words reassure me that I do not overestimate the careful constructions of homes in her work:

I prefer to think of a world-in-which-race-does-*not*-matter as something other than a theme park, or a failed and always failing dream, or as the father's house of many rooms. I am thinking of it as home. "Home" seems a suitable term because, first, it lets me make a radical distinction between the metaphor of house and the metaphor of home and helps me clarify my thoughts on racial construction. Second, the term domesticates the racial project, moves the job of unmattering race away from pathetic yearning and futile desire; away from an impossible future or an irretrievable and probably nonexistent Eden to a manageable, doable, modern human activity. Third, because eliminating the potency of racist constructs in language is the work I can do. Also, matters of race and matters of home are priorities in my work and both have in one way or another initiated my search for that elusive sovereignty as well as my abandonment of the search once I recognized its disguise ["Home" 3–4].

Here, Morrison clarifies the home as a key metaphor for racial construction and deconstruction while also emphasizing the importance of literal homes, along with their representational possibilities, in her work.

While other critics have noted the significance of social resistance in Morrison's novels, they have not typically analyzed the distinctly domestic forms this resistance takes in her post–*Beloved* novels. For example, Jennifer Fitzgerald notes that in *Jazz*, Alice Manfred must acknowledge that "oppressive power engenders resistance"; and Fitzgerald finds that in the novel at large, although "the institutions of supremacy and exploitation hold sway, there is still some space for resistance" (396). However, I find it significant that even Alice Manfred, who runs a tightly controlled home with a particular emphasis on health, cleanliness, wholesomeness, and "proper" behavior, must acknowledge the necessity of resistance. It is Alice, after all, who comes the closest to befriending Violet, also known as "Violent" after her public outbursts, and allows Violet into her home while other members of the community shun her. Although Alice's domestic practice seems to bow to traditional consumerist notions of what a "good" home should be, her interactions with Violet belie her knowledge of institutionalized racial and economic oppression and her will to resist.

In Morrison's work, domestic resistance takes two central forms: social domestic resistance and familial domestic resistance. For these purposes, I define social resistance as resistance to larger social structures of racism, classism, sexism, and other forms of institutionalized oppression through the creation of a homeplace[1] outside these forms of oppression, at least as much as is practically possible. Some characters also enact familial domestic resistance; that is, they resist the internal power structures of the home or community using domestic tools or means. Reading Morrison's work with this focus uncovers domestic resistance as an important, but frequently overlooked form of social protest with roots in slavery. An examination of Morrison as domestic writer also indicates new directions and renewed purpose for the twenty-first-century domestic novel.[2] Morrison expands politicized twentieth-century domesticity to examine the technologies of urban domesticity and the meaning of its contemporary material culture. Just as the home springs to life to mourn violently the tragedies of slavery in *Beloved*, so do the material goods of the home become the tools of twentieth-century social resistance in *Jazz* (1992), *Paradise* (1998), and *Love* (2003).

The African American Domestic Tradition

The idea of domestic resistance in Morrison's recent work, however, remains incomplete unless it is historicized through a brief overview of twentieth-century African American domesticity in literature. To understand African American domesticity, it is necessary to consider its unique features, including its relationship to both slavery and to domestic work for hire. However, one major similarity among domestic *writers* remains. Like their white counterparts, twentieth-century African American domestic novelists run the risk of having their work taken less seriously because of their choice of subject matter. For instance, in "Race and Domesticity in *The Color Purple*" (*African American Review*, 1995), Linda Selzer adds in her first endnote, "By characterizing the novel's point of view as 'domestic,' I mean no criticism, as my paper will make clear" (12). The idea that the term *domestic* might be used as criticism at the end of the twentieth century seems surprising, especially considering the broad scope of works valorizing and reevaluating nineteenth- and twentieth-century sentimental and domestic works, as well as the all-but-final end to separate spheres ideologies.[3] Yet Selzer's disclaimer makes sense given the negative reactions to domestic subjects by some critics, including those she catalogues in reference to *The Color Purple*. Selzer summarizes the critiques of Walker's use of Celie's viewpoint, which suggest that the emphasis on the domestic "may also constrict the novel's ability to analyze issues of 'race' and class," (3) before she goes on to argue for the many ways in which the novel does provide an analysis of race and class, *through* (not despite) its domestic lens.[4]

Selzer's summary of the criticism and one of the issues behind it (the idea that domesticity precludes solid analysis of race and class) suggests one difference in the critical response to white and African American domestic novelists. While white southern domestic novels have been taken to task for ignoring "larger" themes of war, "the land," politics, and large-scale histori-cal movements,[5] they are not usually taken to task for indifference to race, most likely because of the ingrained racist ideologies that view whiteness as a "default" position rather than as a racial position unto itself. Therefore, although white domesticity may be devalued, it is not expected to address racial issues. Just as some Harlem Renaissance writers struggled against the pres-sure to produce works only about race, so do late twentieth-century African American women writers struggle with a double burden (pressure to write "beyond" quotidian concerns and the pressure to analyze race) when they write domestic works.

If both white and African American domesticities have been shunned as "serious subjects," African American domesticity has certainly suffered fur-ther slights as well. In the recent attention to American domesticity, the very term "American" has been aligned most frequently with white women. In *Playing in the Dark: Whiteness and the Literary Imagination*, Morrison explores this problem in terms of the more general disconnect between canonical Amer-ican literature and the African American presence (4–5). African American women's domesticity, along with its intersection of the paid labor force, has received far less attention than white domesticity, not only in its literary man-ifestation,[6] but also in its history.[7] The neglect can be explained, in part, through domesticity scholarship's most recent development: the movement that detonated the ideology of separate spheres. Because "separate spheres" has never been a logical analytical strategy for the culture or the literature of African American domesticity, the attention to "no more separate spheres" risks the exclusion of African American domesticity.[8]

Angela Davis writes that while black women "have seldom been 'just housewives,' they have always done their housework." She also remarks, "They have thus carried the double burden of wage labor and housework — a dou-ble burden which always demands that working women possess the persever-ing power of Sisyphus" (231). Sharon Harley notes that the rise of "day work" (as opposed to "living in") may have intensified the pressures of the "double day" (348). With twentieth-century African American domestic workers mov-ing between white employers' homes and their own homes,[9] with significant social intervals spent on the street and in the world while in transit (Jacque-line Jones 190–193), domesticity was not confined to the inner or private realm. Likewise, attention to one's own private domestic realm did not mean being cut off from the rest of the world. The revelation that the world of the home and the "outside" world are intimately connected is no revelation at all if we use African American rather than white domesticity as our field of inquiry.

Maxine Lavon Montgomery traces "black women's domesticity as being bound within a distinct history traceable to slavery" and remarks that "because of larger social, economic, and political conditions, [black women] have not only had to participate in the workforce, they have had to be good housekeepers as well" (56).[10] It is essential to recognize, as Montgomery does, that the inextricably blended spheres of home and work did not arise in the twentieth century. It goes without saying that under the slave system these blended spheres included endless work, deprivation, and inhumane treatment at every turn, whether in the field, in the home, or somewhere in between. Yet Angela Davis analyzes what she considers a positive aspect of slaves' domestic lives:

> The salient theme emerging from domestic life in the slave quarters is one of sexual equality. The labor that slaves performed for their own sake and not for the aggrandizement of their masters was carried out on terms of equality. Within the confines of their family and community life, therefore, Black people managed to accomplish a magnificent feat. They transformed that negative equality which emanated from the equal oppression they suffered as slaves into a positive quality: the egalitarianism characterizing their social relations [18].[11]

In this sense, African American domesticity as social and political resistance contains a long, rich history, one that echoes through Morrison's novels.

Other historians dispute the focus on egalitarianism: Harley argues that emphasis on "egalitarian domestic relationships" of black women and men contributes to an omission of the roles of gender and class in these relationships (338). Yet Morrison also focuses intently on class and gender differences with domesticity, often giving domestic "clues" as a shorthand code for class status and allowing female characters to analyze openly gender and class conflicts. As Valerie Sweeney Prince comments, Toni Morrison demands "that black female subjectivity be understood as distinct from the black womb," even if this understanding involves "dismemberment and murder" (5). Prince and other African American feminist critics recognize that Morrison openly and frankly interrogates gender conflict and gender identity in her novels, sometimes quite violently. Gender is not, in her work, silent in subjugation to the "larger" topic of race. Instead, racial, gender, and class identities become forever intertwined in realistic ways. In this sense, Morrison moves beyond one of the key theoretical conflicts in African American domesticity: a focus on egalitarian relationships within black families versus a focus on the effects of class and gender difference on those family structures. Her ability to represent the egalitarian nature of some relationships while not shying away from class and gender conflicts uncovers the somewhat false nature of this dichotomy. Like other theorists,[12] Morrison recognizes that race, class, and gender cannot be pulled apart like tangled threads. Rather, they form a tightly woven matrix, even within fictional representations.

Like private, familial domesticity, public or semi-public domesticity as work outside the home offered opportunities for social resistance during slavery, and it functioned similarly during the late nineteenth and early twentieth centuries, when many African American women worked as domestics. In 1900, nine out of ten domestic workers in southern cities were African American women (Jones 128). By 1940, 59.9 percent of employed African American females worked in domestic service (Collins, first edition 55). On one hand, "domestic service recapitulated the mistress-servant relationship" (Jones 127); but on the other hand, domesticity's transformative potential expanded with the increasing freedoms afforded by day labor for hire[13] and property rental and ownership. With domestic work as a primary occupation for African Americans after emancipation (Collins, second edition 54), homes became intimately linked with survival. However, one's own home, unlike and in deliberate contrast to that of the employer, became a site of social resistance in three significant ways: as a source of control over material conditions, as a source of spiritual nurturance and renewal, and as a site for political change.

While twelve- to fourteen-hour days in domestic service provided little time to take care of one's own home and family, this change still marked an improvement over live-in employment. Time in transit, especially on buses, could provide opportunities to bond with others in similar positions and to share vital information (Collins, second edition 58). Family and community enhanced the domestic realm[14]: "The elevated social status denied black domestic workers and laundresses by the larger society and even some members of the black community could be found by them in their families and neighborhoods"; domesticity "provided them with a sense of autonomy and control absent for them in the labor market environment" (Harley 349). Work for oneself (versus the same kind of work for a white employer) took on increased meaning as a source of pride and by providing a sense of community (Jones 4–5; Collins, second edition 46).[15]

Private domesticity also served as a source of spiritual growth and renewal. Maxine Montgomery, in an analysis of Gloria Naylor's fiction, notes the possibility of "transforming the home into a place where women, in particular, experience a measure of freedom, dignity, and creativity" (66). In an essay entitled "Homeplace: A Site of Resistance" in *Yearning* bell hooks writes:

> One's homeplace was the one site where one could freely confront the issue of humanization, where one could resist. Black women resisted by making homes where all black people could strive to be subjects, not objects, where we could be affirmed in our minds and hearts despite poverty, hardship, and deprivation, where we could restore to ourselves the dignity denied us on the outside in the public world [42].

By depicting the home as a key site of nurturing and a site of resistance, in direct opposition to racism and oppression, hooks points to the distinctly political nature of African American domesticity.

While hooks and others point to the political dimensions of using the home as a site of subject identity formation and spiritual renewal, it is important to note that African American domesticity also accomplishes goals more readily and obviously recognized as political in nature. Similarly, the home takes on a political symbolism, especially in the quest for an absent, lost, or idealized future homeplace. Valerie Prince opens her text on the home in African American literature with this idea: "The search for justice, opportunity, and liberty that characterized the twentieth century for African Americans can be described as a quest for home" (1). Yet the actual or present-day home holds political significance as well. The home "has been a crucial site for organizing, for forming political solidarity" (hooks 45) and initiating "positive change within an oppressed black community" (Montgomery 58). In some instances when married African American mothers did not work outside the home and were supported by husbands, this arrangement became "a source of pride" (Harley 346) and may have even been viewed as an act of resistance (Collins, second edition 54). At times, the home signified such a source of positive change that tension arose around the issue of an African American woman working outside the home. However, working outside the home did not necessarily carry a stigma, and "was not a detriment to [the] family's well-being and stability" (Harley 348).

Literary critics, furthermore, note the potential political import of domesticity on an even larger scale in African American women's literature. Examining nineteenth-century works as a precursor to *Beloved*, Denise Rodriguez writes, "For African American women writers, the domestic novel created a framework for working through or reevaluating the contradictions and inconsistencies of slavery—one of the most obvious of which has to do with the status of female slaves in their own home versus in the master's house

(41). Drawing on the work of Margot Anne Kelley, Elizabeth Hayes comments on the complexity of this discourse: "the houses in African American women's literature are often palimpsests of all four kinds of space — architectural, geographic, psychic, and communal — and thus they are multilayered signifiers" (670). In examining texts of the twentieth century, Maxine Montgomery explains that Gloria Naylor uses domesticity to do more than empower; she imbues simple domestic tasks — "cooking, cleaning, and mothering" — with the potential for global liberation of women and men "across time and space" (67). Here, domesticity becomes a key practice linking all women in goals of freedom from all kinds of oppression. This view contrasts sharply with the idea (borne mainly of second-wave, white feminism) of domestic tasks as inherently oppressive. In this sense, literary African American domesticity would seem to point toward some of the most radical political ends associated with any type of domesticity. I would also argue that impulses to depoliticize domesticity, and the tendency to avoid reading twentieth-century African American women's fiction as domestic fiction, risk ignoring much of its associative and historical power, and in that sense, risk capitulation with racist ideologies.

Toni Morrison and Regional Identity

It may seem strange to include Toni Morrison in a study of southern women's writing since, in the strictest sense, Morrison (born in Lorain, Ohio) is not a southerner. However, as Morrison has stated in interviews, "Ohio is right on the Kentucky border so there's not much difference between it and the 'South.' It's an interesting state from the point of view of black people because it is right there by the Ohio River, in the south, and at its northern tip is Canada. And there were these fantastic abolitionists there, and also the Ku Klux Klan lived there" (Stepto 12). In this comment, Morrison makes clear her awareness of her region as a border territory, a contact zone for many of the contrasts that arise in her work. Further, Philip Page remarks that, for Morrison, the "past is rural and South" (*Dangerous Freedom* 29), and Morrison herself has noted, "The first time I went south, it was staggering! It was like going home" (Wilson 136).

Similarly, Morrison's fictional communities insist "upon a knowledge of a Southern past that engendered a Black ethic rooted in slavery and harvested in a desire and a press for intra-racial and universal respect" (Fultz 93). The comments of Page and Fultz seem to apply both to Morrison's own past and to the fictional past of her characters. Morrison experienced a southern family history through her parents and extended family, migrants from the South who kept southern folkways, including "black lore, black music, black language, and all the myths and rituals of black culture," alive in their home (McKay 139). Not surprisingly, as Angelyn Mitchell notes, "Each of her novels engages some aspect of the southern Black experience" (50).[16] A "southern ethos" runs through Morrison's work as well, including associations of the natural world of the South with memories of touchstone erotic, sensual, coming-of-age, and self-identification moments, especially for the female characters (Fultz 80–81). In Morrison's novels, the South comes to represent much of what her characters hold dear and much of what has formed them, even as it represents a haunted, cruel past.[17]

Given the heightened symbolic and narratological importance of the South in Morrison's work, the quick labeling of her work as "not southern" or her person as "not a southern writer" seems arbitrary at best. A kind of anxiety, too, surrounds the question of her regional identity,[18] especially on the part of those exploring the current and future boundaries of southern literature. For instance, she is cited four times in *The Future of Southern Letters* (Humphries and Lowe, 1996). In these instances, the writer distinctly labels Morrison as "not southern": she becomes, instead, "Ohio's Toni Morrison" (11), "a non-southerner" (85), "not from New Orleans," and a "northern black writer" (117). The context of these instances of labeling is equally important. The editors and authors of the collection praise her use of the historical novel ("one of its greatest expressions") in the text's introductory overview of developments in southern historical fiction (Lowe 11) and offer her work as an example of the longed-for "ambitious novel" (in the tradition of Faulkner and Styron) not found in contemporary southern fiction (Fred Hobson, "Of Canons" 85).

Morrison also appears in Lowe's interview with Brenda Marie Osbey, a poet and New Orleans native. Lowe asks, "What do you make of the recent novels by northern black writers such as Toni Morrison and Gloria Naylor that are set in the South?" Osbey replies that "Milkman in *Song of Solomon* becomes more humanized the deeper he descends into the South ... many contemporary black writers see the South as some Harlem Renaissance writers did, as a kind of cultural homeland." In the same reply, Osbey calls *Beloved* "one of the greatest books I've ever read" and adds her appreciation of "the way the South crops up" (117) in black fiction. At the end of this comment, she calls for more work focusing on the Caribbean, stating "the South is also part of the Caribbean world" (118). The interview closes on a statement that leaves the reader with a sense of possibility for the expanding boundaries of southern literature. I find it interesting and potentially significant that Osbey makes this call for expanding boundaries of southern fiction in juxtaposition with, if not in association with, her comments on Morrison's regional identity (the focus of Lowe's question) and Morrison's praiseworthy writing *about* the South (the focus of Osbey's reply).

Each of these mentions of Morrison in *The Future of Southern Letters* evaluates her work in glowing, even superlative, terms: she is known as a master of her craft in historical fiction, in the use of the South in contemporary African American fiction, and in Hobson's own personal category of "ambitious novels." Further, she continually appears as the counterpoint "non-southerner" in discussions of southern writing or as an example of the "non-southerner" succeeding in traditionally southern tropes and modes of writing.[19]

Is part of the anxiety over Morrison's regional identity rooted in a fear that the future of "southern letters" may live and work outside the South? Does the anxiety stem from a fear that critics (such as Hobson) seem to wish that our contemporary southern writers would write about the South as Morrison does? Are critics implying that Morrison has the potential to beat southern writers at what was once their own (exclusive) game? I would argue that these fears seem to contribute to the anxiety surrounding Morrison's regional identity. Without this anxiety, it is unlikely that we would see her name appear so frequently in these discussions as a designated significant "non-southerner." Why else would critics need to repeat the facts of her birth while still including her in the discourse of regional politics?

As I have already mentioned, I am conceiving of this chapter as a springboard to a territory beyond the borders of traditional white southern American domestic fiction of the twentieth century. Because of the anxiety surrounding her regional identity and the border territory she inhabits, Morrison becomes an appropriately "southern but not only southern" focal point for this chapter. Further, just as many of the most radical political uses of domesticity emerge from contemporary African American fiction, many of the most provocative fictional representations of the South now seem to emerge from beyond its physical borders, although clearly not from beyond the region's authentic psychic pull.

"The Home" and "the home": Reading Morrison's Recent Work as Southern and Domestic

If we are to consider Morrison as both a writer of domestic and southern literature by broadening traditional definitions of these categories, how does an analysis of her work change? To address this question, I begin with an overview of Morrison's novels post–*Beloved*, followed by a closer examination of *Jazz*, *Paradise*, and *Love* individually. I choose to explore these three novels because these texts have not been read through domestic and southern lenses as frequently as *Beloved*.[20] Further, domesticity and southern culture play somewhat subtler, although no less important, roles in Morrison's later work.[21] Applying domestic and southern lenses to Morrison's work and fully dissecting the resulting subtleties offer new insights about the subversive potential of African American domesticity as a means of resistance.

Literary critics, including Toni Morrison herself, note the significant status of the home in *Beloved*. The now-famous first sentence "124 was spiteful" casts the home as more than a central object or setting, but as an active, fully realized character exhibiting "haunted" behavior prior to, and prefiguring, Beloved's arrival. In this sense, *Beloved* becomes a type of domestic horror story, in which the home no longer functions as a symbol of "virtue" or "productivity" as in late nineteenth- and early twentieth-century American domestic tradition. Instead, in *Beloved* the home returns as the angry teller of a tale of retribution. Yet the subject of domesticity, whether examined through an angry home or in other ways, is largely absent from the criticism of *Jazz*, *Paradise*, and *Love*, Morrison's first novel after the *Beloved* trilogy.[22] This absence seems strange, especially considering the importance of home, whether as a type of character, a literal location, or as an ideological concept, in all three novels.

An examination of domesticity in Morrison's work cracks open the fault lines of gender politics, revealing as much about the male characters as the female characters. In *Jazz*, *Paradise*, and *Love*, masculinity becomes equated with social and political resistance. Morrison's men are driven: to have a normative middle-class urban experience, to build an entire way of life from scratch, or to provide the entertainment for an emerging African American leisure culture. Although *Paradise* is the title of the final novel of the *Beloved* trilogy, its title conveys what the men of *Jazz* and *Love* (Morrison's first novel after the trilogy) strive to build: an ideal environment for themselves and the families they deem worthy, "like us." The male characters occupy themselves with social resistance (from both progressive and conservative angles), the haunting psychological aftereffects of social resistance, or the conservation of what was won through this type of resistance. Yet Morrison does not portray these struggles as entirely noble. In many cases, the men enact resistance at a great cost. The masculine obsession with "large-scale" resistance leads to the isolation of the male within the family. Always on guard against outside forces, the family man often ignores the parallel resistance mission his wife or partner has set in motion. Somewhat blind to everything but resisting "them," many of Morrison's male characters do not notice a female partner's resistance *to her own familial status quo,* often until it is too late, and a tangible or emotional rift has appeared.

In *Jazz,* generations have fled the post-slavery South for better social and economic opportunities in New York. Violet and Joe Trace decide to leave the farm ways behind them entirely as they embark on a decidedly urban existence. He sells cosmetics door-to-door and she styles hair both in her own home and in the homes of her customers. Although neither Joe nor Violet could be classified as the stereotypical protester or activist, in their own quiet ways, they have chosen lines of work far removed from their former life of subsistence farming. Both attend to the beautification of the body — she, as an unlicensed beautician and he, as a door-to-door cosmetics salesman. It is as if both have chosen to make a living from the more urban image of polished femininity. Yet Joe's long-term resistance to and simultaneous longing for "the old ways" leads him to a growing sense of emotional alienation, one he fails to share with his wife. Instead, he embarks on a disastrous affair with a much younger woman. While the casual reader might expect Joe to become drawn to an urbane, manicured woman, the kind of woman who might represent the target market for his products, the more seasoned Morrison reader knows better. Joe's choice might reveal a new side of his character, but it will not be such a predictable one. Significantly, Joe chooses Dorcas, a teenager plagued with acne, a strict guardian, and an oppressive home life, a young woman he can mold as he could not mold his headstrong wife, and one he can tempt with the empty promises of his beauty products.

Morrison portrays Joe as a man who has failed to notice the cracks in his own house, specifically, in his wife's strange domestic practices. Instead, Joe embraces a private isolationist strategy, acting as if his sense of alienation is the price he must pay for his long-ago move North. Joe's failure to notice the trouble at home contributes to the novel's larger theme of the tension between the individual and the community in urban life, particularly when the urban neighbors have migrated from more rural areas, and are used to a more communal way of life not suited to the carved-up blocks of individual small homes without land.

In *Paradise*, the men of Ruby resist the perils of Reconstruction American life and forge westward to join an all-black community. Rejected because they lack cash, the men suffer their rejection stoically, but angrily. This instance, however, forms a core of resistance and isolationist tendencies that will lead them to build "the all-black town worth all the pain" (5) and to defend it for decades, mandating "a rigidly controlled communal historiography predicated on the subordination of the individual to the group" (Davidson 356). The men maintain their position even when newcomers, adolescents, and women begin to move toward more contact with the outside world. The women, for instance, begin to want goods and services not available in the town of Ruby. They long for greater selection and lower prices, and these desires drive them to the nearby town of Demby. The children, mostly teenagers, leave town to obtain outside goods and pleasures, but they also rebel against their parents' isolationist survival strategies on a more ideological level. While the men of the town maintain an attitude of icy rage toward outsiders and a deep-seated fear of God's wrath against pride and vanity, the young people are interested in the tenets of Black Pride. In the words of their elders they want to "have meetings there to talk about how handsome they were while giving themselves ugly names. Like not American. Like African" (104).

The potent symbol of this struggle is the Oven, formerly a communal source of food, but currently a local hangout for the teens. When a fist, a symbol of Black Pride, is drawn on the Oven, the founding fathers of the town want justice and punishment. One outsider minister, and several of the town women also think that the young people deserve to be heard. Morrison carefully crafts the Oven as a complex symbol invoking the African American domestic tradition, communal domestic practice, and the idea that in a small community, the private (an oven) becomes the public (the Oven). The lack of privacy, anonymity, and, at times, the freedom to explore unorthodox or creative ways of life, are all unspoken prices that must be paid for the "safety" the town provides. Because Morrison portrays the struggle between old and new ways of life in largely domestic terms, the novels are ripe for analysis as domestic novels, yet *Beloved* is still far more likely than *Paradise*, *Jazz*, or *Love* to be read in this way.

Interestingly, in *Love*, Morrison follows a beachside resort proprietor through the heyday of the 1940s to the 1960s when the hotel goes out of business. Bill Cosey, his immediate family, and his workers see a danger in Civil Rights action because it threatens business: seaside leisure seems frivolous, if not extravagant, when activists are dying in the streets. Also, townspeople begin to see Cosey as a man "owned" by whites, and they demand that he give some of his land back to the community. During a rally outside the hotel, one of the protesters covers Cosey in animal waste (149). Cosey chooses this moment, while still covered in waste, to prove his own place in the community, and by association, the townspeople's reliance, and even dependence, on him. Ignoring the stench and the waste dripping from his clothes, he steps down from the hotel property and greets the protesters by name, inquiring about a child's education and the status of a broken truck as he moves through the crowd. Cosey literally repositions himself—he is no longer "the Man"; he is a benevolent father figure embedded in the crowd and in the domestic affairs of his community. It is no coincidence that this section of the novel is ironically subtitled "Guardian."

Despite scenes such as this one, when Cosey manages to contain the resistance to his elitist practices and to earlier scenes of commanding lavish parties and semi-public domestic space, Cosey finds himself undone, but not, as we might imagine, by outside forces. It is the women he lives and works with, mired in their own forms of social resistance to child abuse, class differences, the accumulation of wealth, and the exploitation of the poor, who ultimately ruin Cosey: "First they disappointed him, then they defied him, then they turned his home into a barrel of quarreling she-crabs and his life's work into a cautionary lesson in black history" (201). It is L (or Love, the title character and the narrator of several sections of the novel) who notes the cause of Cosey's downfall in opposition to the town gossip. Interestingly, her interpretation privileges home by mentioning it prior to his life's work, indicating that one of Cosey's chief goals may have been to build himself successful private and public *homes*, rather than simply to succeed in a given business. His misunderstanding of the women in his life (not the larger community or global socioeconomic shifts) and their forms of social resistance, however, ultimately confounds this goal.

Morrison's characters, particularly her male characters, tend to succeed when they are able to recall and employ their roots within *the home* (the current domestic realm, including the relationships embodied there) and their roots within *the Home* (the original homeplace, with all its cultural traditions and folkways, usually set in the South). As Cosey learns when he is confronted by the angry crowd, remembering one's home and one's Home can also become a recovery strategy in a time of crisis, even if the moment of recovery is only temporary.

The House of Jazz: Communal and Individual Domesticity

The opening of *Jazz* quickly shows the interior of an unhappy home, complete with Violet's dramatic act of setting "free" her caged birds (3) and the "poisoned silence" that "floated through the rooms" (5). Yet the background of the Trace family indicates that the recent violent acts of Joe and Violet are not the sole cause of the shadow that has fallen over this home. Instead, their acts may have been the symptoms, not the cause, of larger disappointments.

Both Joe and Violet have chosen jobs that tend to the superficial level of the body, jobs that probably were not available to them in the harsh economic climate of the South during the 1920s. Interestingly, while both jobs seem urban at first glance, they also invite the kind of domestic community usually associated with smaller towns by allowing Joe and Violet into the homes of others on a regular basis. Yet this contact still lacks something; its commercial nature cannot create a true sense of community. Jennifer Fitzgerald views Joe and Violet's occupations as a sign of a deliberately commodified culture, in which "commodities are romanticized and romance is commodified" (382). The theme of lost community ties in urban life runs throughout the book in a subtle way: the characters have friends, but these friendships are easily lost in a time of crisis. Similarly, to Joe, emotions seem to be dampened in their force. Joe realizes that he has lost the level of feeling he experienced before he moved north: "For when Joe tries to remember the way it was when he and Violet were young, when they got married, decided to leave Vesper County and move up North to the City almost nothing comes to mind. He recalls dates, of course, events, purchases, activity, even scenes. But he has a tough time trying to catch what it felt like" (29). The dating of the loss of memory-sensation to the move North indicates that Joe's loss may not be age-related because he does remember: "events, purchases, activity ... scenes" that signal the beginning of a different kind of life. Before he begins his disastrous affair with Dorcas, Joe struggles with a sense of not being able to recall the emotions that have led him to this city life: he cannot remember his original passion for Violet nor his sense of fear at their plans for a new life (29). Morrison creates these motives, rather than a more typical lust, and makes them the plausible rationale behind the affair that sets the novel in motion. In continuing to build a life in resistance to the rural farming life available to him as a young man, Joe has lost sight of his emotional motivation for that resistance, and he misses the signs, embedded in his wife's crumbling domestic practices, that might have told him that she too has reached a crisis that leads her to question their life together.

Instead of examining the domesticity of *Jazz*, critics focus on issues such as race-based identity formation, the identity and characteristics of the novel's sometimes cryptic narrator, the representation of historical events, and the relationship of the narrative's structure to the musical structure of jazz music.[23] My intent is not to subvert the importance of these lines of inquiry, but to suggest that the novel's seemingly trivial domestic details may actually offer valuable insights into these issues as well as others. Rather than addressing the established debates and issues through the lens of the kitchen, I will explore what I view as three main functions of the home in *Jazz* that culminate in a fourth function and overall purpose of the domestic in the novel.

First, homes delineate many sections of the narrative, and second, through their interiors they offer intimate sketches of individuals made visible by the free-floating jazz style of the omniscient narrator. Additionally, homes function as protective socioeconomic borders and as indicators of social status. Finally, when we read the domestic signs in a combination of these three ways, homes and the domestic practices within them begin to represent the tension between new structures of community and new modes of individuality for Morrison's characters. Not surprisingly, the female characters, those with traditionally closer ties to the home, also use the home as a means of enacting resistance to the social status quo. Morrison validates the concept of domestic resistance because it serves as a harbinger of larger social problems in the African American community. If instead, it is read by fellow characters as simply "crazy" behavior, rather than as a form of social protest, disastrous consequences can follow.

The narrative style of *Jazz*, with its omnipresent, self-referential narrator, allows us to see what feels like, at some moments in the reading experience, everything a city has to offer. We witness both its most intimate details of dangling shoes, tipped hats, and snapping fingers, as well as its pulses and heart murmurs of rhythm. Because the narrator or the voice of the book projects him/it/her-self into the crevices of urban life, we do not have the typical narrative closures and pauses of a non-omniscient narrator. That is, no door or window ever closes, leaving us, the readers, along with our first-person narrative guide, out in the cold. Instead, we are pulled (and some readers might say dragged) through doors, walls, streets, under bed covers, and into caves in a way that can be both charming and disarming. It is as if we, along with the narrator, have attained a kind of ghostly presence that allows us to walk through the walls in a manner not available to a typically more humanized omniscient third-person narrator.

Yet even with the peculiarities of a first-person omniscient narrator, delineation in the narrative still exists. We don't walk through a wall without feeling it. Morrison seems to account for the reader's sense of disorientation by offering key domestic details at the beginning of a sudden change in scene. She frequently uses domestic detail to familiarize the reader with new physical surroundings and the characters who inhabit them, but also with our location, teleologically speaking, within the narrative. Similarly, domestic details, even domestic material goods, often combine either literally or through proximity in the narrative, in ways that prefigure which characters, along with which themes and strands of the story, are more deeply linked as well.

The opening of the novel begins with this type of domestic orientation. Early in the novel, the narrator describes a certain type of older person who rejects gossip and interference in others' lives in favor of a more meaningful expenditure of energy: "Sometimes they concentrated on making sure the person they had shared their long lives with had cheerful company and the necessary things for the night" (11). This sentence ends a paragraph, and the new paragraph begins, "But up there on Lenox, in Violent and Joe Trace's apartment, the rooms are like the empty birdcages wrapped in cloth. And a dead girl's face has become the necessary thing for their nights." This object, the dead girl's face, might seem to hold only symbolic import, until we learn that Violet has actually procured Dorcas' (the dead girl's) photograph and placed it on the mantel. Further, the narrator lets us feel the collective rooms themselves (like empty birdcages) rather than simply focusing on the room that Joe and Violet currently inhabit. In only a few sentences, one describing a domestic ideal for old age, followed by a sentence describing an "empty" domestic reality, Morrison's narrator places us squarely in the heart of a conflict that did not end with a murder, but began with one. It is the state of the Trace household, including its boundaries and limitations, as well the narrator's description of its overall atmosphere that cues the reader that this story belongs to Joe and Violet. But it is not theirs alone; the narrative also belongs in a lesser way to "a dead girl," a city with its proper street names and addresses, and to the domestic ideal of old age that Joe and Violet seem, at least at this point in the novel, almost incapable of achieving. Through description of the home, Morrison outlines the broader scope of her fictional territory.

At the end of the novel, we learn that Alice Manfred, who had been Dorcas' guardian before her death, has moved back to Springfield. Another woman has moved into her house. This woman, adds the narrator, seemingly extraneously, "may need a few things": "curtains ... the cheerful company maybe of someone who can provide the necessary things for the night" (222). Once again, this repeated statement of the desire for an ideal of domestic comfort and domestic compatibility ends a paragraph, telling us that the emptiness and want that characterized Joe and Violet's story has now drifted away, coming to rest like a cloud over another home, as a part of someone else's story. Joe and Violet, we quickly learn, have found a new, strange domestic harmony, not resurrected from their past, but created entirely anew from nonnormative sleeping, eating, and working patterns that follow their individual needs for naps and snacks, rather than any external domestic precriptions. Instead of roaming the city, worrying and hunting, now they "stay home figuring things out" (223). Morrison crafts a sense of closure on this narrative through the domestic, but she retains the sense of an open and an open-ended narrative by forgoing the romanticization of any kind of traditional or stereotypical domestic happiness. Conversely, Joe and Violet have forged a new kind of life through resistance to traditional domestic codes.

Before allowing the reader a glimpse of the overall patterns of the community, Morrison invites us into the Trace household to gain an understanding of Violet, including her contradictions and her current progression of rapid changes, as reflected in her domesticity. The novel does not begin with a detailed account of one of the central events of the novel: Violet's desecration of Dorcas' corpse at the funeral. That event is relegated to a meager sentence on the novel's first page: "When the woman, her name is Violet, went to the funeral to see the girl and to cut her dead face they threw her to the floor and out of the church" (3). Much of the opening of the book focuses, instead, on exactly where and how Violet lived, including her first action upon returning from the funeral: she frees her cherished birds, "including the parrot that said 'I love you'" (3). That action alone might be read as Violet's attempt to free herself from an incomplete relationship with her husband or to begin to grieve his recent affair and his murder of a young girl. However, read in its domestic context, the event seems to be an attempt at an even larger grasp for freedom: Violet tries to free herself from the psychic weight of her own life, beginning with its domestic trappings. On the second page of the novel, we read that Violet is rejected as a candidate for aid from the Salem Women's Club, and that she has both tried and given up on "getting herself a boyfriend and letting him visit *in* her own house" (4). In relation to her husband, "washing his handkerchiefs and putting food on the table before him was the most she could manage" (5). In short, in the wake of a disastrous, violent, and life-changing series of events, what Morrison chooses to show us is the interior, not of her characters' psyches, but of their now-disordered domestic lives.

As emotional numbness sets in, so too does Violet's own domestic numbness: "She wakes up in the morning and sees with perfect clarity a string of small, well-lit scenes. In each one something specific is being done: food things, work things; customers and acquaintances are encountered, places entered. But she does not see herself doing these things. She sees them being done" (22). Morrison codes domesticity, and Violet's own work in the homes of other women, as a series of isolated rituals ("a string of small, well-lit scenes"), often performed for comfort and often undertaken in an unfeeling manner ("being done") during a time of crisis. Violet knows that these things must be done, and some must be done in order to avoid public shame. Morrison indicates the public, communal value of these deeds by casting them as "well-lit scenes," seemingly visible to others.

Like Violet, Alice Manfred expresses her emotional state, as well as her emotional history, through her home. Even the food she serves to company remains "a tad skimpy in the portions" and her guests know her to hold "a prejudice against butter" (72). The reader immediately senses the effects of these not-quite deprivations on Dorcas and how they might have made her ripe for an overblown, luxuriant affair full of small gifts and treats. Too, Alice takes on a habit of speaking with Violet every morning when Violet comes to the Manfred house, but only while she irons and mends with a ritualistic attention to detail and perfection. It is as if she must physically place the border of a well-executed domestic task between her own body and Violet's to make their total separation clear to herself.

This pattern of the introduction of characters and their most intimate and complex problems, prejudices, and hopes through the details of their domestic surroundings and practices continues throughout the novel. In a sequence of memories, the reader feels the increasingly horrific effects of Reconstruction as the landowners move from taking the farming implements outside the home and begin to snatch "what was theirs, they said, although we (Violet's family) cooked in it, washed sheets in it, sat on it, ate off of it" (98). Worse, we learn that Violet watched as the landowners tipped her mother, Rose Dear, out of her chair and into the floor in order to repossess both her kitchen chairs and table. Again, these domestic details become a kind of emotional and psychological shorthand, this time, for the intense deprivation that Violet has been subject to for most of her life, even after she thought she had found and made a home with Joe Trace. The emotional and material deprivations Violet felt further connect her to Dorcas, as does her childlike stance when "visiting" Alice.

Images of domestic desperation and abandonment unite Joe, Violet, and Golden Gray, the mixed-race boy who haunted Violet through her grandmother's stories. When Golden Gray searches for his father, Henry Lestory, *Jazz*'s narrator circles back on the tale, allowing Golden Gray to enter his father's empty home, not once, but twice: "This 'double-take' reports the scene with slightly different details from the first version; the fireplace, for example, is now 'clean, set for a new fire' (152) whereas in the first telling it 'has a heap of ash' (147)" (Page 172). Philip Page interprets the "double-take" not in terms of its domestic detail, but as an indication of an unreliable narrator and as a kind of "invitational gap" that invites the reader to participate fully in the construction of meaning (172). However, the changed detail itself, a fireplace, with its synecdochical relationship to the home and its traditional domestic "hearth" symbolism, resonates with the history of African American domesticity as well. Not only does Morrison call into question the reliability of the narrator, she also emphasizes the mutable state of African American domesticity, with its ongoing double consciousness from a history of working within the home of white employers and within personal homes. As Joe Trace mentions when documenting his "seven changes," "The buildings were like castles in pictures and we who had cleaned up everybody's mess since the beginning knew better than anybody how to keep them nice" (127). Perhaps the changing fireplace also indicates the narrator's ability to notice the domestic details and the presence of domestic labor that the privileged Golden Gray cannot. A similarly symbolic depiction of domesticity occurs when Joe finds Wild's "crevice" home. Not only is it filled with golden light, it is also filled with the objects that, if put in context, would unlock the secrets of Joe's, Golden's, and Violet's pasts. And here too, domesticity becomes distinctly mutable, because Joe feels free to rearrange the objects and ponder his past: to "disrupt things, rummage, touch, and move" (184).

Not every domestic image, however, tilts toward abandonment or sadness. At the novel's surprisingly hopeful end, we learn that Joe and Violet have achieved a new brand of peaceful, need-based domesticity. But perhaps even more importantly, they seemed to have arrived at the state largely via domestic practices; they have reinstated their "whispering old-time love" not only through whispering under the covers at night, but also by planning to tear a quilt "into its original scraps" and to "get a nice wool blanket with a satin hem. Powder blue, maybe" (224). Morrison uses domesticity both as an indicator of the internal state of her characters and relationships *and* as a *process* that may hold the capacity for at least some sort of reparation and healing. The exchange of a quilt for a store-bought blanket also indicates that domestic destruction (tearing the quilt into scraps) both mirrors and facilitates the process of emotional healing for the couple. With the phrase "original scraps," Morrison reminds the reader that this is not so much destruction as returning the quilt to its previous state of being, much as Joe and Violet have captured some elements of their original relationship.

Morrison reveals that part of the healing and reparation of marital and personal wrongs, as well as the wrongs suffered under institutionalized racism, can be soothed through the home. The home then, functions as a buffer zone. However, not all characters have access to this type of buffering, and the home marks a socioeconomic boundary between those who can afford a certain kind of home and those who cannot, as well as a layer of insulation, albeit a light one, between her characters and an often cruel urban environment. For instance, in a discussion of "armed" and "unarmed" women and the reasons for the status of each, the narrator asks "Who else were the unarmed ones?" and answers, "those who bought houses and hoarded money as protection and the means to purchase it" (78). In this sense, the home ownership takes on a status as the equivalent of a weapon, a means not only of protection, but also of defense against the easily imagined financial disasters as well as the more shadowy states of disrepair, such as the one that has befallen Violet.

Just as having a home, and owning a home even more so, offers a multifaceted layer of protection, the language surrounding the home creates a border as well. In *Jazz*, when Felice narrates a section of the narrative toward the end of the novel, we learn about her mostly absent parents, seemingly as an explanation for why she might be drawn to Joe and Violet and their nontraditional home. What Felice remembers most about her upbringing is her grandmother's correction when she said that her parents lived in another town. Although Felice saw her parents in the city only every three weeks, her grandmother was quick to note that they *lived* in the city, but they only *worked* in Tuxedo. Yet Felice deconstructs the division that her grandmother holds dear when she says "Just words: Live, work" (198). With this deconstruction, Morrison notes a change from one generation to the next: the grandmother may be resisting the legacy of slavery by insisting that Felice's parents have control over naming their true home place, despite the unequal hours spent in each location. Felice, who does not feel slavery's legacy in the same way as her grandmother, sees only the absence of her parents from her own home. Therefore, Felice must carve out her own protection from the city, as she has in her parents' absence. Without having known the complete comfort of familial domesticity, she may pick a non-domestic form of protection for herself, perhaps one less stable than property ownership or community involvement.

As the narrative moves us backward through time to look at Joe and Violet's separate childhoods, followed by their romance, we find their initial impressions of an unknown city, as well as their impetus for the move. Because of Joe's love of the wilderness, his decision to move surprises many: "It was shocking to his family and friends not when he agreed to marry Violet, but that, thirteen years later, he agreed to take her to Baltimore, where she said all the houses had separate rooms and water came to you — not you to it" (106). It is important to note, first, that this description of the enticements of city life, the comforts of urban domesticity, *precedes* even the promise of new jobs or increased social status. Second, Violet's description privileges the home's separate rooms, and the ability to stay within the confines of the home and receive water, stressing a kind of individuality and independence dependent upon a non-communal style of living. Through her use of the domestic, Morrison unpacks the seemingly simple motivations for migration: simple financial gain was not always the reason, at least for Joe and Violet. Instead, Morrison crafts a matrix of complex reasons for her characters' move — jobs, yes, but also property and the privacy that comes with it, anonymity coupled with a sense of community — and she frequently uses the home and its complicated contents as the chosen form of representation of that matrix.

Morrison describes an individual's or a family's domesticity as a way of letting us know that we are exiting one life and entering another in what would otherwise be a very confusing narrative structure. She also makes productive, intimate thumbnail sketches of each character's mindset through what they do (or do not do) in the home. But homes also *act* in *Jazz*, sometimes as nearly personified entities, armoring individuals for personal and institutional battles. In this last way, the state of the home gives the readers clues not only to the character's mindset, but also to what she might see as her most formidable opponent and how she intends to conduct her battle.

Yet frequently, there are allies in the battle. Morrison's characters are engaged in a form of domesticity that glorifies both individuality and privacy, while also depending upon and valorizing the conveniences and solidarity of community. In the opening of the novel, even a grocery list becomes a creative, collective endeavor:

> Up in those big five-story apartment buildings and the narrow wooden houses in between people knock on each other's doors to see if anything is needed or can be had. A piece of soap? A little kerosene? Some fat, chicken or pork, to brace the soup one more time? Whose husband is getting ready to go see if he can find a shop open? Is there time to add turpentine to the list drawn up and handed to him by the wives? [11].

Here, the rhythm of the questions and requests called from door to door emerges. The occupants of these apartments are individuated and comforted by separate rooms, decorated and cared for along the lines of individual tastes, but they are still part of a fabric of a community. They may not meet at a shared water source, but they will still meet and support each other, even through the smallest of domestic details. Morrison constructs a significant portion of the jazz structure of the novel — its tension between individual and group performances, between personal needs and accountability to the community — through the very homes themselves. The jazz aesthetic "is characterized in particular by the tension between an element of controlled collective improvisation and the emergence of the soloist as it figured prominently in jazz styles that were contemporary to the novel's action" (Ludigkeit 169).

In many ways, the homes of *Jazz* are haunted with the past and present secrets of their inhabitants, though more quietly so than *Beloved*'s 124. The narrative structure of the novel, evocative of jazz music, allows Morrison to see the intimate details — the parrot cages, the dolls hidden under the bed, the hair singed in the kitchen, the poorly and the well-hemmed dresses and coats — of multiple sites of domesticity. Whereas 124 unravels to tell a violent tale of the slavery, migration, and the aftermath of both, the many townhouses, apartments, and houses of *Jazz* combine their contained violent and secretive acts to weave an urban fabric of African American life that includes the foundation of new communities. Through her use of homes and urban domestic detail within the jazz structure, Morrison heralds the development of a culture of clearly delineated individuals, with the walls of each home representing and exaggerating the importance and the glamour of each individual. Yet the novel's unexpected ending, in which a chain of tragedies brings individuals into homes they had never planned to enter, valorizes community solidarity. In short, Morrison uses a jazz-based narrative structure to perform much the same work as jazz music: through the creation of a new African American urban domestic genre, Morrison highlights both the individual performances within each home, as well as the group improvisation of homes that forms her fictional African American communities.

Cold Ovens and Scandalous Convents: *Paradise's Subversive Domesticity*

With *Paradise*, Morrison introduces an original approach to the domestic novel. Instead of traditional associations with (usually white) single-family dwellings and their individual household practices, or icons such as "the angel in the house," Morrison takes a sweeping, wide-angle view of the theories, ideologies, legends, historical events, and emotional crises that form the home and the large-scale communal domestic practices of a particular community. In many ways, large-scale domestic resistance, enacted by a group in the face of socioeconomic and historical circumstances, forms the core of *Paradise*. The forefathers of the novel's original all-black town, Haven, Oklahoma, created it in response to racism and rapidly diminishing career opportunities after Reconstruction. Decades later, a smaller group of those founding families resists the economic damage to the town post–World War II and sets out to establish a new home elsewhere in Oklahoma. However, "the Disallowing," the rejection of their cash-poor group because of their lack of resources and, according to some, their dark skin tone, psychologically wounds them in ways that will emerge for the next eighty years. This rejection occurs at the hands of light-skinned and more prosperous African Americans in already-established towns, and is heightened by what looks like pity: a small cash offering, blankets, and some food (193–95). At this point, the families of Haven, including several children and pregnant women, are hungry, exhausted, and seared by the rejection at the hands of other African Americans, something they had not imagined in their own context of banding together for survival.

Having faced racism at the hands of whites, world war, the collapse of their former town, poverty, and outright rejection, the former Havenites take up rejection as their rallying cry and vow to build an entirely self-sufficient way of life, no matter what the cost. In the new town of Ruby, they build a communal life on the principle of social resistance. The rigidity of the male founders' resistance, however, leads them to ignore the signs of familial resistance: many of their wives and children have begun to doubt their men's beliefs and the high costs of "the one all-black town worth the pain" (5). Although most literary critics do not categorize *Paradise* as a domestic novel,[24] both the social and the familial resistance take numerous *domestic* forms, including rethinking the town's symbol of communal domesticity (the Oven), changing domestic practices within individual homes, and ultimately, attacks on outsiders who threaten to introduce new ways of being in the home and in the world.

Given the scale and the scope of *Paradise*'s perspective on domesticity, we might expect Morrison to work in large brushstrokes, sketching out the major historical conflicts of the "big novel." Instead, she balances both large and small, frequently using domestic details to flesh out the quotidian realities of a well-known historical event, and thus refuting the most common criticism of domestic novels: that they overlook the larger, historical picture. She performs this balancing act using three main arenas: the town's Oven, the private kitchens of Ruby residents, and in marked contrast, the Convent's kitchen. Morrison tightly weaves these three arenas together, despite some characters' active resistance to the associations among them. Further, the entanglement of the Oven, the private kitchens, and the Convent kitchens resists and even rejects the town's central, founding principle of isolated self-reliance. Several of the town's women seem to encourage this entanglement, individuating from their families and "mixing" with the Convent women, other towns, and each other's private lives. Some of the women encourage other forms of blending the town's rigid borders by mixing domestic items and ideas: combining old and new, store-bought and homemade, as well as "inside" and "outside" goods. For instance, Dovey uses canned peas rather than home-grown, and spices them with hot peppers from the Convent. Some of the male characters do their own mixing as well, but it tends to be more covert and to involve people rather than goods, as with Deek's affair with Connie from the Convent, K.D.'s affair with Gigi, and Reverend Misner's meeting with the town's young people. In general, the insider male characters violently resist, at least publicly, the women's mixing with outsiders, as well as their incorporation of outside goods, ideas, and practices. This fear of domestic mixing becomes intimately linked with their anxiety about racial purity — the fear of mixing the pure "8-rock" blood with whites or lighter-skinned blacks like those who performed the Disallowing.

The Oven represents and acts as the site of many of the "mixing" practices the town fathers fear. A large brick structure originally built in Haven, then moved to Ruby, the Oven was built as a site of communal domesticity, a place for townspeople to gather, cook, and eat. But even with the moderate effects of industrialization in Ruby (in the late 1970s the town has electricity and private kitchens, but rejects television), a communal space of this type falls into disuse. Morrison writes, "A utility became a shrine ... and, like anything that offended Him, destroyed its own self," indicating that the Oven became overloaded with symbolic value, even as its use value declined (103–4). The loss of community through industrialization and the resulting scramble to reinscribe a sense of community, sometimes at any cost, becomes a theme for Morrison, also seen in *Jazz*'s isolated city dwellers, and to a lesser extent in *Love* and the attempts to recapture the mystique of an all-black vacation resort.

Morrison imbues the Oven with the history of African American slavery, including domestic resistance:

> Maybe Zechariah never wanted to eat another stick-roasted rabbit, or cold buffalo meat. Maybe, having been routed from office by whites, refused a homestead by coloreds, he wanted to make a permanent feature in that open land so different from Louisiana. Anyway, while they set up temporary quarters — lean-tos, dugouts — and hauled wood in a wagon with two horses the State Indians lent them, Zechariah corralled some of the men into building a cook oven. They were proud that none of their women had ever worked in a whiteman's kitchen or nursed a white child. Although field labor was harder and carried no status, they believed the rape of women who worked in white kitchens was if not a certainty a distinct possibility — neither of which they could bear to contemplate. So they exchanged that danger for the relative safety of brutal work. It was that thinking that made a community "kitchen" so agreeable. They were extraordinary [99].

This passage contains echoes of the pride of domesticity, the true *homemaking* found outside a slave owner's kitchen, or later, outside a white domestic employer's kitchen. Without the threat of whites, the Haven residents craft this pride into a communal, public pride and a public act of domestic resistance to their past. However, when the private becomes public, what is to become of individual homes and kitchens, now divested, at least in part, of their earlier anti-oppression historical and sociological import?

One answer lies in the women's resistance to the Oven itself, its literal physicality, dating from the time of the move from Haven to Ruby. In a scene of kitchen meditation reminiscent of Ellen's cake-baking scene in *Delta Wedding*, Soane Morgan contemplates the Oven's significance while brewing her herbal menopause tea:

Minus the baptisms the Oven had no real value. What was needed back in Haven's early days had never been needed in Ruby. The trucks they came in brought cook-stoves as well. The meat they ate clucked in the yard, or fell on its knees under a hammer, or squealed through a slice in its throat. Unlike at Haven's beginning, when Ruby was founded hunting game was a game. The women nodded when the men took the Oven apart, packed, moved and reassembled it. But privately they resented the truck space given over to it — rather than a few more sacks of seed, rather than shoats or even a child's crib. Resented also the hours spent putting it back together — hours that could have been spent getting the privy door on sooner. If the plaque was so important — and judging from the part of the meeting she had witnessed she, supposed it was — why hadn't they just taken it by itself, left the bricks where they had stood for fifty years? [103].

Here Soane recognizes what may have been the beginning of the rift between many of the town's women and men, as well as the seemingly practical, domestic roots of the rift. The women, unlike the men, recognize that part of the town's progress, part of the evidence of its economic success, lies in the privatization of home life — the growing of one's own food and livestock rather than the need for a group hunt and a communal cooking session. Instead of using truck space on a symbolic piece, they would prefer to amass the material goods that would sustain the town, thus proving its mission a worthy one. Similarly, Morrison heightens this conflict by showing the women's secret to-do list: "getting the privy door on sooner." This example of their resentment toward the Oven indicates that the women feel exposed to their neighbors in even their most private acts because of the men's insistence on rituals and appearances of communitarianism.

Meanwhile, as she ponders the history of the Oven, Soane participates in the type of mixing the town fathers condemn: the remedy she brews and sips as she thinks about the Oven was created at the Convent, from Convent herbs. (Later, Deek arrives home and expresses his disapproval of this formula, even though Soane refuses to tell him what it is [105].) During her meditation, she stands under "newly installed fluorescent light" that prevents her from seeing "into the darkness outside as she waited for the kettle to boil" (100), so that technology trumps her former connection with the natural world through her home. Further, in the very moments while Soane mixes new technology, mysterious Convent herbs, and thoughts of the town's symbol of its past, her husband, Deek, hunts quail, mimicking the town's former patterns of survival long after these practices are truly needed. Morrison frames Soane's kitchen meditation about the Oven in a setting of new-meets-old and inside-meets-outside, heightening these conflicts and casting them in a distinctly domestic light.

In her kitchen, Soane also thinks about the all-important Oven plaque, with its debated message that reads either "Beware the Furrow of His Brow" or "Be the Furrow of His Brow." The confusion over the plaque's message serves as the most overt sign of conflict between the younger and the older townspeople. The youth, using the tenets of Black Pride, proclaim their own strength as well as God's presence within all human life, and push for a "Be the Furrow" interpretation (84–85), thus showing that they have been influenced by the social consciousness and perhaps the popular culture of the 1970s through outsiders such as Richard Misner and pseudo-outsiders, such as Anna Flood.[25] The town elders, in a more authoritarian but less ideologically clear position, argue for "Beware the Furrow," adamantly proclaiming God's divine will for the town and the need for obedience (87). More subtly, however, they seem to allow for a double meaning, directing the "Beware" at those who had done the Disallowing (195). The location of the plaque on the Oven, the former center of public domesticity, places the entire ideological debate literally within the realm of the domestic symbolism, and Morrison heightens the significance of domesticity by representing "the outside" through details such as going to Demby for better household goods and hospital births. In this sense, the older generation and the younger generation argue over the town's entire way of life and the meaning of its original mission: Will they "Be the Furrow" by boldly venturing into neighboring towns and beyond or will they continue to "Beware" all "outside" ways of life not sanctioned in Ruby? Morrison's use of domestic details to exemplify this battle foreshadows the domestic nature of the novel's ultimate conflict: the violence at the Convent.

Morrison inextricably connects the Oven and the Convent's kitchen. The circularly structured novel opens with the conclusion of the narrative: nine of the 8-rock men have arrived at the Convent to "save" the town from the Convent women. Yet their motivations once they are in the house seem to shift. As they invade the house, one of the men[26] touches the stove's hood, "admiring its construction and power." He notices that "it was the same length as the brick oven that once sat in the middle of his hometown" (6). Since the Oven remains in Ruby, the phrase "once sat" appears to refer to its positioning as spatially and metaphorically central to the town. Here, a subtle depiction of the man's envy emerges: the Convent women do not need the town, nor its Oven; they are "women who chose themselves for company, which is to say not a convent but a coven" (276). Further, unlike Ruby's relationship to the Oven, the Convent oven remains central to the women's lives and their well-being; they have been gathered around it preparing breakfast and lunch together when the men invade (5). The women's access to communal, meaningful domesticity, more than their reputation for "evil," seems to drive the men's violence once they have entered the Convent.

Other implications of the men's envy arise as they survey the room and its contents more closely: "The kitchen is bigger than the house in which either man was born. The ceiling barn-rafter high. More shelving than Ace's Grocery store. The table is fourteen feet long if an inch" (5). The men also notice abundant, gorgeous food that the women have grown themselves: "scallion piled like a handful of green confetti nestles brilliant disks of carrot, and the potatoes, peeled and whole, are bone white, wet and crisp" (5). While the "bone white, wet and crisp" imagery prefigures the violence about to occur, the food also contains other potent associations. The Convent women provide for themselves, and they provide for the town of Ruby, long after its residents have come to rely on the convenience of canned foods (made palatable with Convent peppers),[27] much like Lee Smith's Appalachian characters who recognize the affluent way of life represented in "store-bought" food. Even though the men claim that they are at the Convent to root out "evil ways" and "whores" destroying the community, the domestic details imply that their resistance to the women lies at a far more primal level: they cannot feed their families in the abundant, communal, self-sufficient style of the Convent, even though they possess far greater economic resources. But to admit their failure to provide on this domestic-spiritual level, and to admit their failure to remain self-sufficient, would be tantamount to a third Disallowing[28] for the men.

Interestingly, one of the men admires the stockpot: "His mother bathed him in a pot no bigger than that. A luxury in the sod house where she was born" (5). He traces this memory back to Haven, its failure as a town, then remarks, "That is why they are here in this Convent. To make sure it never happens again. That nothing inside or out rots the one all-black town worth all the pain" (5). The language of "rot," like the labels used to describe the women just before the invasion — "bitches," "witches," and "sluts," among others (276) — contrasts sharply and ironically with the scene of calm domesticity they find in the actual Convent kitchen and their envy of common domestic goods.[29]

After the women have been killed by the nine 8-rock men, their bodies mysteriously disappear from the Convent house and grounds. Richard and Anna, significantly, are out of town for a conference when the violence occurs. Doubting "the convenient mass disappearance of the victims," they venture to the Convent on their own (303). As outsiders, they witness the interior of the Convent with a kinder eye, seemingly viewing it as a home rather than a cradle of evil. Finding in the cellar the women's drawings of their own bodies and their deepest troubles, Anna "saw the terribleness K.D. reported, but it wasn't the pornography he had seen, nor was it Satan's scrawl. She saw instead the turbulence of females trying to bridle, without being trampled, the monsters that slavered them" (303). Anna recognizes the drawing as a kind of coping mechanism, as a way of working through trauma. Strangely, both Anna and Misner also sense something unreported by the rest of the community. Each feels the sensation of some kind of opening in the yard: she believes it to be a door, he a window, although "there was nothing to see" (305). They laugh as they discuss it, playfully debating its form and meaning. Although this portion of the text remains dense and leans toward the mystical, Morrison implies that Anna and Misner are able to understand the nature of the disappearance as a joyful escape rather than as a shameful, violent end. Because of their outsider status, Richard and Anna have the ability to recognize a "way out" of Ruby, even an invisible one.

Morrison proves Anna and Misner correct, perhaps about their idea that the town's young people deserve to be heard, but much more definitively about the fate of the Convent women. The final passages of the text feature the women revisiting key figures in their lives, often in the context of eating or sharing a meal. In these encounters, the women seem exempt from their former familial and domestic woes: each remains slightly aloof, as if occupied with a sense of purpose, perhaps even ghostly, perhaps very much alive (Morrison provides details of their physical forms). I would argue for two distinct interpretations of this ending. First, Connie's domestic and spiritual rituals have been successful. By adopting her program, the women have transcended their problems. In this sense, the nontraditional, female-centered domesticity of the Convent prevails over the isolationist, communitarian domesticity of Ruby. Second, the Convent women, a racially mixed group, prevail over the 8-rock philosophy and promise, as stated by Pat Best: "Suddenly, Pat thought she knew all of it. Unadulterated and unadulteried 8-rock blood held its magic as long as it resided in Ruby. That was the recipe. That was their deal. For Immortality.... In that case, she thought, everything that worries them must come from women" (217). The men of Ruby, in the end, were justified in their worry about the Convent women, but not for the reasons they proclaimed. Ironically, just as the women seem to have found a recipe for domestic strength and tranquility, they have also found what they may not have been seeking: the immortality coveted by the town of Ruby. As some of the residents of Ruby had learned, the key to immortality lay in applying a creative, individualized approach to the very concept of maintaining a home. And as Pat Best, the town's unofficial historian, points out, "Home is not a little thing" (212).

"The House Nailed Down in Your Dreams and Nightmares": The Emotional Politics of Mutable Domesticity in Toni Morrison's Love

> Then home: a familiar place that, when you left, kept changing behind your back. The creamy oil painting you carried in your head turned into house paint. Vibrant, magical neighbors became misty outlines of themselves. The house nailed down in your dreams and nightmares comes undone, not sparkling but shabby, but even more desirable because what had happened to it had happened to you. The house had not shrunk; you had. The windows were not askew — you were. Which is to say it was more yours than ever.
>
> — Toni Morrison, Love

In the three novels prior to Love, Morrison offers her readers the home literally haunted by the devastation of slavery (Beloved), the home grieving for dead and unrealized loves (Jazz), and the women's communal home that ends in violence (Paradise). While Morrison carefully maps the details of each dwelling, the novels do not read solely as social commentaries on African American domestic life in various historical moments. Instead, Morrison lingers over the physical and emotional characteristics of each home over a span of many chapters, lining her descriptions with subtle significance and symbolism often more noticeable on a second reading, once the reader anticipates the intricacies of each plot. In this sense, the home operates in her recent fiction as more of a fictional *character* than as a setting. The homes of Love, even more so than the homes of Beloved, Jazz, and Paradise refuse to remain static, no matter how desperately their owners might want them to. Like the characters inhabiting them, homes change via their material cultures, but also through their rapidly changing emotional microclimates, which the most savvy of Morrison's characters read carefully — and others ignore at their own peril. In Love in particular, the home, in both its private and public manifestations, becomes more than a macabre background for unbelievable events. The home takes on a mutable consciousness of its own, acting as a repository for a set of complex emotional politics — the personal psychological agendas that shift and reformulate to fit the available resources and to map onto the available material objects. When she writes about the home, Morrison does not merely return to a favorite setting or theme; she explores the development of a recurring character in her fiction.

If one views the label "domestic fiction" through its nineteenth-century connotations of texts written by white authors that promote the social and moral value of a healthy, loving home, indeed, *Love* hardly fits the description. Yet domesticity — if by that we mean simply "all things home-related" — is a key issue in the novel. *Love*'s central crisis revolves around the value of a home, the question of who can or cannot own that home, even whether or not a home can be owned at all, and if not, which homemaking actions might equate with property ownership. Christine condenses these themes into an angry conversation with her lawyer, who suggests that Christine's long absence from her childhood home does not support her case for ownership of the property. Christine responds angrily: "If you don't know the difference between property and a home you need to be kicked in the face, you stupid, you dumb, you cannery trash! You're fired!" (95). The intensity of Christine's outburst, as well as Heed's own intensity in her struggle to maintain ownership, suggest that this difference — between the material culture of property ownership and the implied emotional content of the concept of "home" — informs the novel's central conflict.

Morrison proposes that a home place, whether a public or private dwelling, bears a cultural, but possibly more importantly, an emotional legacy, as well as a set of past and present emotional politics. While emotional politics might be taken for granted as a feature of every home, real or fictional, Morrison implies that they are worthy of closer examination. Anissa Janine Wardi points out that "In *Love*, Morrison continues her exploration of this topic by literalizing love not merely as an emotion, not what one purportedly feels towards another; rather, she portrays love as an act, leading to the question: how does one 'do' love?" (202). While some critics and reviewers have remarked that the novel would be more aptly titled "Lust" or "Hate," Morrison clearly chooses "love" for its variety of costumes and disguises, for the depth of its resulting emotional politics.

On the surface, the linkage of "love" and "home" sounds like a return to the nineteenth-century connotations of the term "domesticity." Yet the way that Morrsion links these concepts seems, instead, to question the very connection between home and love. For the characters of *Love*, home certainly does not symbolize a single type of familial or domestic love because home does not have the same representational paradigm from moment to moment. Christine's musings on the home she has never had showcase this mutability as not only a feature of her background of constant domestic upheaval, but also as a characteristic of her *concept* of home: "The house nailed down in your dreams and nightmares comes undone, not sparkling but shabby, but even more desirable because what had happened to it had happened to you" (86). Here, Christine notes not only the inevitable fact that one's home physically changes, but also that the significance of home (the concept and the physical place) changes for the individual. The physical changes in the home, combined with its environment of mutable emotional politics, give the home the semblance of a life of its own. Like a double of its inhabitants, it changes physically and emotionally, and for Christine, the ability to understand and interpret these mirrored changes, not a deed or a will, signifies ownership. While a home that alters itself to fit its inhabitants might sound cozy, for Christine it becomes anything but: for her, the mutability of the home as double has the properties of "dreams and nightmares." I would argue that Christine's emotional politics of domesticity construct the home as a nightmarish double to reflect her experience with Heed, her childhood best friend who inexplicably becomes her step-grandmother. Heed, once Christine's double, sharing her ice cream from the same spoon and wearing her bathing suit, morphed into a representation of Christine's confusion and horror at her discovery of the seamy side of adult sex. Heed becomes a part of this domestic nightmare by marrying Christine's grandfather at a young age. Because Heed has, in effect, removed Christine from every home that she has ever known, Christine conceives of home as a double for the self ("what had happened to it had happened to you") that distorts itself to accommodate its inhabitant's emotional disfigurement ("The windows were not askew — you were.") (86).

While the fight for ownership of the Cosey family home forms the central conflict of the novel, the fight for the home cannot be understood without delving into images of the Cosey hotel in its heyday. Morrison crafts the history of the emotional politics of domesticity through scenes of the now-abandoned hotel. Yet the hotel does not function as a public realm far from the concerns of the domestic. Rather, the hotel represents an increasingly politicized and public way of domestic life. It recreates the domestic experiences — all the preparations necessary for eating, sleeping, and relaxing comfortably — as a mass-market experience. Nowhere is the whole spectrum of domestic activity more public than in a hotel. As Susan Strasser has noted, early twentieth-century housing reformers worried about the effects of both boardinghouses and hotels on the "cherished ... privacy of the nuclear family," citing increasing intimacy between strangers as a moral problem (156).

Strasser's comments underscore the hotel's status as a domestic sphere, although a more public one with an increasingly complex set of emotional relationships between the owner, the owning family, hired domestic workers, and guests. Lawrence Veiller, a leading housing reformer of the early 1900s, commenting on boardinghouses, expanded on the dangers of semi-public living in close quarters: "It means the undermining of family life; often the breaking down of domestic standards. It frequently leads to the breaking up of homes and families, to the downfall and subsequent degraded career of young women, to grave immoralities — in a word, to the profanation of the home" (qtd. in Strasser 156). Strasser, however, reads between the lines of the reformers' claims, mounting a convincing argument that their deeper worry was not about domestic conditions, but about the unification of the labor force living in "safe places" for planning sabotage. Strasser's argument recalls the downfall of the Cosey resort at the hands of the new police chief during the Civil Rights movement (186–67), as well as the scene of local reformers demanding Cosey land for community centers (149), and May's insistence on storing provisions against the "acting up" she despised (82). As Heed tells Christine near the novel's close, "the new [police chief] upped the fees" (187). Like the housing reformers, Boss Silk, the police chief, was not really concerned with an African American resort and its "grave immoralities" of group living. Instead, he may have wanted to destroy a potential site for political unification and organization during the 1960s.

In this way, falling domestic standards became historically linked to immorality, and the powerful combination was used as a cover for deeper anxieties and as a substitute for fears that could not be publicly named or discussed. Much the same process takes hold in *Love*, especially when May and Christine claim to have legitimate complaints about Heed's qualifications as a wife, "lady," and business manager. May and Christine engage in constant criticism of the newly married Heed: "her speech, hygiene, table manners, and thousands of things Heed didn't know. What 'endorse a check' meant; how to dress a bed; how to dispose of sanitary napkins; how to set a table; how to estimate supplies" (76). Interestingly, this catalogue of Heed's shortcomings intertwines the deeply personal and bodily habits with domestic acts and business skills. In the litany, all the actions take on a kind of equal weight, as proof of Heed's definitive outsider status. The intertwining and equal weighting of these skills indicate the extent of the blending of the private and the public in hotel life. The setting of the hotel offers more opportunity for criticism of Heed, because it is unlikely that May and Christine would know of her intimate habits without the space of the semi-public hotel home, and because, as her fellow workers, they are privy to her business shortcomings.

However, it is not Heed's habits that truly anger and worry mother and daughter. As Morrison states, "Thoughts of Papa and her together in bed drove the two of them to more and newer meanness" (76). Yet Heed's marriage to Christine's grandfather acts as merely the external impetus for the criticism of Heed's every move. Hidden in domestic concerns and outrage over the "immorality" of the marriage lies another hidden fear. Mother and daughter seem to share an unasked question: If "Papa" could see Heed, a preteen, in a sexual light, what kept him from seeing his own granddaughter in that same light? As Heed and Christine cling to each other at the end of the novel, Morrison implies that Christine was a victim of her grandfather's sexual appetites, even if he didn't pursue her as he had pursued Heed: "It wasn't the arousals, not altogether unpleasant, that the girls could not talk about. It was the other thing. The thing that made each believe, without knowing why, that this particular shame was different and could not tolerate speech — not even in the language they had invented for secrets.... Would the inside dirtiness leak?" (192). After scenes of the two fighting wildly, plotting against each other, and silently seething at opposite ends of a home, the denouement of their reconciliation comes as something of a surprise to the reader. The revelation that they shared a sense of "dirtiness" — one that Christine and May tried frantically to ascribe to Heed alone in her domestic and hygienic habits — explains their simultaneous revulsion and devotion toward each other. Christine indicates her ability to read the imprint of sexual shame on the house itself since her childhood, beginning the day Cosey molested Heed and unknowingly masturbated in front of Christine: "When she went to bed that night, his shadow booked the room. She didn't have to glance at the windows or see the curtains yield before a breeze to know that an old man's solitary pleasure lurked there. Like a guest with a long-held reservation arriving in your room at last, a guest you knew would stay" (192). Here, Christine proves her ability to "read" the changes in her home, the ability to interpret the changing emotional climate that, in her adult mind, signals rightful ownership. The realization, in the novel's final scenes, that she and Heed shared this ability to interpret a home's constantly changing emotional climate, leads to their reconciliation. If both can read the home's hidden emotional politics in its material culture, then both are rightful owners.

The final section of the novel, narrated by L, or Love,[30] reveals that she has engineered much of this war. She casually confesses to having killed Cosey with foxglove, "a beautiful plant that is as medicinal as it is deadly" (Wardi 214) and to having destroyed his real will, which would have left everything (except a boat) to Celestial, his mistress (200–201). About the will she forged on a menu, Love comments, "My menu worked just fine. Gave them a reason to stay connected and maybe figure out how precious the tongue is" (201). Love, the character, has authored the entire property dispute, the resulting emotional dependence, and the final resolution of the conflict. Significantly, she has created the conflict using a material cultural artifact of public domesticity, the hotel menu, as if to offer up a "menu" of options for interpretation, ensuring that Heed and Christine remain locked in their bond as they work their way through the menu/will's possible meanings. Through Love's confession Morrison implies that the emotion of love, including the ability to interpret its many guises (the ability to "figure out how precious the tongue is") trumps legal property ownership, even as love — and its demise or absence — paradoxically creates the home. After taking the fall that will eventually kill her, Heed asks herself why she ever wanted to own the hotel. Still seeing the wallpaper's forget-me-nots even after she closes her eyes, she answers her own question: "Home, she thinks. When I stepped in the door, I thought I was home" (183).

L's final narrative implies that the sense of home Heed feels stemmed not from Cosey or from a feeling of emotional or financial security, but from the hotel's original context in her life, as the home of her childhood friend Christine. Significantly, Love indicates that this is where the two children fell in love with each other in a way that only children can:

> It's like that when children fall for one another. On the spot, without introduction.... If such children find each other before they know their own sex, or which of them is starving, which well fed; before they know color from no color, kin from stranger, then they have found a mix of surrender and mutiny they can never live without. Heed and Christine found such a one [199].

Love's list of the qualifying factors reads as a description of the kind of childhood innocence the children share when they meet, but also as a list of the factors that tear them apart as they age. A subtle critique of Cosey runs through this catalogue as well, since he directly or indirectly contributes to the girls' knowledge of sexuality, socioeconomic class, and race. Love's meditation on the girls' friendship ends with direct indictment of Cosey: "I blame May for the hate she put in them, but I have to fault Mr. Cosey for the theft" (200). The unnamed object of "the theft" would seem to expand Cosey's culpability: he has stolen both innocence and a friendship. Interestingly, Love seems to dismiss Cosey at this point, turning her final gaze on Junior, Christine, Heed, and Celestial. In this way, Morrison reveals that Cosey may have been little more than a catalyst in the woman-to-woman relationships that form the substance of the novel, despite the chapter titles bearing Cosey's roles: Portrait, Friend, Stranger, Benefactor, Lover, Husband, Guardian, Father, and Phantom. Although two of these titles bear masculine associations, the women have also played these roles for each other, or for themselves. The framed structure of the novel, with L's voice represented in two longer italicized passages at the beginning and ending of the work, also emphasizes the women, not Cosey, as the novel's true subject. If, as readers, we focus on the female characters and their relationships to one another as much as the myth of Cosey, then the novel becomes less a tale of failure and betrayal, and more a tale of interpretative strategies, survival strategies, and redemption. Because the women struggle to interpret their various homes, to maintain their homes, and to redeem themselves so as to appear as "rightful owners" of these homes, a focus on the women also highlights the work's status as a new kind of domestic novel.

In Morrison's most recent texts, domestic resistance *is* resistance to social oppression, and it becomes as important within families and communities as the publicly recognized forms of activism. Much like other authors in this work, Morrison presents domesticity as a subtly subversive force; however, Morrison's characters typically face more oppression than their white counterparts and are more likely to employ even more complex strategies of domestic resistance. Throughout this project, I have added my voice to other critics of domestic literature who argue that the domestic narrative does not exist alongside an ideologically "big" narrative; instead, the domestic narrative *is* the big narrative, told from an equally valuable viewpoint. The domestic narrative does more than quietly brush against or interact with the worlds of politics, technology, feminism, and economics. Instead, domesticity, in both its real-world forms and its literary representations, has a hand in the creation of many American ideologies and institutions. To overlook its roles is to hold an incomplete picture of the world.

Chapter Six

BETTY CROCKER, BETTY FRIEDAN, AND THE TECHNO-SOUTHERN BELLES
Reading the Online Kitchen

From the beginning of the twentieth century, new home technologies have resulted in corresponding changes in the ways that women perceive their roles in the home. As perceptions of domesticity have changed, southern women novelists have chronicled how homemakers, often burdened with the responsibility for maintaining a sense of domestic "tradition" in both gender roles and practical production, have coped with the changes in the kitchen. This project of tracking domestic change has often led to corresponding innovations in narrative form — narrative innovations that function as technologies in their own right — as well as new types of spatial depiction for the physical kitchen.[1]

Gas lines and indoor plumbing, along with a domestic worker shortage in the early 1900s, led to a new breed of middle-class housewife who often occupied the kitchen alone. Ellen Glasgow tracks this trend at the end of the nineteenth century, not only in the content of her novels and stories, but with her insistent use of a claustrophobic form of third-person narration. Her characters, particularly the women encumbered by domestic duty, carry on simultaneous monologues rather than conversations with their families inside houses that close in on them, beginning with the kitchen.

The 1920s ushered in an entirely new way of thinking about home design, one that emphasized a flow between nature and home, rather than the home as claustrophobic castle. This mode of thinking was symbolized by "the bungalow craze" (Clark 171). The home was no longer a bulwark against an invasive, dangerous outside world, but a structure meant to mediate both indoor and outdoor life. The bungalow design incorporated the "symbolic use of a spacious front porch and low-pitched roof to create a harmonious relationship to outdoor life" (Clark 173). Within this structure, "modern" was the word of the day for the kitchen; built-in cupboards saved steps and space, and the introduction of the electric refrigerator in the late twenties meant that "housewives no longer had to keep a watchful eye on the drip pan of the old-fashioned icebox" (Plante 230). In short, the innovations of the 1920s and 1930s made the kitchen a less isolating space, and one that did not require a homemaker to separate herself from family and guests, as evidenced by the addition of new kitchen features such as the "breakfast nook" (Plante 225). Writing *Delta Wedding* (set in the 1920s) during the 1940s, Eudora Welty reflects on these changes in the home and kitchen through a narrative style that entangles women's voices through multiple meshed narrative points of view and in the physical spaces they occupy throughout the novel. Though the Fairchilds live without all the modern conveniences, their mode of expansive living encompasses the domestic theory of the day. The domestic role expands to include new kinds of work and multiple "kitchens," or feminine centers of creativity, both inside the physical home and on the surrounding grounds.

The concept of domestic mobility and expansion continued to influence writers in the latter half of the twentieth century. With the already well-documented technological changes in the 1950s kitchen came a powerful new wave of isolation for homemakers, one Betty Friedan called "the problem that has no name." Middle-class white women who tried to embrace "the feminine mystique," an ideology that encouraged them to derive identity and fulfillment from home-based roles, were left with an overwhelming sense of emptiness. Although the idea of the feminine mystique held at least some power throughout the latter half of the twentieth century, it is important to note that Friedan uses only a small sample of middle-class white women in her research and that some researchers question the scientific rigor of her methodology. Despite the limitations of her study, the feminine mystique persists, as evidenced by "stay-at-home mom" movements, including pro-housewife, anti–ERA public statements by Phyllis Schlafly (Douglas 232–23) and Danielle Crittenden's 1999 publication of *What Our Mothers Didn't Tell Us: Why Happiness Eludes the Modern Woman*. While Friedan obviously urges women to work against the power of the feminine mystique, both Schlafly and Crittenden urge women to find happiness first and foremost in their own lives, as individual mothers and wives, and certainly not as parts of cohesive women's movements.

Given the political tension surrounding issues of women and the home in the late twentieth century, novels published during this period but set in the first half of the century take on a special significance, as they, willingly or not, draw parallels between current and past states of American domesticity. For instance, in *Oral History*, Lee Smith takes on a narrative format that consists of multiple, fragmented sites of narration. This format can be seen as a type of technological innovation itself since such a format would not have been possible without the advent of a postmodern culture that tends to question all types of unity, including narrative and ideological unity. Further, Smith portrays a combination of rugged mountain individualism and feminine community that allowed Appalachian culture to survive the 1930s Depression. In the light of 1980s feminism and the "mommies at home" movements, Smith seems to call for both individual creativity within the home and within communities that include and validate the feminine embodiment of occupations such as homemaker, folk healer, artist, and even witch. Both the narrative structure of individual, fragmented monologues, as well as the women's physical treks up and down mountains so that they might convene in kitchens, emphasize the kitchen's mobility and permeability in 1930s Appalachia (a place not as influenced by the bungalow craze or by many of the 1920s home technology developments). Yet Smith's novel also bears traces of her own 1980s moment, as indicated in her postmodern method of representing an oral history: her novel offers a portrait of the 1930s period that is tinged with feminist idealism and hope for women in the 1980s because it validates the voices of a wide variety of women.

The concept of the kitchen as a mobile, multimodal, multivocal communal enterprise has continued into the present, but was amplified most dramatically by the boom in Internet use during the 1990s. Far from Glasgow's depiction of domestic claustrophobia and isolation, the kitchen of the late twentieth century (at least according to popular magazines) was brightly lit, often connected to the rest of the house through a design that eschewed dividing walls, and most of all, wired for communication. The physical space of the kitchen comes to matter less and less (even as design features allowed the kitchen to mesh with the rest of the house) as women around the world participated, and continue to participate, in communal online kitchens. In this chapter, I will examine the rise of personal home and kitchen web sites in the late 1990s along with the problematic nature of the relationship between regionality and Internet technologies, including the unique features of kitchen-themed hypertexts by southern women. I focus on Internet domesticity in the late 1990s as a way of concluding a project concerned with expanding definitions of twentieth-century domesticity, but also because of the atmosphere of experimentation and optimism surrounding Internet culture at that moment. Just as some 1950s housewives hoped that new appliances might save time and human energy, some 1990s homemakers seem to have hoped to connect to others and share the significance of their domestic experiences via the Internet.

Few would deny that, despite technological advances such as the Internet and increasingly specialized formats in television, many popular and mass media portrayals of women remain problematic. The phenomenon can be explained in part by "cultural lag theory," developed in the 1960s to explore the gap that often exists between real life gender roles and gender roles depicted in popular culture.[2] While cultural lag theory is important, a brief look at the history of gender criticism of the media indicates more endemic problems in many cultural representations of women. In the 1970s, the first cultural critics to examine the images of women in the mass media in a comprehensive way often found women, at least in any substantive form, completely absent from television, magazines, and newspapers.[3] During the 1970s and 1980s, media studies turned to quantitative methods of analysis, examining nudity, "attractiveness," and general sexism both in print and on television.[4] Other 1980s and 1990s studies focused on the multiple meanings that popular media can be used to convey, or the meanings that readers sometimes use to subvert the messages they find to be sexist or otherwise offensive.[5]

Later research, however, takes a slightly different direction, pointing to advertising that takes a more neutral approach, often overlapping gender roles, showing men and women with similar jobs and performing similar tasks.[6] In essence, many critics now characterize portrayals of women as "fractured" or "contradictory" rather than wholly stereotypical or wholly progressive.[7] Interestingly, this approach often examines both current and earlier twentieth-century media, refuting the claims of Betty Friedan and other second-wave feminists who saw 1950s and 1960s women's magazines as entirely detrimental to the well-being of women. For instance, Nancy Walker notes that "precisely in the contradictory messages that the magazines frequently conveyed is it possible to see the domestic as a contested and negotiated concept rather than a proscribed and stable one" (*Shaping Our Mothers' World* vii).

Walker's concept of the domestic as "contested and negotiated" draws us into one hotbed of the media's gender stereotyping: the home, and more specifically, the kitchen. Given the current critical focus on gender in contemporary film and television, and the newer, overlapping and less stereotypical portrayals of women, it might seem that turning to 1950s and 1960s magazines would be the primary way to study gender, sexism, feminism, and the home. The kitchen, however, acting as a hub of the home, has undergone a late twentieth-century revival that extends into the twenty-first century, incorporating both traditional and more progressive portrayals of women, and less frequently, men, in pitches for the omnipresent "new and improved" domestic goods. What distinguishes the twenty-first-century kitchen sales pitch from its 1950s predecessors is that specialty cooking stores such as Williams-Sonoma, direct selling organizations such as The Pampered Chef, and the corporate conglomeration known as Martha Stewart, as well as many others, now sell the kitchen not as a warm and homey space for cooking, but as an all-encompassing way of life.

The sales pitches of these organizations are indeed fragmented, seemingly drawing on a 1950s-style domestic "guilt," but also on a 1980s spirit of overindulgence and consumption, and even on the 1990s quest for "simplicity."[8] In short, the message seems to be that if you buy the products, you can avoid feeling guilty for not providing for the family, you can indulge yourself with fancy gadgets and fancier food, and you can live the simple life by cooking everything from scratch. But the new consumer kitchen culture does not stop at advertising itself in print and on television. Like most twentieth-century enterprises, kitchens can be purchased online. And like the participatory structures Walker and others have examined within magazine culture, the kitchen web sites boast a subversive, personal side as well. In fact, because kitchen-themed *personal, noncommercial* web sites (usually created from home, by a single author) often pre-dated their commercial cousins, it might be said that the Internet incorporates far more participatory structures within its medium than women's print magazines could ever offer. Precisely because of the Internet's opportunities for self-publication and subversion of dominant gender-based imagery, more work on electronic media in the area of gender studies remains to be done. This chapter examines a small group of southern personal and commercial kitchen web sites at the close of the twentieth century in light of their fragmented and contradictory gender portrayals of women in relation to the domestic realm and in relation to computer technology itself.

The shifting locations and meanings of the home make the notion of region an especially problematic one. For example, an online kitchen creator may face difficulties in expressing the traditions and the community surrounding regional recipes and cooking styles. These difficulties often lead to the potential for an additional layer of stereotyping, as readers and creators struggle to understand their own domestic customs as part of a rapidly changing American culture. These problems seem especially acute in the American South, as southern women often report feelings of responsibility for maintaining a sense of domestic tradition in both gender roles and practical production. Nonetheless, a wide variety of southern kitchen web sites prevail, even as southern men and women confront the loss of a distinct regionality due, in part, to the reach of mass cultural forces. Southern kitchen web sites, then, come to represent a crucible of conflicting images of gender and region, often seen through a lens of larger technological, cultural, and historical changes. Though the creators may claim to be "just" southern belles posting recipes, their sites provide significant glimpses of the clashes of old and new American foodways and gender roles.

"Comes in Five Colors to Match Your Kitchen": The Personal Computer as Kitchen Appliance

1990s American trends in home design reflected the rise of a cult-like brand of domestic technology. Products such as the Advantage 2000 by CMI and the Screenfridge by Electrolux offered an Internet-ready, flat-screen PC, already installed in the door of a deluxe-model refrigerator. The touch-screen monitors (or water-washable keyboards) allowed one to monitor the contents of the refrigerator, the expiration dates on food, and even offered recipes based on recent food purchases. In short, every type of food-oriented text, from scribbled reminder, to grocery list, to cookbook, suddenly had its hypertext counterpart and became further linked to a comprehensive interplay of the intensely personal and the public.[9] Smaller digital kitchen components, such as Audrey from 3Com, which was advertised as coming "in five colors to match your kitchen,"[10] tried, and failed, to market to women. In 2000, 3Com advertised Audrey as an appliance that would organize the family beyond the capabilities of notes, lists, and invitations posted on the refrigerator and could sync with personal digital assistants (PDAs), but 3Com dropped this product after less than a year due to lack of public interest.

The failure of products such as the Audrey and the simultaneous rise in kitchen-themed personal web sites at the turn of the century suggests that many homemakers were more interested in producing their own bodies of kitchen knowledge than in buying new products to organize the information flow. To this end, in between the public realm of kitchen marketing and the private realm of the family refrigerator, vast semi-public online spaces for hypertext discourse on domestic matters appeared. Most of these sites focused on the sharing, exchange, or sale of recipes. Although recipes were the focal point of the sites, the sites presented themselves as real southern family "kitchens,"[11] full of personal narrative and dialogue, not as databases.

Because of their narrative-based structures, the 1990s online kitchen bore more resemblance to a domestic novel than to a typical commercial or research-oriented site. New media raise new interpretive challenges. If online kitchens were more like their physical world counterparts than databases or archives, then how did they account for regional differences? How would a homemaker and web site creator in Georgia distinguish her online kitchen from one in New Jersey, if at all? Perhaps most importantly, the reader of these sites might ask if they were simply technological outgrowths of existent regional domestic communities or new kinds of communities that transcended physical boundaries?

In a 1999 press release for the Screenfridge, Bob Lamson, CEO of CMI Worldwide, acknowledged the significance of the physical kitchen as a part of his sales pitch: "We know that the kitchen is the heart of the home, and the area that has the most activity, the highest traffic and the place that some of the most important and meaningful occasions occur" (qtd. in "A True Internet Appliance," *AllNetDevices*). Lamson's statement raises the question of whether the kitchen, a traditionally feminized space infused with specific types of texts and domestic narratives, has gained corporate recognition only as a target market for new, expensive technological equipment.[12] Are the creators of domestic sites, both past and present, and the users of products such as the Screenfridge (which unmistakably targets women in its marketing) liberating themselves from the overwhelming responsibilities of running a home or are they merely pawns for devices designed to keep them in their homes and constantly concerned with home-based consumption?[13]

To affirm the latter and more cynical view on this question suggests that the kitchen has been co-opted at a new level by American capitalism and that the kitchen as a physical location may be losing some of its feminine, subversive power as well as some of its regional flavor. Kitchen web sites allow home managers (and others) to connect a physical kitchen to an online "space" offering access to the theory, information, and practice behind literally millions of other kitchens worldwide. Because of this increase in information accessibility, the physical kitchen, in combination with the home computer, is now the ultimate site for the expansion of domestic narratives. The kitchen-themed web site, like nineteenth-century home management manuals, dictates a new standard of an American home, and more specifically, what an American kitchen "should" be. Hypertext domestic narratives proliferate, not only in the form of requests for recipes, but in intensely personal meditations on what it means to feed others and to preserve vital cultural history, even while utilizing technology. In the case of the southern kitchen hypertext, these personal meditations seem to take on even greater importance and a more prominent textual position. Many of the writers of 1990s southern kitchen hypertexts, unlike their counterparts in other regions, were also engaged in specific projects of valorizing their region and its traditions. The southern cyberdomestics often belonged to web-based organizations that explicitly promoted the image of the southern belle.[14] The southern kitchen site creator, then, placed herself in an interesting bind: Can one promote southern "heritage" and "tradition" (including the implication of a home-based role for women) while engaging in a technological project whose effect is to establish a feminine community that is not home or region based, but is, in fact, everywhere and nowhere at once?

The advent of the personal computer as kitchen appliance indicates that some women may have used the Internet to replace the traditional feminine communities that revolved around the kitchen. But could these technologies duplicate the sense of community (the sharing of practical, historical, and emotional narratives) found in the earlier twentieth-century kitchen, and particularly in the southern kitchen? Independent kitchen web sites repositioned the kitchen as a site of technological know-how and mass self-selecting communities rather than a site of unskilled labor and chance bonding. The communities were self-selecting because their members actively searched out communities interested in both the kitchen and the computer as an aid to the kitchen, as a kitchen appliance.[15] Chance meetings and the borrowing and lending of supplies did not play a role in the formation of hypertext kitchen communities, as they might in the random formation of physical kitchen communities. Instead, being a part of an online kitchen required an acute sense of one's double role as cyborg[16] and homemaker.

The guest books often included in these sites seemed to indicate that, despite the vexed nature of the cyborg-homemaker role, users of the sites felt bonded to their regions as well as their "communities" through their online kitchen experiences. Without the physical element — no cup of sugar to borrow and no recipe card to share — something else had to function as a bonding tool in the kitchen. The sites usually contained recipes, family lore, autobiographies of the authors, a chat or bulletin board element, and kitchen imagery. While the kitchen imagery provided a sense of the familiar in what was an unfamiliar realm for some, it was the self-negating, autobiographical narratives within the texts of these web sites that were positioned as the primary bonding tool. The narratives of self-negation created communities indirectly through a lack of technical intimidation. The personal narratives these sites contained, wedged in between recipes and household tips, seemed to say, "Don't mind me. I'm not really good with computers and the Internet, but I just *had* to share this recipe with you!"

Unlike the creators of academic or corporate pages, cyberdomestics seemed to take no pride in their technological savvy. What evolved, instead, was a new type of narrative structure designed to create bonds among women, a narrative that functioned as a powerful subversive tool by negating the site creator's own technological expertise in a way that encouraged participation in the creation of the site, validating *kitchen experience as technological experience*. The emotional tenor of these narratives was reminiscent of the opening of Betty Friedan's *The Feminine Mystique*, when Friedan discusses the women who responded to her surveys about the quality of their home lives with surprising passion, often offering far more information than the original survey form could contain. Friedan writes,

> The problems and satisfactions of their lives, and mine, and the way our education had contributed to them, simply did not fit the image of the modern American woman as she was written about in women's magazines, studied and analyzed in classrooms and clinics, praised and damned in a ceaseless barrage of words since the end of World War II. There was a strange discrepancy between the reality of our lives as women and the image to which we were trying to conform, the image that I came to call the feminine mystique. I wondered if other women faced this schizophrenic split, and what it meant [7].

The women of 1990s online kitchens clearly felt a specific form of this schizophrenia in their dual roles as cyborgs and homemakers. And like the respondents to Friedan's survey, they may have begun by simply posting a few recipes, but in the process, many of the sites produced an analysis of the changing forces in the kitchen, including a specifically "southern" rhetoric of new and old foodways, of roasting one's own pig versus copying a Cracker Barrel Recipe, and of valorizing the role of southern homemaker, even while broadcasting the details of this role in a new form of mass media.[17]

A further similarity between Friedan's feminine mystique and the "mystiques" of other eras lies in the effects of the introduction of new technology. In *The Feminine Mystique*, Friedan famously claims that "even with all the new labor-saving appliances, the modern American housewife probably spends more time on housework than her grandmother" (230).[18] But given the ongoing waves of new domestic technology, the feminine mystique begins to emerge as not a period-specific or one-time phenomenon but a powerful historical cycle with cultural impact. That is, each new wave of home-based technology, be it the icebox, the vacuum, or the Internet, spikes both consumer behavior and time spent managing the home for women. While one might debate the inclusion of the Internet as "home-based technology," in its current incarnation, the Internet has been used as a corporate vehicle (as with the Screenfridge and Audrey) to re-market the kitchen to American women. Further, this type of "re-marketing" is not new, but has roots in the 1890s New Woman movement. While the New Women fought for better education, "rational" dress, jobs outside the home, and involvement in athletics, sales of domestic goods plummeted. The home was then reconfigured as "a microcosm of the sciences" in an effort to promote a new, "professional" type of homemaker[19] (Marks 42). A similar re-marketing occurred in the face of the servant crisis in the 1900s and 1910s, when upper-middle-class women were encouraged to re-learn domestic skills (and to buy new domestic products) as former servants became employees of new factories.[20]

The ultimate effect of such marketing, whether for women of the 1890s, 1950s, or 1990s, is increased time spent at home, followed by a type of "backlash" movement where women reach out to one another to discuss the "problem that has no name" of the day. As we have seen, this backlash can take a variety of forms, including domestic novels, a sociological study like Friedan's, or online narratives. Yet these types of narratives are rarely read as a cohesive whole, as a chronological historical response to changes in women's perceptions of home culture. Nor are the narratives read as responses to prevalent technologies; they are more often read as period-specific oddities, chastised for chronicling "minutae." Read within its cultural context, however, the minutae form a historical record of the changing and often symbiotic relationships between women and technology.

Bug Bite Soup and Cracker Barrel Casserole: The Southern Kitchen Goes Online

While not as widespread as the use of the icebox in 1900 or the vacuum cleaner in 1950, the use of the computer as a tool for home management during the 1990s certainly increased, expanding to include tasks such as household budgeting or searches for recipes. In retrospect, we might also ask if computers, like other appliances before them, may have played a role in confining homemakers to the physical home, albeit in the role of "household expert." Yet a computer, of course, does far more than any previous home appliance. While the home computer and Internet technology undoubtedly have the capacity to confine, unlike the vacuum cleaner or the icebox, computer technology also has the ability to unite women. In other words, women do not have to search out a medium, such as a novel, a survey, or a sociological study, to unite and analyze the changes they are noticing in their own homes and their prescribed roles. The technology itself becomes the medium of response.[21]

Within the web sites examined here, women read the site as containing the communal aspect of a kitchen in part because of its appearance. Many 1990s sites contained nineteenth-century kitchen imagery or an image map that appeared as one wall of a kitchen, where visitors click on the stove, the shelf, etc.[22] More importantly, women may have been drawn into the sites because of creation narratives in which the writer explained why she decided to open her physical kitchen into an Internet interface — what might be called the cyberkitchen apologia.

The cyberkitchen apologia is an apology, an assertion, and a family history all at once.[23] These narratives do more than defend the institution of the cyberkitchen. The writers negate their own expertise in their chosen medium even while employing technological skills; they apologize for the creator's technological savvy by remarking on the necessity of the site.[24] For example, Mimi Hiller remarks that she created her page, *Mimi's CyberKitchen*, in part, to pass along the Jewish recipes of her grandmother and her friend's grandmother. Only when all kitchens had access to these recipes would she feel that she had done justice to the women's memory. She reads her own site not as a creative act or an established community for women, but as a memorial, and thus, she does not have to take responsibility for the power she might wield as a woman capable of both domestic and intellectual creation and as a leader among cyberdomestic workers.[25]

The phenomenon of the cyberdomestic apologia evokes Myra Sadker and David Sadker's sociological research on women in the college classroom. The Sadkers remark that women learn "to preface [their] speech with phrases like 'I'm not sure if this is what you want' or 'This probably isn't right but'" (Sadker and Sadker 171). These statements negate the women's responsibility for the correct answer, but they also avoid the problem of seeming pushy or dominant. Women are able to create community indirectly, through a lack of intimidation. They engage in self-negating behavior even as they use technology to unite other women under the banner of domesticity, an ideology historically thought to have confined women. The creators, however, seem aware of the radical nature of a project that repositions the kitchen as a site of technological know-how and mass self-selecting communities rather than a site of unskilled labor and chance bonding. They feel the necessity of using certain narrative strategies to resist conflicts, both within the communities they establish and in response to their own image as a strange new breed of cyberdomestics, no longer confined to the kitchen, but connected to kitchens worldwide.

Domestic web sites produced in the American South with an eye toward showcasing their "southern-ness" compound the paradigm of technological know-how encased in the apologia. The pervasive image of the helpless southern "belle" as a kind of ideal for young women adds to the existent anxiety over taking a traditional role (that of female homemaker) into a nontraditional medium. Southern cyberdomestics face an amplified bind of both the constricting role of homemaker as well as that of southern woman. Some southern women, even if they are not homemakers in the traditional sense, feel that they have been socialized to be less assertive than other women and this trait, in the form of the "belle" image, is acknowledged within the web sites. Therefore, if a cyberdomestic worker without a regional focus needs to tell you why she has invaded a "masculine" technological realm with her recipes, then we can imagine that a "southern belle" cyberdomestic worker may feel an even greater need to justify her presence. In this sense, the southern domestic narrative is far from dead, and southern cyberkitchens may be read as following in the tradition of southern domestic novels, novels that have always borne the criticism of being overly concerned with the mundane details of family life.[26]

As independent, noncommercial web sites, both *The Southern Kitchen* and *Mother Red's Southern Country Kitchen* display a certain level of identity anxiety through their kitchen-centered graphics, "down-home" language, and general de-professionalization of the role of household cook, combined with comparatively technically sophisticated sites. In the world of the cyberkitchen, content and technique have little common ground; that is, "Miz Angel" of *The Southern Kitchen* will recount how to roast a pig in a narrative form ("the pig must be very fat, nicely cleaned, and not too large to lie in the dish"), but she does not tell you where she learned the basics of web design or how one can enter the creative side of the Internet and what it feels like to be in that position as a southern woman. In many of these cyberkitchens, the content, through its "homey" narrative style, apologizes for the technical expertise, as if to say, "Even though we can create and manage web sites, we are just regular 'good ole gals' ready to make iced tea and barbecue at any given moment."

The Southern Kitchen is not a *Southern Living*-style cookbook. Nor does it present itself as an archival collection of recipes from a by-gone grandmother's era. In the midst of the narrative on how to roast a pig and the recipes for "Good Pone Bread," "Sweet Potato Pie," and "Molasses Gingerbread," lurks an oddly contemporary recipe/call-to-arms for "Southern Sweet Iced Tea":

> We in the south make the best iced tea you'll find. Maybe it's how it's done, or maybe it is the water in the south, or maybe it's just that a southern belle has put a lot of TLC into making the tea. Who knows! We recommend Luzianne Tea Bags if available. Place the two cups of water in a pot and add the tea bags. Bring to a boil, do not continue boiling. Remove from heat and let steep. Pour warm tea into empty pitcher. Add the sugar and stir until the sugar is dissolved. Fill remaining pitcher with cold water. Optional — some women say they use less water and add ice to the tea.

This recipe, despite its specific brewing instructions, invites several questions: Do men in the South make iced tea? Should the cook feel anxious about the outcome of the tea if she does not have access to a southern belle heritage? Or will this recipe allow her to "pass" as a belle? Aside from these obvious and immediate questions, one wonders about the genre of the site at this moment. Why is this contemporary recipe, advocating a major national brand of iced tea, mixed with the "grandmother"-style recipes that have few or no measurement units?

How do the seeming anachronisms mirror the cyberkitchen creator's anxiety over her own technical creation? Here, the old-style recipes, rather than serving as a mark of authenticity (in terms of both the author's southernness and her cooking skills and background) act as a type of compensation for the ultra-contemporary medium of the hypertext. In other words, instead of a prolonged apologia, such as a story of a dead relative and an expressed "need" to pass the recipes on, Miz Angel, *The Southern Kitchen's* creator, uses nineteenth-century graphics (mostly of women near ovens) as well as fleur-de-lis details as a kind of shorthand connection to the past and denial of her own technological knowledge. It is as if enough old-fashioned images, combined with captions such as "Well, of course, everyone knows the best cooks are Southern girls" will erase the somewhat radical intent of her project, which is to promote the kitchen and its content as important enough to enter a relatively new medium. In this project, the kitchen is no longer a basic support structure to other enterprises, but a microcosm with its own content and politics. It is important to note that Miz Angel is supporting a specific political agenda as well. Her site was a part of the Dixieland WebRing and she self identifies as a member of the B.R.I.T.S. or Belles Raised in the South and as the Web Mistress for a group called "The Magnolias" in the Geocities WebRing entrance to her kitchen site. Like the Southern Agrarians before her, she supports a "back to basics" mode of traditional production, but unlike the Agrarians, she is willing to use the new technologies to promote her ideology.

A second web site, *Mother Red's Southern Country Kitchen*, offers a more overt apologia couched in the southern vernacular, rather than in slick presentations or "authentic" recipes. For instance, many of the recipe category headings are phrased in the following manner: "Stuff for Breakfast," "Stuff for Lunch," and "Chicken and Beef and Stuff." In contrast to *The Southern Kitchen*, Mother Red's site does not pretend any links to the deep past, and many southern recipes are for items such as "taco salad" or a "copycat recipe for Cracker Barrel Hashbrown Casserole."[27] Yet here, too, lies a political agenda. While Mother Red appears to have no desire to return to the days of roasting one's own pig, she is interested in promoting the New South in its current incarnation, as witnessed in her references to Cracker Barrel and Tex-Mex cuisine. It is as though she is saying that this, too, is a southern kitchen culture, and one worth documenting.

Mother Red continues to express her dual placement between two cultures — those of the New and Old South, as well as those of the physical and hypertext kitchen community within the narrative of "Bug Bite Soup." Rhonda Squires, Mother Red's niece and site collaborator, writes,

> For years I've pondered why it is that we find it so hard to accept change in the human race. We groom ourselves in a particular way, we eat certain foods, we tend to buy things routinely; same toothpaste, same toilet paper, certain brands of shoes, clothes, even our vehicles. We get used to something and far be it to ever change! Which brings to mind my story of bug bite soup.

As first glance, Squires' text seems to be an informal defense of cultural materialism. The detritus of domestic life — the toothpaste, the toilet paper — is, in fact important; it tells our history. The actual narrative continues to tell the story of how Squires' own mother made a "mockery" at her grandmother's soup recipe, "tarnish(ing) it forever" by cutting the vegetables into overly uniform, neat pieces. In the grandmother's words, the soup contained pieces "small enough for a bug to eat" rather than the whole pods of okra and the misplaced entire carrot that sometimes characterize homemade soup. In this way, the narrative speaks to the importance of history in both the individual rituals of the kitchen, as well as the rituals of a region. The mother is chastised not only for her attention to detail, but in a subtext, for buying into a national domestic culture that recommends perfection, à la Martha Stewart and Heloise, as well as countless other self-proclaimed kitchen gurus who urge women to strive for perfection in food presentation, taste, and hygiene.

As an ending to the bug bite soup narrative, Squires contemplates her own position in the "ongoing controversy." She asks herself, "Do I make my mom's bug bite soup? Do I make my grandmother's old fashioned soup?" then concludes, "What to do... what to do... Maybe someday I'll figure it out." Here Squires catalogues the tension between the old and new ways of producing food in the southern kitchen, but negates her position as a new type of southern homemaker. Squires wonders "what to do" only in a rhetorical sense. She has played her part in the documentation of kitchen changes to its fullest extent not only by cataloguing the clash between new and old rituals, but by choosing her own "new way" of being a homemaker in the form of the kitchen hypertext. Instead of tiny "bug bites" of soup, she has produced tiny computerized bytes of information while battling the technological "bugs" of web site creation, and she has taken her kitchen into a new public arena while creating a historical record of the late twentieth-century southern kitchen. Yet, even here, she must apologize for this project, as she hopes, "Maybe someday I'll figure it out."[28]

The creators of hypertext kitchens have already figured it out. With the communal nature of the kitchen a thing of the past due to work outside the home, bedroom communities, and other challenges of a technologically oriented country, women who cook, and especially women who like to cook for sustenance (rather than in a gourmet tradition), may feel that they are becoming relics. The solution then becomes both obvious and revolutionary — to use the technology that often distances women from their kitchens and the kitchens of other women to form an entirely new breed of kitchen that is both everywhere and nowhere at the same time. Homemakers may sit at their own kitchen computers and remain spatially disparate but ideologically united. In this sense, hypertext kitchens form the ultimate feminist southern domestic narrative: one that is in constant flux, documenting and often preserving the past, urging its members not to be contained by household technologies, but to use those technologies to create communities that are not subject to the constraints of where one makes one's home.

Beyond the cyberdomestic apologia, perhaps the most interesting aspect of the online southern kitchen is its mediation of the belle image. Many of the web creators discussed here are all explicit in their self-identification as "southern belles," either in the language on their pages or in their posted hyperlinks to online "belle" organizations. Arguably the most common use of this image in southern literature has been for instructive purposes, to show what may happen to women when they choose to adopt or refute the "belle" role. The southern online kitchen, however, touts a new type of belle, one who opens her interface, not her front door, with smiling southern hospitality. In this way, the site creators maintain that asserting oneself in the form of participating in worldwide mass communications is acceptable; one can publicize the private without violating the code of southern ladyhood. As Miz Angel puts it, "All you techno–Southern Belles just come on down and join right in! We may be prim and proper, but we're smart, too!" (*Southern Belles Web Ring*). Interestingly, this is one of the few statements that works against the idea of the apologia by claiming intelligence as a part of the southern cyberdomestic identity. Despite the contradiction that lies between the content and the politics of these sites, southern online kitchens post a subtle recipe for resistance to the role of demure southern belle.

Southern Culture for Sale: Commercial Hypertext Kitchens

The marketing ploys designed to promote the Screenfridge, the Advantage 2000, and the Audrey signaled that the target market of homemakers had already linked the computer and the kitchen as a part of its own subculture by the 1990s. In the case of southern homemakers, this linkage became problematic, as this group tried to negotiate the boundaries of the roles of belle and cyborg, with the apologia as a bonding tool for establishing online communities.

Yet it should be noted that not all southern kitchen-themed sites from this era contain an apologia. In the sites that encompass a strange middle ground between the commercial and the personal, as well as in the blatantly commercial, such as the web sites of *Southern Living* and *Southern Accents* magazines, the raison d'etre is quite simply a question of financial gain, and no apologia is needed. Corporate sites repackage the culture of the online southern culture in a slick format, one that obviously remediates print culture rather than the technology of a physical kitchen (e.g., the graphics of ovens). Jay David Bolter and Richard Grusin note the replication of earlier or later technologies, or remediation, as a common phenomenon in new media.[29] They cite the printed *USA Today*'s layout's resemblance to a "multimedia computer application" as an example of this phenomenon, a way of expressing "the tension between regarding a visual space as mediated and as a 'real' space that lies beyond mediation" (Bolter and Grusin 40–41). But perhaps any hypertext "space" focusing on southern culture faces this tension on an even more basic level. Southerners, online and off, often find themselves in the process of questioning the South itself — its culture, people, and physical boundaries — as either "mediated" or "real." That is, southerners, academic and not, question what constitutes the "real" South and what acts as simple icon, easily transported, then mythologized or sold. The South is already a mediated culture because "southern-ness" is continually packaged and sold back to those who consider themselves either southerners or aficionados of southern culture. The packaging and mediation of southern culture takes the form of many of the institutions mentioned here, including *Southern Living* magazine and the Cracker Barrel chain of restaurants. In this way, computerized mediation may seem oddly familiar and comfortable to the young contemporary southerner, having grown up in what amounts to a virtual South.

More commercial web sites created in the 1990s, such as About.com, revisit the problem of a mediated or virtual South. While perhaps refreshing in their lack of self-deprecation, theses sites situate themselves at the nexus of southern cultures, foodways, and technological cultures in an even more problematic way. The commercial sites depersonalize the southern kitchen to such an extent that it becomes sterile — an environment not suited to the formation of a community. Further, the people/personae linked to these sites have little voice. While many of these sites boast numerous authorities that one may consult, the viewer of these sites has no way of connecting with the site's "personality" precisely because of the lack of personal information.[30] Instead of allowing for the messy apologia, replete with inconsistent graphics and dialect, some corporations write canned biographies for their experts.

Many of the contrasts between the personal and the commercial sites are to be expected in the way that a store selling kitchen gadgets would be likely to be less friendly and less communal than a recipe-exchange party at the house of a neighbor. However, three specific, subtler aspects of this contrast appear upon closer inspection. First, while the concept of gender in an online world is shaky at best, 1990s-era corporate southern kitchen sites seem to assign gender at a visual level that corresponded to information as much as it did to people or online personae. By processing each frame of the site as an image, readers could gather information about the corporate ideology of the "assigned gender" of the information presented based on the look of the hypermedia — the combined tone of graphics, print, and hyperlinks. In this context, non-commercial recipe-sharing sites became "feminine," surrounded by more graphics and a more "flowery" visual style.[31] Information related to buying and selling became "masculine," often presented only in a straightforward block of text or link of hyperlinks. Within his analysis of the evolution of the image from European painting to television culture in *Ways of Seeing* (1977), John Berger emphasizes the notion that "*men act* and *women appear*":

> Men look at women. Women watch themselves being looked at. This determines not only most relations between men and women but also the relation of women to themselves. The surveyor of woman in herself is male: the surveyed female. Thus she turns herself into an object — and most particularly an object of vision: a sight [47].

While these assumptions are often challenged by contemporary artists, feminists, and others, the association of the feminine and the spectacle as well as the masculine and action (or hypermedia information) is at work in these sites. The overall look of the commercial sites resembles print culture in its lack of graphics as well as the consistency of print size and font styles. Gender comes into play in other ways as well, as those identified as "feminine" in some contexts self-identify as a masculine persona in other, more "serious" (often more commercial) roles on the same site.

In combination with these gender politics, the corporate sites boast an emphasis on the professionalization of the homemaker role. While the online kitchen creators eschew any notion of themselves as professional cooks or professional web designers, the "expert" personae of corporate sites reiterate their qualifications, as well as their standards for professional participation in their forums and live chats. The magazine sites take this emphasis in a different direction: they seem to say that if one completes the following tasks (including everything from complicated remodeling to Christmas crafts), using the following products, then one can become a professional homemaker, thus validating the choice *not* to pursue other options — presumably those options outside the home.

As an "expert" and an online homemaker, Diana Rattray held, and still holds, an unusual and liminal position between the realms of personal and commercial web sites, enmeshed in the politics of gender, professionalization, and reader response. At first glance, it would appear that Rattray functions online in two distinct roles: that of About.com's "guide" (their term for their online experts in endless fields of interest) to *Southern U.S. Cuisine* as well as the creator/manager of *Diana's Kitchen*, a personal web page established in 1995. Yet because of About.com's incorporation of Rattray's materials, many of the hyperlinks featured in *Diana's Kitchen* take the user directly to About.com's site on the topic. In this way, we have the incorporation of a personal online kitchen into a corporate forum, complete with its "sponsored links" to eBay, a magazine subscription service, and several online kitchen stores.[32] Therefore, any kind of extensive navigation of Rattray's personal site unavoidably results in an interaction with About.com's superengine and advertisements. Is this linkage a progressive medium where a southern woman hones her homemaking skills into a wide profit margin? Based on the rhetoric of gender and professionalization, it seems that *Diana's Kitchen* has been co-opted by About and serves only as a kind of placemarker, as a piece of "evidence" to assert Rattray's "expert" status as granted by About.com.

In the 1990s, *Diana's Kitchen* differed in appearance from About.com in a number of ways. It included "flowery" graphics (literal flowers included), as well as food icons, though the site was far less graphics-heavy than the personal kitchen sites previously examined. It is interesting to note that the two sites are far less distinguishable as of this writing, more than ten years after Rattray created her own site. While the 1990s About.com version's left text-box column contained recipes that linked to other pages on the personal site, the headline links, as well as the larger, right column all hyperlinked to About.com. It is also interesting to note that at the close of the twentieth century, this site's "update line" read "This kitchen established October, 1995. Revised October, 2000." Most lines of this sort give only the most recent update information. Here, Rattray emphasizes the invention of her site, possibly because it predates About.com by several years. (About was not established in its current form until 1999.) She also emphasizes her site as a "real" and communal space; she calls it "this kitchen" rather than "this page" or "this kitchen web site."

In the 1990s version, linking to the About.com's *Southern U.S. Cuisine* (which happens when the hypertext reader uses the majority of the links in *Diana's Kitchen*) transformed the continuity (or what Bolter and Grusin would term the "immediacy" of the hypertext experience) in that the graphic interface changed abruptly. The soft blues and greens of the personal site gave way to red and black graphics, with small print and multiple text boxes, in a format that resembled a newspaper. Interestingly, as of this writing, the blue and green color scheme has been replaced with the red and black text and graphics, creating an almost seamless transition between the two sites. In the 1990s version, however, a revolving banner advertised everything from online travel agents to Stouffer's frozen entrees. Once "inside" the About site, Rattray appears not as the owner of a successful personal page, but as a hired "expert" who happens, incidentally, to have her own site as well. In this vein, when one enters *Diana's Kitchen* through the About topic site, *Diana's Kitchen* appears with an "About" banner at the top. The About banner has two buttons that read "Back to the topic site" and "Turn off this top frame." The first button implies that About is both the "true" authority and that About is also the proprietor of *Diana's Kitchen*. A traditional literary narrative "frame" implies that the persona narrating the frame has some type of authority, or at the very least an insider perspective, and the graphic device of a web frame performs much the same function. Yet the second button — "turn off this top frame"— implies a phantasm, an omniscient authority that cannot be truly subverted, only "turned off" for the time being. The "kitchen" appears to be co-opted by the commercial site, and may even appear to be an integral part of the About site to some, despite its stand-alone capacity and the fact that it predates About's enterprise.

Further, no 1990s apologia exists; in its place we receive a biography of Rattray that includes her grandfather's experience as a chef and her collection of southern cookbooks as evidence of her expertise. The final line of the biography mentions Rattray's own site, "which recently [as of 2001] won *Windows Magazine*'s award for Best Personal Web Page." Clearly, in the case of the commercial biography, *public recognition*, not an enthusiasm for subject, nor an unheralded web site of one's own, nor an ethic of community building, validates one's position as an expert.

The way that commercial sites bestow expertise is reminiscent of the hygiene movement of the 1930s, when women were trained as household experts either by food corporations, hospitals, or the government. During the Depression-era 1930s, the government and corporations sought to make the kitchen a public space that operated efficiently for the "good" of family and country. Yet in the 1930s, a good kitchen, according to their standards, was one that bought the products that needed to be sold, just as a good kitchen, in the eyes of some corporate sites in the late twentieth century, was one that supported a web-based economy.[33] The effect of the corporate attempt to take over web kitchens, much like the effect of 1930s government experts, was to standardize home practices and to professionalize the homemaker, effectively silencing the homemaker's own personal meditations on her practices and their ties to her own familial cultural history.

In About.com's 1990s idealized version of the southern kitchen, the only notion of Rattray's voice can be found in the last section of the bio, subtitled "From Diana Rattray." This type of demarcation seems to indicate About's desire to contain and mediate Rattray's voice. The section reads, "Here, you'll find frequently updated topics, links, and recipes. I welcome and encourage everyone's participation in Southern American Cuisine so please suggest topics, ask for recipes, and share your own favorite recipes and techniques." Interestingly, Rattray first invites us to participate in the *cuisine itself* (complete with capital letters), not in a communal *discourse about the cuisine*.[34] While she does invite participation, she also delineates the appropriate ways in which one should participate (suggest topics, share recipes and techniques) just as About proscribes the format and content of Rattray's site.[35] Notably, she does not ask for personal narratives, cultural histories, or anecdotes. The brevity and "canned" tone of this statement "from Diana Rattray" is a far cry from the personal narrative of "Bug Bite Soup," yet Rattray unintentionally makes a similar point to that of the "Bug Bite Soup" story. It is possible to make southern food indistinguishable from that of any other region when the person in the kitchen favors tiny, uniform pieces rather than messy, personalized pots of soup or narrative forms.

Similar to its anxiety over the professionalization of the homemaker in general and Rattray's expertise specifically, the personal and the commercial sites also feature a certain amount of gender anxiety. Read together, the two sites form a commentary on what roles are and are not appropriate for women in the world of kitchen commercialism. It is important to note the commercial influence of this prescription of roles, of course. If women feel validated as home "professionals," then they are likely to continue to work in the home and to participate in home-based consumption of goods. The idea of creating a personality to ensure that women feel positive about the homemaker role is nothing new: Betty Crocker was conjured up by the Washburn-Crosby (later General Mills) advertising department in 1926 and she continued her heyday into the 1950s as Majorie Husted, her "real" executive persona, sought to combat women's sense of being "uncertain, anxious, and insecure" in the housewife role (Levenstein 33, 132). The "Betty Crocker" image has continued throughout the late twentieth century, both as a disembodied face on a product label, and in its current twenty-first century incarnation as the name on a spoon-shaped product logo.[36]

Rattray's 1990s persona exists within a highly constructed gender code. Even when one moves from page to page within the former version of *Southern U.S. Cuisine*, the top frame that contains Rattray's name and photograph remains in place. The frame genders the advice, recipes, and advertisements beneath it, reminding the viewer that despite the site's "professional" level of information and information management, there is, in fact, a "real" woman in this hypertext. The anxiety seems to lie in the notion that the reader may not believe this as a woman's site (minus the "feminine" visual reminders of an elaborate color scheme or multiple graphics) without Rattray's photo as a constant reminder.[37]

The emphasis on the presence of a "real" person continues through the "Contact Guide" hyperlink underneath About's top banner. This banner is obviously transferable to and identical to About's proclaimed "over 700 sites" (circa 2000), hence the phrase "contact guide" rather than "contact Diana Rattray." While in one sense this link de-personalizes Rattray, it also places her in About's "elite" group of guides, thus further professionalizing the role of homemaker and home expert. Rattray herself (or her production team at About) seems to acknowledge the anxiety over the de-personalization evident in the link. The linked page begins with frequently asked questions about southern foods, but it ends with the following phrases: "Like all the Guides at The Mining Co, I'm a real person. You can email me at *southernfood.guide@ about.com*." Again, Rattray reiterates her professional status by placing herself within the group of "all the guides at The Mining Co." (About's former moniker). Yet the second sentence stresses her status as "a real person." The anxiety over the real reveals the fear of the assumption that a homemaker could not possibly possess this type of archival knowledge, nor could she manage it in an online form. Rattray's statement also stresses the tension between the roles of cyborg and homemaker — the notion that an online persona cannot or may not be a real homemaker. Like Martha Stewart, or the other professional homemakers, she may have an extensive staff to do what she recommends that women do alone, in a series of "easy steps."[38] Like the apologia of the personal online kitchens, the About site seems to feel the need to explain the presence of a homemaker online, or perhaps to explain the fairly new combination of kitchen lore and computer technology.

While we may assume that Rattray's persona is genuine, or at least as genuine as any other online persona, the two sites are not always so clear about who does what in the kitchen. For example, *Diana's Kitchen* features a hyperlink that reads "Have questions? Having a debate with a friend or co-worker and need help to find an answer? Ask Uncle Phaedrus for an answer." At first it is not even clear that this hyperlink is food-related. It seems, on the surface, to invite questions of any sort. Closer investigation reveals the same "Uncle Phaedrus" in the About.com site, though here, the persona takes a different form. Under a link for "copycat recipes," the About site identifies Gloria Pitzer as "the Recipe Detective," who offers to find recipes that have been lost (using a general description of the recipe) or to find/create "copycat" recipes that produce food similar to that served at favorite restaurants. A cross-reference with *Diana's Kitchen* reveals that there, the "recipe detective" is also known as Uncle Phaedrus. What is interesting about this exercise in persona-morphing is that in *Diana's Kitchen*, the "detective" is decidedly male—Uncle Phaedrus—while on About, the "detective" is female—Gloria Pitzer. Here, we may read the gender-swapping as indicative of About's anxiety that a site about food "appear" or "feel" feminine.

If the corporate site needs to present a plethora of female personae, then why does the personal site bill the detective as masculine? The logic of the apologia seems to be, at least in part, at work in this kitchen as well. While a southern homemaker may feel the need to explain her presence online (or to validate it with "credentials"), a female who presents as a male is not likely to feel such a need. Further, Uncle Phaedrus/Pitzer is not presenting as a homemaker, but as a seeker and finder of lost things, a less feminine role than that of food expert. Most importantly, perhaps, is that in the absence of masculine, corporate authority (like that of About's site), women may present themselves as, and to link themselves to, imposter sources of masculine authority. In the personal sites, there is no corporate big brother to expose the masculine persona as a fraud, nor is there an integral "masculine" source of authority to lend the site credibility. Therefore, a woman posing as a man who offers to recover recipes solves two problems at once: she does not need to explain her presence online, and she may even lend the site a kind of credibility in the eyes of those who bring their own gender biases to the site.

The twentieth-century online kitchen came not only in many colors, but also in many versions of what was public and what was private. We see these variations in a spectrum of sites, from those that were quite obviously created in private homes, using mass-produced graphics and "web page in a box" tools or w.y.s.i.w.y.g (pronounced "wizzy-wig," an acronym for "what you see is what you get") software. It is also important to note that even many of the least sophisticated personal sites offered, and still do offer, advertisements in the form of links to larger corporates sites, links that presumably provided income for the creator of the personal site.[39] But just as a kitchen that is copied from a magazine design plan will still become personalized to a certain degree, so do these "personal" sites retain their own voices, despite the widely available building tools and advertising links they have in common. While other types of web sites contain personal narratives, online kitchens produce narratives that seem more similar to their literary counterparts — domestic novels — with an emphasis on narrating the sights, smells, tastes, and communal nature of a real-world kitchen. While other types of sites focused more and more on graphics and sophisticated interactive tools in the 1990s, personal online kitchens continued to rely on the narrative form to preserve cultural history and to create the virtual kitchen, complete with its complex history of rigid gender roles.

Commercial sites, or pseudo-commercial sites like Rattray's, can boast original graphics and slick layouts designed exclusively for the corporation by a team of Internet professionals. Yet without the personal narratives of family lore, the recipes replete with marginalia about when to serve a certain food, or which age groups/genders are likely to prefer it, commercial sites do not often create a communal feel. While a for-profit site may strive to hide its reason for being, the personal site states its mission again and again, creating a greater likelihood of feminine community with little technical intimidation.

Always New and Improved: From Betty Crocker to Betty Friedan

Because of their different aims, 1990s commercial and personal online kitchens handled the issue of gender in very different ways. While not overtly feminist, late twentieth-century personal sites were engaged with an important variety of recovery work — the recovery of thousands of recipes that were threatened by our move away from a print culture. Yet perhaps more importantly, the personal sites attempted to recover the emotional fabric that surrounds foodways, and particularly southern foodways, including generational conflicts. Commercial sites, on the other hand, and not surprisingly, promoted a corporate culture, with "copycat" and "quick crockpot" recipes, as well as with hundreds of links to kitchen-related e-businesses. What is interesting about the commercial sites is their return to a 1920s Betty Crocker marketing mentality. Just as General Mills sought to prove that there was a real woman behind the technology of the family radio, so do the commercial sites seek to prove the reality of their experts. In this way, not only do the sites re-package and sell food culture and southern-ness, they are also engaged in a process of selling gender, of re-packaging a palatable version of techno-femininity. But in this case, the commercial sites become much more of a threat to feminism than Betty Crocker ever was. While many people had access to the receiving end of a radio, an appliance marketed to women as a domestic tool in the 1920s (Carlat 116), very few were broadcasting to a mass market. In contrast, with the Internet as technological tool, many have access to both the production and reception ends of web sites, and hence, the pro-duction and reception ends of both popular and mass culture.[40] The corpo-rate sites, through their process of co-opting online kitchen culture, seek to offer a few women as "examples" or "experts" on the web, with the majority of the "real" women in the kitchens, and not in control of the content and process of their own online kitchens. This positioning, of course, makes for the best kind of passive consumer. An "active" web homemaker, one who controls her own web site, might also decide to set up her own type of econ-omy that extends beyond the exchange of recipes and folklore, and ultimately beyond corporate control and strictly dictated market tastes.

Technology, then, continued to be a very mixed blessing for the home-maker who did not work outside the home. Each new round of devices pur-ported to "help" her also brought a new round of accessory products to buy, as well as new kinds of costly mechanical maintenance services. Additionally, as Betty Friedan claims, housework does expand to fill the available time. Yet not, as has been claimed, because domestic workers are willing to fight bore-dom with vacuuming, but because new appliances will always engender new standards of aesthetics, family care, and hygiene for the homemaker. These standards are then marketed as editorials of a sort, claiming that the "right way" to do things in the home has been found.[41]

Though not typically examined as such, the feminine mystique is an ongoing process, with each new technology adding a new layer of anxiety to the role of homemaker. Clearly, the ideal kitchen of 1990s contained its own set of anxieties. Through personal and commercial kitchen web sites, we discover that this anxiety often centered on who controls the technology of the kitchen, as well as who is authorized to speak as a kitchen authority. A similar issue of authority has already been addressed within the field of American literature, by critics who argue that domestic novels should be included within the canon. As many critics, including Jane Tompkins and Ann Romines, have already argued, domestic novels and women's fiction should not be cast aside because of an emphasis on detail and household ritual. Instead, we should preserve this literature for its record of not only material culture but also of social movements and social change. Because of extensive feminist recovery work, nineteenth- and early twentieth-century women's fiction and domestic fiction now meet with critical acceptance on most fronts, including canonization. Although sometimes counterintuitive, feminist recovery of Internet materials is essential, and web sites such as Internet Archive make it increasing possible.[42] Recovery work becomes even more essential when we arrive at the intersection of the domestic, the South, and the machine. Each of these areas contains vital and ongoing struggles in the areas of race, class, gender, and sexuality. As one of the least theorized area in terms of the critical work on contemporary southern domestic literature, hypertext and new media studies must be examined in light of gender politics. Further investigation into the race, class, and sexual politics is needed as well. The loss of online kitchens with no critical examination is the loss of pieces of domestic, southern, and technological culture.

This environment of newer and better domestic supplies and information is a part of a much older pattern.[43] Its cycles encompass imaginary figures such as Betty Crocker and social critics such as Betty Friedan, as well as endless new appliances and endless forms of escaping homes filled with appliances, including cycles of vague ailments and new drug "cures" for the homemaker. With these cycles in place, and with the corporate attention the domestic arena receives, it is not difficult to imagine the kitchen of the future. Its spatial boundaries will continue to expand, making the kitchen look more and more like an integrated section of a technologically wired home, with the narratives about this space expanding in form, genre, and medium correspondingly. What becomes more difficult is to imagine how, without more extensive critical attention to women's webs — those of real kitchen, those of domestic literature, those of technologies not yet imagined, and hybrids of these forms — we will record and analyze our "kitchen selves" for posterity, as well as for their valuable commentary on region, ritual, gender, and feminism.

AFTERWORD

In the preceding chapters, I have pointed toward the importance of a renewed interest in domestic novels, histories, and technologies. Such a renewed interest begins with the freedom to categorize a text as "domestic" without the fear of an implied insult. I see this project as inherently feminist and in the same spirit of the second-wave recovery of women's texts and the third-wave reclamation of words such as "bitch" and "girl." It has been my project to reclaim the label "domestic" as it applies to twentieth-century literature by women of the American South and to explore the many worlds the home can contain, as well as the many identities it shapes. All of us draw some parts of our social, sexual, political, financial, emotional, and other identities from our homes, both current and past. Those of us who claim literature as another kind of "home" form our identities through our reading as well. When we read about homes, we gain a privileged glimpse into the intimate details and rituals of survival: at the most basic level, we learn how others eat, sleep, and maintain a shelter. From there, the rituals and ideologies that surround these activities take on astounding proportions, so much so that some of the rituals seem entirely divorced from recognizable basic needs.

When we open a text concerned with domesticity, it is as if we walk along a street at dusk, peering in open windows, watching the preparations for the evening meal. Each scene appears as a stage set, with well-lit scenes of actors arranged around a common domestic centerpiece: a boiling kettle, a set table, or the blue light of a television screen. What is compelling about these scenes is the combination of the quotidian and the unique: we see both ourselves and the Other, sometimes at the same time. The fascination, however, lies in the knowledge that our brief glimpse of domestic ritual only hints at the vast complexity of the lives within.

CHAPTER NOTES

Chapter One

1. I am indebted to Kevin Hinton, a student in my Southern Women Writers class, for mentioning the connection between "Dare's Gift" and *Beloved* as haunted homes.

Chapter Two

1. Pamela Matthews also refers to Glasgow's disability as a metaphor, but a metaphor for "her alienation within a tradition of male selfhood" (201) in *Ellen Glasgow and a Woman's Traditions*.

2. Disability studies prides itself on its position as a political, social, and cultural studies movement. On the political side, the movement fought for the Americans with Disabilities Act, which was successfully passed in 1990 and guarantees civil rights to those with disabilities. This political victory has brought to the field an increased interest on the part of many scholars, especially within the humanities. For a thorough history of the field, see Lennard J. Davis' introduction in *The Disability Studies Reader* (1997).

3. The capitalization of "Deaf" is used as the signifier for the cultural community of deaf persons.

4. It is important to note that I am not promoting a "separate spheres" variety of domestic criticism. Glasgow's own characters—most notably, women such as Mrs. Payson and Abby Goode, who are quite active beyond the home domain, make such a critique insupportable. Instead, I am interested in the ways that the modes of narration interact with motifs of insularity, interiority, illness/dis-

ability, and the kitchen. Also, it is important to remember that Glasgow stresses the voluntary nature of Virginia's confinement. Virginia continually refuses opportunities for interactions outside the home and Glasgow's narrative ultimately works as a cautionary tale, punishing Virginia for her self-entrapment.

5. See Linda Wagner's *Ellen Glasgow: Beyond Convention* (1982) and Lynette Carpenter's "The Daring Gift in Ellen Glasgow's 'Dare's Gift'" in *Haunting the House of Fiction* (1984).

6. Other critical approaches to Glasgow's short stories include an emphasis on the way she "came to terms with the psychological knowledge that began, after 1910 or so, to be more and more the central concern of fiction" (see Julius Raper's "Invisible Things: The Short Stories of Ellen Glasgow"). Edgar MacDonald also remarks on the influence of psychology, namely in the form of Glasgow's personal relationship with "noted New York psychiatrist Dr. Bailey." MacDonald focuses on Henry Anderson's long-term influence on Glasgow's writing as well ("From Jordan's End to Frenchman's Bend"). Both of these critical views imply that Glasgow was, in many ways identifying herself with men and under their professional influence at this time. While Glasgow was undoubtedly aware of the rise of psychology of her time, I would argue that the "alienist" and "doctor" figures of her stories often serve as foils to women who are waging psychic battles with the ideology that controls their homes, and winning, largely through their own resources and creative solutions.

7. For an overview of the popular cultural images of "Mammy" during this time period,

see "'Now Then—Who Said Biscuits?': The Black Woman Cook as Fetish in American Advertising, 1905–1953" by Alice A. Deck in *Kitchen Culture in America: Popular Representations of Food, Gender, and Race*, edited by Sherrie A. Inness.

Chapter Three

1. In her essay "'Making a Scene': Some Thoughts on Female Sexuality and Marriage in Eudora Welty's *Delta Wedding* and the *Optimist's Daughter*" (*Mississippi Quarterly*, Fall 1995), Danielle Fuller takes a different view of Dabney's proclamation of independence. Fuller writes, "Dabney's dreams of self-possession and her sensuous longing for sexual fulfillment and the control of her own life are enmeshed in the mores of the Fairchilds even as she tries to define herself against them. Her sexual self, although vibrantly awakened, is not free from the constraints and limits of her Fairchild upbringing, and hence her vision, like her glimpse into the whirlpool, incorporates the known and the mysterious, tantalizing possibility and the threat of danger" (302). While I would agree with Fuller that the Fairchild upbringing may necessarily limit a complete sense of sexual agency, I am interested in the ways that Dabney (and other Welty characters) are able to combine and articulate the "known and mysterious" (or sexual and domestic) in a way that their predecessors in southern women's literature are not.

2. Louise Westling and Ann Romines provide helpful readings of certain aspects of female sexuality in conjunction with domestic acts. These readings appear in the context of arguments for the power of the feminine role in Welty's work. For discussions of fertility and community, see Westling's *Eudora Welty* in the Macmillan Women Writers series. Westling also explores the themes of motherhood, fertility, feminine ritual, and sexual imagery in *Delta Wedding*, often in comparison to *To the Lighthouse* (See *Sacred Groves and Ravaged Gardens*). In *Fiction of the Home Place*, Helen Fiddyment Levy focuses on Welty's rewriting of "her American history, the narrative of the woman's home" (168). Her discussion centers on time, cycles, and "the female artist's memory" (175), but she

finds that the "harsh environments" of "man-made modernisms" and "the undomesticated natural world" "allow neither the feminine emotion nor the female sexuality full and safe expression" (166). While I agree that Welty's characters do not feel safe expressing every emotion and sexual desire, I argue that especially the younger generations of Shellmound women especially show signs of progress in their freedom of expression. I am also interested in the ways that sexuality and domesticity become narratalogically and thematically fused, a topic that has yet to be further analyzed.

3. Fuller, for instance, privileges sexuality, arguing that "Welty's female characters subvert, question, and re-present female sexuality in ways that reveal the power imbalances involved in heterosexual relationships" (292). I would add that Welty's female characters often employ domestic acts and rituals in much the same way. Ellen's cake-baking narrative simultaneously interrogates imbalances in both domestic power and heterosexual relationships. Ellen questions the relationships between George and Robbie Reid and the relationship between Dabney and Troy, even as she questions her own ability to bake a "nice" cake and to continue binding the family together (32–33). In a discussion of what she terms "empowering pleasures," Suzan Harrsion analyzes sexual imagery and pleasure in language in *Delta Wedding* (See "'The Other Way to Live': Gender and Selfhood in *Delta Wedding* and *The Golden Apples*," *Mississippi Quarterly*, 44:1 [Winter 1990–1991] 49–57). Romines, on the other hand, clearly privileges the domestic in *The Home Plot*, reading domestic rituals that sometimes have sexual content and symbolism, and sometimes do not. In her wide-ranging study of Welty's work, Ruth Vande Kieft describes the "variety of resonances even the word *home* has in Eudora Welty's fiction" (52) as well as the "most simple and primitive rituals of the home, or the private rituals that come from a repeated performance of an action of love" (59). Yet in reference to the cake-baking narrative, she finds "nothing in the language of this passage to weld the two different areas of experience [the outer and the inner life]" (80).

4. For early feminist readings of *Delta Wedding*, see essays by Jane Hinton, Elizabeth

Kerr, and Margaret Jones Bolsterli in *Eudora Welty: Critical Essays* (1979), edited by Peggy Whitman Prenshaw, as well as Prenshaw's essay "Woman's World, Man's Place: The Fiction of Eudora Welty" in *Eudora Welty: A Form of Thanks* (1979). In *Serious Daring from Within: Female Narrative Stategies in Eudora Welty's Novels* (1990), Franziska Gygax builds on these works in her feminist study of narrative patterns in Welty's work. Her chapter on *Delta Wedding* examines various forms of female initiation, including sexual initiation.

5. See Prenshaw, "Sex and Wreckage in the Parlour," *The Southern Quarterly* 33:2–3 (Winter–Spring 1995), 107. Helen Fiddyment Levy connects Welty's interest in women's voices and narratives to this section of *One Writer's Beginnings* (See *Fiction of the Home Place* 162). Gail Mortimer finds evidence of how Welty learned to "explore her beliefs about the nature of knowledge" in the visual construction of several scenes from "Listening" (See *Daughter of the Swan: Love and Knowledge in Eudora Welty's Fiction* 5–7).

6. For another example of Dabney's sexualized performance of the bride role, see the opening of Chapter 2: "Dabney came down the stairs vaguely in time to the song Mary Lamar Mackey was rippling out in the music room — 'Drink to Me Only with Thine Eyes.' 'Oh, I'm a wreck,' she sighed absently" (34). Here, the act of descending the stairs to music prefigures the wedding march, with both the song and Dabney's manner indicating a languorous, sensual performance of the bride role.

7. Ellen expresses this type of disapproval of female sexual desire, especially within the context of cross-class marriage: "They [George and Robbie Reid] lay there smiling and worn out, but twined together — appealing, shining in moonlight, and almost — somehow — threatening, Ellen felt" (31). When Ellen mentions her memory of this evening to Battle, he remarks, "You mean when they put on the Rape of the Sabines down at the Grove?" (75). While Battle characterizes George as the aggressor in this comment, the phrase "they put on," as well as Battle's sarcasm, would seem to implicate Robbie Reid as partially responsible for an overtly sexualized performance as well.

8. Welty writes, "The women it was who inherited the place — or their brothers, guiltily, handed it over." In this section of *Delta Wedding*, Robbie Reid notes that the women seem to recognize the need for masculine performance of land ownership: "In the Delta the land belonged to the women — they only let the men have it, and sometimes they tried to take it back and give it to someone else" (190). Robbie Reid's narrative also catalogues various specific transfers of property that conform to these Delta gender conventions. In an interview with Jo Brans, Welty notes the power of the Delta matriarchy, commenting on women who "ruled the roost" (See *Conversations with Eudora Welty* 304).

Chapter Four

1. See Michaels, "Local Colors" 744.

2. This shift in thinking — from the home as relatively self-sufficient to the train as essential provider — could, at times, result in an intense competition for household goods, particularly directly following World War II. J.R. Hefner, a longtime Appalachian resident and World War II veteran, remarks that it was common practice for residents of North Carolina mountain towns to watch the goods unloaded at the depot on an almost daily basis. The addresses of large boxes that could be identified as kitchen appliances were noted, and residents often tried to beat the merchandise to its destination in order to purchase the limited post–War goods, such as ovens and refrigerators. J.R. Hefner, personal interview, Blowing Rock, N.C., 5 January 2001.

3. Here, I am indebted to Walter Benn Michaels for his naming of a narrative that works toward a cultural reconceptualization as a "technology." In *Our America: Nativism, Modernism, and Pluralism*, Michaels names numerous modernist and nativist narratives of the 1920s as the technologies for "reconceptualizing and thereby preserving the contours of racial identity" (13).

4. See Lora Romero's *Home Fronts* and also the "No More Separate Spheres!" special issue of *American Literature* (September 1998).

5. The categories listed here are from Susan Goodman's 1998 biography of Ellen Glasgow. Yaeger cites Goodman's categories

in her prologue to position her work as opposed to these categories because of their limited application to the "peculiarity of southern women's fictions across racial boundaries" (ix).

6. Edward Ayers notes a similar blending of public and private that had already occurred in terms of plantation life. Planters and freedmen, once accustomed to producing nearly all their own goods, might purchase everything from the country store (frequently on credit based on newly planted crops) during the 1860s and 1870s. The availability of a wide range of goods meant that planters could focus on a single profitable crop, usually cotton.

7. A notable exception, of course, is Amy Richter's *Home on the Rails: Women, the Railroad, and the Rise of Public Domesticity*.

Chapter Five

1. Here I am using bell hooks' term for an African American place apart from oppressive forces. (See *Yearning: Race, Gender, and Cultural Politics* 41–49.)

2. William Hogue argues that postmodern African American writers "are looking for new forms in which to represent the African American" (169). I would add that for Morrison, the domestic novel is one of these forms.

3. See Amy Kaplan, "Manifest Domesticity," Cathy N. Davidson and Jessamyn Hatcher (Eds.), *No More Separate Spheres!: A Next Wave American Studies Reader*. For information on British domestic novels, see Nancy Armstrong, *Desire and Domestic Fiction: A Political History of the Novel*.

4. Related to the debate about the use of the domestic perspective in *The Color Purple* is the controversy over Walker's "negative" portrayal of black men. For further discussion of this issue and how it played out in popular media, see bell hooks' *Yearning: Race, Gender, and Cultural Politics*, Chapter 8, "Representations: Feminism and Black Masculinity."

5. Fred Hobson in *The Southern Writer in the Postmodern World* seems to fault pre–1980s southern domestic literature for ignoring "the sweep of history" in favor of "concrete details" (78).

6. For a recent (2005) examination of literary African American domesticity, see Valerie Sweeney Prince's *Burnin' Down the House: Home in African American Literature*. Prince reconfigures Houston Baker's blues matrix to trace the concept of the home through the city, the kitchen, and the womb, as "sites that specifically inform our understanding of an African American sense of home" (3).

7. For more on this omission, see Sharon Harley's "For the Good of the Family and Race: Gender, Work, and Domestic Roles in the Black Community, 1880–1930." Harley notes the abundance of "sweeping generalizations and unfounded stereotypes" even when examining the history of black working women (336). In *Labor of Love, Labor of Sorrow: Black Women, Work, and the Family from Slavery to Present*, Jacqueline Jones notes that historical scholarship on work not performed by white men (often domestic in nature) has focused on black men or white women.

8. Sharon Harley writes that "Blacks had reasons for supporting separate spheres for women and men that were unique to their history." Included in these reasons are a newfound status in "gender-defined work" for those "one generation out of slavery." Sex segregation could also shelter black women "from charges of immorality" (347). I would argue that the political support of separate spheres differs from experiencing separate spheres as a static, lived reality.

9. For specific statistics on the numbers of American black women working as domestics during various eras, see Davis (*Women, Race and Class*), Jones, and Harley.

10. Here Montgomery draws on the work of Jacqueline Jones.

11. This passage is drawn form Davis's larger argument denouncing the mythology of the dominating African American wife and mother, as well as the mythology of the matriarchical and matrilineal society. Davis points out that slave societies were matrilineal only to the extent that the slaveholder and the state imposed this structure upon them through "the principle of *partus sequiter ventrem*— the child follows the condition of the mother" and through birth records that recorded only matrilineage, thereby hiding the true lineage of slave children fathered by slaveowners (12). This mythology survived

well into the 1960s and was legitimized in the eyes of many through the 1965 government "Moynihan Report," which blamed African Americans for social ills caused by this "matriarchal structure" (qtd. in Davis 13). For more information on the Moynihan Report and the response of the Black Power movement to its propaganda, see Jones 312–13. For a discussion of the dangers of "black mother worship," see hooks 45. For further literary analysis of this issue, especially as it relates to Morrison, see Prince 5.

12. For an analysis that argues for the interlaced nature of these categories and, even more interestingly, against the fixed nature of the categories of race and gender themselves, see Robyn Wiegman's *American Anatomies: Theorizing Race and Gender*.

13. It's essential to note that the end of slavery did not necessitate an immediate improvement in material conditions for many African Americans in the South. For a discussion of post-emancipation physical and economic abuses, see Davis, especially 127–46. Sexual harassment and rape also continued. See Collins, second edition 56.

14. Betsy Klimasmith, in *At Home in the City: Urban Domesticity in American Literature and Culture 1850–1930*, usefully points out that domesticity's oldest definition, according to the Oxford English Dictionary, encompasses a *group* of dwellings in a community, village, or town, rather than referring only to a single dwelling, as in most contemporary concepts of domesticity.

15. In contrast, in Chapter 13, "The Approaching Obsolescence of Housework: A Working-Class Perspective" of *Women, Race, and Class*, Angela Davis urges all women to recognize housework as a waste of time and to lobby for socialist solutions such as teams of subsidized workers who would perform housework at a price affordable for working-class women. It's also essential to note that Collins characterizes "unpaid family labor" as both "confining and empowering" (second edition 46).

16. See Angelyn Mitchell's "'Sth, I Know That Woman': History, Gender, and the South in Toni Morrison's *Jazz*" for a complete account of how the South, especially southern African American women, appears in each novel.

17. Catherine Carr Lee explores the role of the South in *Song of Solomon*. Of Milkman Dead, the protagonist, she writes, "Central to both his maturation and his healing is Milkman's recognition that the cultural past of the African-American South continues to create his twentieth-century present in ways that are not constraining but liberating" (43). See "The South in Toni Morrison's *Song of Solomon*: Initiation, Healing, and Home" in *Toni Morrison's Song of Solomon: A Casebook*.

18. While Morrison does not seem to feel any anxiety about her own regional identity, she does admit that she has never felt firmly rooted in one particular regional identity: "I know that I never felt like an American or an Ohioan or even a Lorainite. I never felt like a citizen. But I felt very strongly — not much with the first book; more with the second; and very much with the one I'm working on now — I felt a very strong sense of place, not in terms of the country or the state, but in terms of the details, the feeling, the mood of the community, of the town" (Stepto 10).

19. Book critic Jonathan Yardley writes, "Toni Morrison is not a Southern writer, but she has located place and community with the skill of a Flannery O'Connor or a Eudora Welty" (quoted in a 2006 reconsideration of *Sula*; the original quotation is from Yardley's initial 1973 review of the book. Yardley notes that "there is no reason to alter that judgment today.") For a different kind of comparison of the use of place by Welty and Morrison, see Anne-Marie Paquet-Deyris's "Toni Morrison's *Jazz* and the City."

20. For a reading of *Beloved* as a domestic novel see, for example, Denise Rodriguez's "'Where the Self that had No Self Made Its Home': The Reinscription of Domestic Discourse in Toni Morrison's *Beloved*." Elizabeth Hayes also analyzes *Beloved* through the lens of African American domesticity in "The Named and the Nameless: Morrison's 124 and Naylor's 'the Other Place' as Semiotic *Chorae*."

21. Although the criticism of her work does not usually combine these perspectives, Morrison comments specifically on the relationship between feminine domesticity and a sense of place: "Also, I think some of it [the sense of place in the novels] is just a woman's strong sense of being in a room, a place, or in a house. Sometimes my relationship to things in a house would be a little different from, say

my brother's or my father's or my sons.' I clean them and I move them and I do very intimate things 'in place'" (Stepto 10–11).

22. Stephen Knadler, however, does address the topic of domestic *violence* in *Jazz*. Magali Cornier Michael provides a feminist reading of the material culture of the Convent, including the food, shelter, and folk remedies it provides (655) in "Re-Imagining Agency: Toni Morrison's *Paradise*," but she does not analyze these aspects in the framework of domesticity scholarship.

23. See, for example Michael Nowlin's "Toni Morrison's *Jazz* and the Racial Dreams of the American Writer," Angelyn Mitchell's "'Sth, I Know That Woman': History, Gender, and the South in Toni Morrison's *Jazz*," and "Off the Record: *Jazz* and the Production of Black Culture" by Patricia McKee. For a detailed discussion of a jazz aesthetic, see Dirk Ludigkeit's "Collective Improvisation and Narrative Structure in Toni Morrison's *Jazz*."

24. Instead, other critical approaches focus on "national and individual identity building" (Fraile-Marcos), American exceptionalism (Dalsgård), repetition (of communal history) *without* difference (Krumholz), the cycle of life and death (Aguiar), religion (Channette Romero), and parallels between the difficulties of reading the nonlinear narrative and the difficulties of communication the characters face (Kearly, "Toni Morrison's *Paradise* and the Politics of Community;" Page, "Furrowing All the Brows").

25. Anna Flood moved away from Ruby to live in urban areas, then returned to run the family store. She seems to bring "outsider" ideas with her and she aligns herself with Misner, a distinct outsider.

26. In the version of this scene in the opening of the novel, Morrison obscures the characters' identities. At the end of the novel, the identities are clearer, although differences in the two versions of the same scene cause difficulties in aligning the revealed identities and the actions of "the men" of the opening. This method implies that the men are an anonymous threat at the beginning of the novel, and that their reasoning for the violence can only be explained through the town's history.

27. Dovey adds Convent peppers to canned peas (supposedly because Steward's taste buds have been numbed by tobacco) and

thinks that "Convent peppers, hot as hellfire, did all the cooking for her" (81).

28. The second Disallowing occurred when the World War II veterans among the men returned to Haven in the face of racism and the town's general decline. At this point, they decided to move west to found a new town, the town that would become Ruby, the novel's setting (194).

29. The men do register disgust at the messy conditions of many of the rooms, although they admit that "these rooms are normal," as they look at the bedrooms (8). Little evidence exists of the sexual deviance they imagine.

30. L confirms her own name when she remarks, "If your name is the subject of first Corinthians, chapter 13" (199) during a meditation on different types of love.

Chapter Six

1. Here, I am indebted to Walter Benn Michaels for his naming of a narrative that works toward a cultural reconceptualization as a "technology." In *Our America: Nativism, Modernism, and Pluralism*, Michaels names numerous modernist and nativist narratives of the 1920s as the technologies for "reconceptualizing and thereby preserving the contours of racial identity" (13). In my examination of the effects of household technology on domestic narratives, I will also explore the ways in which narrative acts as a form of technology.

2. For a discussion of the cultural lag theory — the gap that exists between developments in gender roles and media recognition of such developments — see Ogburn, W.F., *On Culture and Social Change*.

3. For one of the earliest works to give a broad overview of the portrayals of women in television, women's magazines, and newspapers, see Tuchman, *Hearth and Home: Images of Women in the Mass Media*. Tuchman claims that during the 1960s and 1970s, women were subjegated to a "symbolic annihilation" by the mass media.

4. For quantitative approaches to evaluating sexism in media, see Pingree et al., "A Scale for Sexism," *Journal of Communication*.

5. For a discussion of the contested

meanings of popular media, including the dynamics of the "preferred" readings of the producers versus the "less preferred" readings that may be established by consumers, see Fiske, *Understanding Popular Culture*.

6. In "The Portrayal of Women in Television Advertising," Carolyn Lin discusses the gender "overlap" of advertising, in which the defined roles for men and women become "less distinguishable." This phenomenon is even more noticeable with electronic media, as the gender of the author or speaker is easily, and many times, intentionally, eschewed.

7. In the introduction to *Mediated Women*, Marian Meyers responds to Tuchman's concept of "symbolic annihilation" of women in 1970s mass media portrayals in light of the effects of third-wave feminism, claiming that 1990s images still cling to stereotypes, but also offer varying levels of progressive images as well, leading to "fractured ... multiple and often contradictory images."

8. The first decade of the twenty-first century will undoubtedly have its own manner of responding, via various media, to the realm of the domestic, possibly with an emphasis on comfort, balance, and natural foods as current domestic ideals.

9. A later version of the "intelligent" refrigerator, LG's "Side by Side with HD Ready LCD TV and Weather & Info Center" has a slightly different set of capabilities, including one television screen and an additional screen devoted to local weather forecasts. It also boasts "pre-stored" recipes and storage space for digital photos. In this newer 2006–2007 model, the Internet is no longer a focus, nor is the ability to track food purchases (http://us.lge.com). The newest developments in computer technology in the kitchen seem to be in the form of the personal digital assistant (PDA). PDA software now allows for the downloading and storage of recipes, including nutritional analysis. Although these kitchen technologies might seem to "do it all," the kitchen still retains its function as a meal preparation space that requires human labor. Despite turn-of-the-century feminist cries for "kitchenless homes" by writers such as Zona Gale and Charlotte Perkins Gilman, these products reiterate the kitchen's longstanding status as the center of the home. For a discussion of the proposals of Gale and Gilman in this context, see Scanlon, Jennifer

in *Inarticulate Longings: The Ladies' Home Journal, Gender, and the Promises of Consumer Culture.*

10. Interestingly, despite the technological advances in the wired refrigerator, much of the advertising seems to rely on standard pitches, such as vague references to technology and the future, as well as the all-too-familiar dazzling array of colors. Valerie Korinek notes the initial enthusiasm for "fashion colors" in the kitchen with the 1960s McClary "Refrigerator of the Future" — available in "white, palomino, coppertone, avocado, and as illustrated, verd antique" (Korinek 157). Although the Audrey failed as a kitchen appliance, hacker communities quickly co-opted the technology and continue to do so today. See audreyhacking.com. This development would seem to indicate that early marketing strategies were ineffective, and that 3Com may have targeted the wrong audience.

11. The idea of a kitchen as a metaphorical space representing the communities established by women-centered media is not new. In her analysis of *Chatelaine*, a Canadian women's monthly, Valerie Korinek quotes the magazine's current editor, Rona Maynard, as referring to the cultural community created by the magazine as "the biggest kitchen table in the country" (23).

12. Not all advertisements for high-tech products depict women as empowered users of their products. Jane Caputi points to a type of "extraordinary representation of this normative sadism linked not only to sexual violence (represented by these fragmented and dehumanized women) but to a porno-technological power over nature" in a 1993 ad for Eclipse fax machines, which features a woman with all her visible orifices jammed with pipes and electronic equipment and the line "If It Were Any Faster, You'd Have to Send and Receive Your Faxes Internally" ("The Pornography of Everyday Life" [71]).

13. Jane Hobson notes that the type of advertising used for appliances carries over into other markets as well; for instance, greeting card manufacturers often refer to the greeting card as a "product that will ease increasing burdens on women." "Non-occasion Greeting Cards and the Commodification of Personal Relationships" in *All the World and Her Husband: Women in Twentieth Century Consumer Culture*, 239–52.

14. Shelley Budgeon notes the phenomenon of this type of individualism divorced from history or politics in her essay on fashion magazine advertising: "Fashion Magazine Advertising: Constructing Femininity in the 'Postfeminist' Era." The cyberdomestics do make historical references — as to the "belle" image — but these references often concern the individual and her habits, not her place within a wider historical or political realm, possibly in unconscious imitation of much of the advertising found in "women's" media that strongly advocates this type of individualism.

15. Carolyn Lin refers to a similar type of self-selection that happens in the context of a "'500 channel' digital multimedia environment." In the context of television advertising and broadcasting she refers to this increasing fragmentation as "narrowcasting," speculating that television will come to emulate "the specialized offerings that we associate with the magazine industry and online computer database services such as America Online and Prodigy" (264). Obviously, even since the late 1990s publication of *Mediated Women*, the Internet's capacity for "narrowcasting" has reached far beyond the database stage.

16. I am drawing on Donna Haraway's definition of a cyborg as "a cybernetic organism, a hybrid of machine and organism, a creature of social reality as well a creature of fiction," a phenomenon that "changes what counts as women's experience in the late twentieth century" (149).

17. Both Friedan and Naomi Woolf have faced criticism for supporting the "myth" that magazines and other forms of media are "bad" for women in that they reinforce gender-role stereotyping to encourage home-based consumption. For example, Korinek counters that the content of such magazines has always been more subversive than it was thought to be by many cultural critics (10).

18. Nancy Walker refutes Friedan's tendency to view women's magazines and much of women's popular culture as monolithically supportive of the homemaker role and its primacy within domestic consumption. Walker notes a variety of "needs, tastes, and values" addressed within different publications and within the same issue of a single magazine (vii).

19. For a discussion of "scientific" house-keeping and "the new housekeeping" as portrayed in women's magazines, see Scanlon, 65–69.

20. *Ladies Home Journal* featured several articles to help women deal with this problem, including "Back to the Kitchen: But How?" and "I'm Glad My Servant Left" (Scanlon 59).

21. George Landow discusses the breakdown of the author-reader boundary in terms of hypertext in the final chapter of *Hypertext 2.0*: "The Politics of Hypertext: Who Controls the Text?"

22. I am especially interested in the way that *Mimi's Cyber Kitchen* uses a cartoon-style wall of a kitchen as the interface for the site. For instance, one clicks on the shelf for information on cookbooks, the refrigerator for information on buying food, and the stove for recipes. I find this type of interface interesting, as it does not correspond to other types of web sites. Amazon.com, for instance, does not craft its interface to resemble the shop front or interior of a physical bookstore. This type of mediation of the interface seems to operate on the assumption that cyberdomestics will feel more comfortable with the presence of kitchen icons (as well as forms of technology) with which they are already familiar. David Bolter and Richard Grusin refer to this style of media as "hypermediacy": " a style of visual representation whose goal is to remind the viewer of the medium" (272). The hypermediacy of *Mimi's Cyber Kitchen* is vexed by its inclusion of an apologia as well as the text box entitled "Kalling All Kitchen Klowns." Hiller simultaneously reminds us of her skilled use of new media while not so subtly positioning her content, kitchen advice and instruction, as somehow not worthy of its technological format. Interestingly, of the purely personal southern kitchen web sites examined in this chapter, only *Mimi's Cyber Kitchen* survives as of 2007, although Rattray's more personal site (in a different form) still links to her About.com expert page. Although not a kitchen site, the Southern Belles WebRing can also still be found online at http://www.geocities.com/BourbonStreet/Delta/1337/soubelles.html.

23. In the twenty-first century, kitchen web logs (blogs) seem to have surpassed their personal web site siblings in popularity, as evidenced by the decline of some of the sites

mentioned in this chapter (see n. 22). Perhaps the most famous kitchen blog of the twenty-first century is Julie Powell's *The Julie/Julia Project* (*http://blogs.salon.com/000 1399/*), which led to the 2005 book *Julie and Julia: 365 Days, 524 Recipes, 1 Tiny Apartment Kitchen.* The blog dynamic, with its near-constant updates and interaction via comments, obviously differs from the web site dynamic in its immediacy. For kitchen blogs, this increased immediacy heightens the potential for unification and community in the virtual kitchen. Interestingly, in southern kitchen blogs, the apologia element seems to disappear. The absence of the apologia makes sense because many blogs are created using preexisting templates. Given the rise in the popularity of blogs and the ease with which they can be created and updated, southern cyberdomestics would seem to have little to explain and nothing for which to apologize. These developments underscore the unique qualities of cyberkitchen culture during the 1990s, when going online, perhaps especially as a southern homemaker, was a pioneering act. For examples of early twenty-first-century southern kitchen blogs and southern culture blogs, see *Southern Kitchen http://www. southernkitchen.blogspot.com/, The Kitchen Madonna http://kitchenmadonna.blogspot.com/, Ramblings of a Southern Goddess http://ladybel-lagrace.blogspot.com/,* and *A Southern Girl's Guide to Almost Anything http://southern-born-and-bred.blogspot.com/2006/08/everything-but-kitchen-sink_25.html.*

24. Temporality becomes a problem in the analysis of Internet materials. Some of the sites I will discuss do not exist today, while others live on in altered or similar forms. I also want to point to what I see as a unique moment in Internet culture that has now passed. Therefore, I typically use the past tense when referring to general 1990s trends, but I retain the literary convention of writing in the present tense when analyzing specific texts/hypertexts.

25. Yet at first glance, it appears that Hiller does, in fact, recognize her own place as a leader among cyberdomestics. A brightly colored text box beneath her own logo asks, "Want to start your own recipe web site? Don't know how?" and it seems as though Hiller is on the verge of both acknowledging and sharing her expertise. However, the text box title

reads "Kalling all Kitchen Klowns," a phrase that hardly allows for the valorization of the cyberdomestic. Also, the hyperlink leads to an advertisement-supported site that offers a one-size-fits-all template for sharing recipes online, an approach that Hiller herself eschews.

26. Nancy Walker notes that the term *domestic* has often been used in women's magazines in a broad sense, particularly during the World War II era, to mean "that which was not foreign," a meaning the "techno-belles" would seem to promote through their emphasis on region (viii).

27. It may be that women find the kind of "pleasure mixed up with anxiety" that Naomi Woolf notes in *The Beauty Myth* (62) when looking at recipes and home "ideas" online rather than at pictures of women's bodies and women's fashion, in addition to the house-wifely guilt brought to our attention largely by Friedan in the 1960s. That is, women may derive a great deal of comfort and pleasure from perusing not only recipes, but also intimate narratives of home life. However, like fashion magazines, these web pages also induce guilt, a feeling of domestic unworthiness, as opposed to beauty- and body-related unworthiness. It is important to note, however, that the interactive nature of these web sites seems to support, at least in theory, a greater degree of agency for readers, as well as a greater degree of interpretative freedom than other forms of media, because of their highly malleable physical form. An offending page of a web site, can, with a click of the mouse, be made to disappear without changing the document's integrity.

28. Marian Meyers notes the current tendency of feminist scholars to remark on the contradictions of late twentieth-century popular culture representations of women, to acknowledge that "single texts are rarely uniformly regressive or unvaryingly progressive" (11). Squires' narrative would seem to warrant this type of critique as well, as it documents women's culture even while constructing an apologia.

29. Korinek notes the tendencies of earlier forms of media to act as the precursors to electronic communities in reference to the Canadian women's magazine, *Chatelaine*: "Oftentimes, the letters page resembled a print precursor of e-mail correspondence, as women who had met only through letters re-

sponded to each other and, perhaps, took their relationship outside the magazine's perimeters" (9).

30. I use the term "personality" and "persona" interchangeably, but in contrast to the creators of personal sites, to indicate that the women of corporate sites are "marketed" along the lines of a "Dear Abby" figure, complete with a boxed photo next to their names. There seems to be a sort of gender anxiety behind the photo as well, as if there is a need to prove that "real" women have created, at the very least, their own columns and articles within the "masculine" space of these sites. As Sherry Turkle notes, "the preoccupation in MUDs (multi-user domains, a type of hypertext 'virtual' environment) with getting a 'fix' on people through 'fixing' their gender reminds us of the extent to which we use gender to shape our relationships" (437).

31. For further methods of reading specific signifiers within the world of "women's" popular culture, see Ellen McCracken's *Decoding Women's Magazines: From* Mademoiselle *to* Ms.

32. Ellen Garvey traces this type of "fragmented" combination of advertising and editorial copy in magazines to the late 1910s. Prior to this time, ads and copy were strictly divided, with ads only at the front and back of the magazine. Garvey links this mixing of ads and copy to the development of the department store, an arena in which shoppers and sellers realized that distraction could serve as a pleasant (and presumably economically effective) force (*The Adman in the Parlor* 4–5).

33. For a historical perspective on domesticity and changing economic cultures, see David Abrahamson's *Magazine-Made America: The Cultural Transformation of the Postwar Periodical.*

34. Jennifer Scanlon points out the discouragement of democratic participation in mass culture, specifically in *Ladies' Home Journal.* A side-by-side comparison of women's magazines in hypertext forms to individual kitchen web sites would seem to emphasize this point. As the individual sites rarely make reference to the periodicals (and their hypertext versions), it is difficult to know if the hypertext creators see their work as resistant to mass culture, and more specifically, to mass culture aimed at women (Scanlon 4–5).

35. It would be interesting to compare *Diana's Kitchen* in its current incarnation with the *Diana's Kitchen* that existed prior to the advent of About.com.

36. For feminist discussions of the disembodiment of women in advertising, see Brownmiller, *Femininity* and Dworkin, *Woman Hating.*

37. The importance of female persona in attracting women is not a new concept. Scanlon notes that as early as 1889, Edward Bok portrayed "Ruth Ashmore" in a monthly feature called "Side Talks with Girls" in *The Ladies' Home Journal* (Scanlon 50).

38. For a historical perspective on the roles of kitchen "experts," see, for example, "'How to': The Experts Speak" (Walker 145–88).

39. For another type of text that draws on commercial advertising, but is ultimately composed by the supposed consumer, see Ellen Garvey's discussion of nineteenth-century trade card scrapbooks ("Readers Read Advertising into Their Lives: The Trade Card Scrapbook" in *The Adman in the Parlor* 16–50).

40. See Michael Kammen's *American Culture, American Tastes: Social Change and the Twentieth Century* for his helpful remarks on the distinction between popular and mass culture, as well as the rise of mass culture between the 1930s and the 1960s.

41. For an informative, feminist perspective on "complimentary copy" in women's media, see Gloria Steinem, "Sex, Lies, and Advertising" in *Moving Beyond Words.*

42. Maggie Andrews and Mary Talbot note that the "significant part that consumption plays in so many women's live justifies its study by feminists." I would add that when women's personal narratives and advertising become as tightly intertwined as they have in the web sites I have examined (without as much of the third-party intervention of an editorial force as in magazine culture), the study would seem to hold particular importance to feminist scholars (1–22).

43. Luigi Manca and Alessandra Manca characterize these type of "better life" images in advertising as utopian rather than political. While I would argue that the images are often both utopian and political, I agree that the advertisements tend to offer "a multitude of fragmented and diverse appeals" to consumers rather than an overarching societal vision (1).

WORKS CITED

Abrahamson, David. *Magazine-Made America: The Cultural Transformation of the Postwar Periodical.* Crosshill, NJ: Hampton Press, 1996.

Aguiar, Sarah Appleton. "'Passing On' Death: Stealing Life in Toni Morrison's *Paradise.*" *African American Review* 38.3 (Fall 2004): 513–19.

Andrews, Maggie, and Mary Talbot. *All the World and Her Husband: Women in Twentieth-Century Consumer Culture.* London: Cassell, 2000.

Armstrong, Nancy. *Desire and Domestic Fiction: A Political History of the Novel.* New York: Oxford, 1987.

Asch, Adrienne, and Michelle Fine. "Nurturance, Sexuality, and Women with Disabilities: The Example of Women in Literature." *The Disability Studies Reader.* Ed. Lennard Davis. Routledge: New York, 1997. 241–49.

Audreyhacking.com. 11 June 2007. Audrey Hacking Wiki. 1 Nov. 2007 audrey hacking.com.

Audrey by 3Com. Advertisement. *Better Homes and Gardens* (November 2000): 176–77.

Austen, Jane. *Pride and Prejudice.* New York: Oxford, 1990 (first published 1813).

Ayers, Edward. *The Promise of the New South: Life after Reconstruction.* New York and Oxford: Oxford University Press, 1992.

Bakhtin, M. M. *The Dialogic Imagination.* Austin: University of Texas Press, 1981.

Bane, Lita. "Reading Your Character in Your Kitchen." *Ladies' Home Journal* 50 (March 1933): 34, 110.

Barnhill, John, and Ernest Wales. *Principles and Practice of Modern Otology.* Philadelphia: W. B. Saunders Company, 1907.

Batchelder, Ann. "What a Difference Color Makes." *Ladies' Home Journal* 53 (October 1936): 38–39.

Baynton, Douglas. "'A Silent Exile on This Earth': The Metaphorical Construction of Deafness in the Nineteenth Century." *The Disability Studies Reader.* Ed. Lennard Davis. Routledge: New York, 1997. 128–50.

Beecher, Catharine E., and Harriet Beecher Stowe. *American Woman's Home: Principles of Domestic Science.* New Brunswick, NJ: Rutgers University Press, 1975 (first published 1869).

Berger, John. *Ways of Seeing.* London: Penguin, 1977.

Bernstein, Irving. *The Lean Years: A History of the American Worker, 1920–1933.* Boston: Houghton-Mifflin, 1960.

Bolter, Jay David, and Richard Grusin. *Remediation: Understanding New Media.* Cambridge: MIT Press, 1999.

Branson, Stephanie. "'Experience Illuminated': Veristic Representation in Glasgow's Short Stories." *Ellen Glasgow: New Perspectives.* Ed. Dorothy Scura. Knoxville: The University of Tennessee Press, 1995.

Budgeon, Shelley. "Fashion Magazine Advertising: Constructing Femininity in the 'Postfeminist' Era." *Gender and*

Utopia in Advertising: A Critical Reader. Eds. Luigi Manca and Alessandra Manca. Lisle, IL: Procopian Press, Benedictine College, 1994. 55–70.

Bunting, Charles T. "'The Interior World': An Interview with Eudora Welty." *Conversations with Eudora Welty.* Ed. Peggy Whitman Prenshaw. Jackson: University Press of Mississippi, 1984. 50.

Burke, Fielding [Olive Dargan]. *Call Home the Heart.* Longmans: New York, 1932.

Brans, Jo. "Struggling against the Plaid: An Interview with Eudora Welty." *Conversations with Eudora Welty.* Ed. Peggy Whitman Prenshaw. Jackson: University Press of Mississippi, 1984. 304.

Brownmiller, Susan. *Femininity.* New York: Simon & Schuster, 1984.

Caputi, Jane. "The Pornography of Everyday Life." *Mediated Women.* Ed. Marian Meyers. Cresskill, NJ: Hampton Press, 1999.

Carlat, Louis. "'A Cleanser for the Mind': Marketing Radio Receivers for the American Home, 1922–1932." *His and Hers: Gender, Consumption, and Technology.* Eds. Roger Horowitz and Arwen Mohun. Charlottesville: University Press of Virginia, 1998. 115–37.

Carpenter, Lynette. "The Daring Gift in Ellen Glasgow's 'Dare's Gift.'" *Studies in Short Fiction* 21 (1984): 95–102.

_____. *Haunting the House of Fiction.* Knoxville: University of Tennessee Press, 1991.

Chesnutt, Charles. *The Marrow of Tradition. Three Classic African-American Novels.* Ed. Henry Louis Gates, Jr. New York: Vintage Books, 1990 (first published 1901).

Clark, Clifford Edward. *The American Family Home, 1800–1960.* Chapel Hill: The University of North Carolina Press, 1986.

Collins, Patricia H. *Black Feminist Thought: Knowledge, Consciousness, and the Politics of Empowerment.* Boston: Unwin Hyman 1990.

_____. *Black Feminist Thought: Knowledge, Consciousness, and the Politics of Empow-*

erment. 2d ed. New York: Routledge, 2000.

Cook, Sylvia Jenkins. *From Tobacco Road to Route 66: The Southern Poor White in Fiction.* Chapel Hill: The University of North Carolina Press, 1976.

Crittenden, Danielle. *What Our Mothers Didn't Tell Us: Why Happiness Eludes the Modern Woman.* New York: Simon & Schuster, 1999.

Cussler, Margaret, and Mary L. de Give. *'Twixt the Cup and the Lip: Psychological and Socio-Cultural Factors Affecting Food Habits.* New York: Twayne, 1952.

Dalsgård, Katrine. "The One All-Black Town Worth the Pain: (African) American Exceptionalism, Historical Narration, and the Critique of Nationhood in Toni Morrison's *Paradise.*" *African American Review* 35.2 (Summer 2001): 233–48.

Davidson, Cathy N., and Jessamyn Hatcher, eds. "No More Separate Spheres!" *American Literature, Special Issue* (September 1998).

Davidson, Rob. "Racial Stock and 8-Rocks: Communal Historiography in Toni Morrison's *Paradise.*" *Twentieth Century Literature: A Scholarly and Critical Journal* 47.3 (Fall 2001): 355–73.

Davis, Angela. *Women, Race, and Class.* New York: Random House, 1981.

Davis, Lennard. "Introduction." *The Disability Studies Reader.* Ed. Lennard Davis. Routledge: New York, 1997. 1–6.

Davis, Thadious. "Women's Art and Authoriship in Southern Region: Connections." *The Female Tradition in Southern Literature.* Ed. Carol S. Manning. Urbana and Chicago: University of Illinois Press, 1993. 15–36.

Deck, Alice. "'Now Then — Who Said Biscuits?': The Black Woman Cook as Fetish in American Advertising, 1905–1953." *Kitchen Culture in America: Popular Representations of Food, Gender, and Race.* Ed. Sherrie A. Inness. Philadelphia: University of Pennsylvania Press, 2001. 69–93.

Dickinson, Emily. "I like to see it lap the miles." *The Complete Poems of Emily*

Dickinson. Ed. Thomas H. Johnson. Boston and New York: Little, Brown, 1960.

Dickinson, Robert Latou, and Louise Stevens Bryant. *Control of Conception: An Illustrated Manual*. Baltimore: The Williams and Wilkins Company, 1931.

Dickinson, Robert Latou, and Lura Beam. *A Thousand Marriages: A Medical Study of Sex Adjustment*. Baltimore: The Williams and Wilkins Company, 1931.

_____. *The Single Woman: A Medical Study in Sex Education*. Baltimore: The Williams and Wilkins Company, 1934.

Dixieland Web Ring. 14 August 1996. Yahoo Geocities. 15 Nov. 2007 http://www.geocities.com/bourbonstreet/2757/.

Douglas, Susan. *Where the Girls Are*. New York: Random House, 1994.

Drake, Kimberly. "Women on the Go: Blues, Conjure, and Other Alternatives to Domesticity in Ann Petry's *The Street* and *The Narrows*." *Arizona Quarterly: A Journal of American Literature, Culture, and Theory* 54.1 (Spring 1998): 65–90.

Du Maurier, Daphne. *Rebecca*. New York: Literary Guild, 1938.

Dworkin, Andrea. *Woman Hating*. New York: E.P. Dutton, 1974.

"Electrolux Previews Internet Refrigerator." *AllNetDevices: News*. 1999. AllNetDevices. 21 Oct. 1999 *http://devices.internet.com/news_archive/q199/990212elux/990212elux.html*.

Ellis, Havelock. *Essays in War-Time: Further Studies in the Task of Social Hygiene*. Boston and New York: Houghton Mifflin, 1917.

_____. *Psychology of Sex: A Manual for Students*. New York: Emerson Books, Inc., 1937.

_____. *Studies in the Psychology of Sex*. 7 vols. London: Watford, The University Press, 1897–1928.

Fiske, John. *Understanding Popular Culture*. Boston: Unwin Hyman, 1989.

Fitzgerald, Jennifer. "Signifyin(g) on Determinism: Commodity, Romance and Bricolage in Toni Morrison's *Jazz*." Lit: *Literature Interpretation Theory* 12.4 (Dec. 2001): 381–409.

Fraile-Marcos, Ana María. "Hybridizing the 'City upon a Hill' in Toni Morrison's *Paradise*." *MELUS: The Journal of the Society for the Study of the Multi-Ethnic Literature of the United States* 28.4 (Winter 2003): 3–33.

Friedan, Betty. *The Feminine Mystique*. New York: Dell, 1970 (first published 1963).

Fuller, Danielle. "'Making a Scene': Some Thoughts on Female Sexuality and Marriage in Eudora Welty's *Delta Wedding* and *The Optimist's Daughter*." *Mississippi Quarterly* 48 (1995): 291–318.

Fultz, Lucille P. "Southern Ethos/Black Ethics in Toni Morrison's Fiction." *Studies in the Literary Imagination* 31.2 (Fall 1998): 79–95.

Fussell, Betty. *My Kitchen Wars*. New York: North Point Press, 1999.

Garvey, Ellen. *The Adman in the Parlor*. New York: Oxford University Press, 1996.

Glasgow, Ellen. *The Collected Stories of Ellen Glasgow*. Ed. Richard Meeker. Baton Rouge: Louisiana State University Press, 1963.

_____. *Life and Gabriella*. New York: Doubleday, Page, 1916.

_____. *The Woman Within*. Charlottesville: University of Virginia Press, 1954.

_____. *Virginia*. New York: Doubleday, Page, 1913.

_____. *Virginia*. New York: Penguin, 1983 (first published 1913).

Goodman, Susan. *Ellen Glasgow: A Biography*. Baltimore: Johns Hopkins University Press, 1998.

Gordon, Sarah H. *Passage to Union: How the Railroads Transformed American Life, 1829–1929*. Chicago: Ivan R. Dee, 1996.

Gray, Richard. *Southern Aberrations: Writers of the New South and the Problems of Regionalism*. Baton Rouge: Louisiana State University Press, 2000.

Gygax, Franziska. *Serious Daring from Within: Female Narrative Strategies in Eudora Welty's Novels*. New York: Greenwood Press, 1990.

Hamilton, Patrick. *Angel Street.* New York: Samuel French, 1942.

Haraway, Donna. "A Cyborg Manifesto: Science, Technology, and Socialist-Feminism in the Late Twentieth Century." *Simians, Cyborgs, and Women: The Reinvention of Nature.* New York: Routledge, 1991.

Harley, Sharon. "For the Good of Family and Race: Gender, Work, and Domestic Roles in the Black Community, 1880–1930." *Signs* 15.2 (Winter 1990): 336–49.

Harrison, Suzan. "'The Other Way to Live': Gender and Selfhood in *Delta Wedding* and *The Golden Apples.*" *Mississippi Quarterly* 44:1 (Winter 1990–91): 49–67.

Hayes, Elizabeth T. "The Named and the Nameless: Morrison's 124 and Naylor's 'the Other Place' as Semiotic Chorae." *African American Review* 38.4 (Winter 2004): 669–81.

Hefner, J. R. Personal Interview. 5 January 2001.

Helmholtz, Hermann. *Sensations of Tone.* New York: Dover, 1954 (first published 1863).

Herion-Sarafidis, Elisabeth. "Interview with Lee Smith." *The Southern Quarterly* 32.2 (Winter 1994) 7–36.

Hiller, Mimi. *Mimi's CyberKitchen.* 1997. 2 October 1999. http://www.cyber-kitchen.com.

"History of the U.S. Postal Service." *United States Postal Service.* 31 December 1998. United States Postal Service. 8 January 2001. *http://www.usps.gov/history/his2.htm.*

Hobson, Fred. *The Southern Writer in the Postmodern World.* Athens: University of Georgia Press, 1991.

———. "Of Canons and Cultural Wars: Southern Literature and Literary Scholarship after Midcentury." *The Future of Southern Letters.* Eds. Jefferson Humphries and John Lowe. Oxford: Oxford University Press, USA, 1996, 72–86.

Hobson, Jane. "Non-Occasion Greeting Cards and the Commodification of Personal Relationships." *All the World and Her Husband: Women in Twentieth Century Consumer Culture.* Eds. Maggie Andrews and Mary Talbot. New York: Cassell, 2000. 239–52.

Hogue, W. Lawrence. "Postmodernism, Traditional Cultural Forms, and the African American Narrative: Major's *Reflex,* Morrison's *Jazz,* and Reed's *Mumbo Jumbo.*" *Novel: A Forum on Fiction* 35.2–3 (Spring 2002-Summer 2002): 169–92.

hooks, bell. *Yearning: Race, Gender, and Cultural Politics.* Boston: South End Press, 1990.

Hubbard, Freeman H. "Southern Railway System." *Encyclopedia of North American Railroading.* McGraw-Hill: New York, 1981.

Humphries, Jefferson, and John Lowe, eds. *The Future of Southern Letters.* Oxford: Oxford University Press, USA, 1996.

Internet Archive. 1996. 1 Nov. 2007. http://www.archive.org/index.php.

Irvine, Janice. "Sexology." *The Reader's Companion to U.S. Women's History.* Boston: Houghton Mifflin, 1998.

Jones, Anne Goodwyn, and Susan Donaldson. *Haunted Bodies: Gender and Southern Texts.* Charlottesville: University Press of Virginia, 1997.

Jones, Anne Goodwyn. *Tomorrow Is Another Day: The Woman Writer in the South, 1859–1936.* Baton Rouge: Louisiana State University Press, 1981.

Jones, Jacqueline. *Labor of Love, Labor of Sorrow: Black Women, Work, and the Family from Slavery to Present.* New York: Basic Books, 1985.

Kammen, Michael. *American Culture, American Tastes: Social Change and the Twentieth Century.* New York: Knopf, 1999.

Kaplan, Amy. "Manifest Domesticity." *American Literature: A Journal of Literary History, Criticism, and Bibliography* 70.3 (Sep. 1998): 581–606.

Kearly, Peter R. "Toni Morrison's *Paradise* and the Politics of Community." *Journal of American & Comparative Cultures* 23.2 (Summer 2000): 9–16.

Kornasky, Linda. "Ellen Glasgow's Disability." *Mississippi Quarterly: The Journal of Southern Culture* 49.2 (Spring 1996): 281–93.

King, Caroline. "Witches' Fêtes, Druids' Feasts." *Ladies' Home Journal* 50 (October 1933): 31.

Klimasmith, Betsy. *At Home in the City: Urban Domesticity in American Literature and Culture, 1850–1930.* Hanover: University Press of New England, 2005.

Knadler, Stephen. "Domestic Violence in the Harlem Renaissance: Remaking the Record from Nella Larsen's *Passing* to Toni Morrison's *Jazz*." *African American Review* 38.1 (Spring 2004): 99–118.

Korinek, Valerie. *Roughing It in the Suburbs: Reading* Chatelaine *Magazine in the Fifties and Sixties.* Toronto: University of Toronto Press, 2000.

Kreyling, Michael. *Inventing Southern Literature.* Jackson: University Press of Mississippi, 1998.

Kristeva, Julia. *Revolution in Poetic Language.* New York: Columbia University Press, 1984.

Krumholz, Linda J. "Reading and Insight in Toni Morrison's *Paradise*." *African American Review* 36.1 (Spring 2002): 21–34.

LG: Life's Good. 2007. LG Electronics Worldwide. 1 Nov. 2007. http://www.lge.com/.

Landow, George. *Hypertext 2.0.* Baltimore: Johns Hopkins University Press, 1992.

Lane, Harlan. "Construction of Deafness." *The Disability Studies Reader.* Ed. Lennard Davis. Routledge: New York, 1997. 153–71.

Lee, Catherine Carr. "The South in Toni Morrison's *Song of Solomon*: Initiation, Healing, and Home." *Toni Morrison's Song of Solomon: A Casebook.* Oxford, England: Oxford University Press, 2003. 43–64.

Levenstein, Harvey. *Paradox of Plenty: A Social History of Eating in Modern America.* Oxford University Press: New York, 1993.

Levy, Helen Fiddyment. *Fiction of the Home Place: Jewett, Cather, Glasgow, Porter,* Welty, and Naylor. Jackson and London: University Press of Mississippi, 1992.

Lin, Carolyn. "The Portrayal of Women in Television Advertising." *Mediated Women.* Ed. Marian Myers. Cresskill, NJ: Hampton Press, 1999. 253–70.

Lowe, John. "Introduction." *The Future of Southern Letters.* Eds. Jefferson Humphries and John Lowe. Oxford: Oxford University Press, USA, 1996. 3–19.

Ludigkeit, Dirk. "Collective Improvisation and Narrative Structure in Toni Morrison's *Jazz*." *Lit: Literature Interpretation Theory* 12.2 (June 2001): 165–87.

MacDonald, Edgar. "From Jordan's End to Frenchman's Bend: Ellen Glasgow's Short Stories." *Mississippi Quarterly* 49 (Spring 1996): 319–32.

Manca, Luigi, and Alessandra Manca. *Gender and Utopia in Advertising: A Critical Reader.* Eds. Luigi and Alessandra Manca. Lisle, IL: Procopian Press, Benedictine University, 1994.

Manning, Carol. "Introduction: On Defining Themes and (Mis)Placing Women Writers." *The Female Tradition in Southern Literature.* Ed. Carol S. Manning. Urbana and Chicago: University of Illinois Press, 1993. 1–12.

Mark, Rebecca. *The Dragon's Blood: Feminist Intertextuality in Eudora Welty's* The Golden Apples. Jackson: University Press of Mississippi, 1994.

Marks, Patricia. *Bicycles, Bangs, and Bloomers: The New Woman in the Popular Press.* Lexington: The University Press of Kentucky, 1990.

Matthews, Pamela. *Ellen Glasgow and a Woman's Traditions.* Charlottesville: University of Virginia Press, 1995.

McCracken, Ellen. *Decoding Women's Magazines: From* Mademoiselle *to* Ms. New York: St. Martin's, 1993.

McDowell, Deborah. "Reading Family Matters." *Haunted Bodies: Gender and Southern Text.* Eds. Anne Goodwyn Jones and Susan V. Donaldson. Charlottesville: University Press of Virginia, 1997.

McHaney, Pearl Amelia. "Introduction." *A*

Writer's Eye: Collected Book Reviews. By Eudora Welty. Jackson: University Press of Mississippi, 1994. xiii–xxviii.

McKay, Nellie. "An Interview with Toni Morrison." *Conversations with Toni Morrison.* Jackson: University Press of Mississippi, 1994. 138–55.

McKee, Patricia. *Producing American Races: Henry James, William Faulkner, Toni Morrison.* Durham: Duke University Press, 1999.

Meeker, Richard K. *The Collected Letters of Ellen Glasgow.* Baton Rouge: Louisiana State University Press, 1963.

Meyers, Marian. Introduction: "Fracturing Women." *Mediated Women.* Ed. Marian Meyers. Cresskill, NJ: Hampton Press, 1999. 6–7.

Michael, Magali Cornier. "Re-Imagining Agency: Toni Morrison's *Paradise*." *African American Review* 36.4 (Winter 2002): 643–61.

Michaels, Walter Benn. "Local Colors." *MLN* 113.4 (1998): 734–56.

Michaels, Walter Benn. *Our America: Nativism, Modernism, and Pluralism.* Durham: Duke University Press, 1995.

Mintz, Steven, and Susan Kellogg. *Domestic Revolutions: A Social History of American Family Life.* Macmillan: New York, 1988.

Mitchell, Angelyn. "'Sth, I Know That Woman': History, Gender, and the South in Toni Morrison's *Jazz*." *Studies in the Literary Imagination* 31.2 (Fall 1998): 49–60.

Montgomery, Maxine Lavon. "Good Housekeeping: Domestic Ritual in Gloria Naylor's Fiction." *Gloria Naylor's Early Novels.* Gainesville: University Press of Florida, 1999. 55–69.

Morrison, Toni. "Home." *The House That Race Built.* Ed. Wahneema Lubiano. New York: Pantheon Books, 1997. 3–12.

_____. *Beloved.* New York: Knopf, 1987.

_____. *Jazz.* New York: Knopf, 1992.

_____. *Love.* New York: Knopf, 2003.

_____. *Paradise.* New York: Knopf, 1998.

_____. *Playing in the Dark: Whiteness and*

the Literary Imagination. Cambridge: Harvard University Press, 1992.

Mortimer, Gail. *Daughter of the Swan: Love and Knowledge in Eudora Welty's Fiction.* Athens and London: University of Georgia Press, 1994.

Moss, Elizabeth. *Domestic Novelists in the Old South: Defenders of Southern Culture.* Baton Rouge: Louisiana State University Press, 1992.

Mother Red's Southern Country Kitchen. 1 October 2000. DB Tech Personal Pages. 3 November 2000. *http://web.dbtech.net/-suncastl/kitchen.htm.*

Nowlin, Michael. "Toni Morrison's *Jazz* and the Racial Dreams of the American Writer." *American Literature: A Journal of Literary History, Criticism, and Bibliography* 71.1 (March 1999): 151–74.

Ogburn, W. F. *On Culture and Social Change.* Chicago: University of Chicago Press, 1964.

Ong, Walter. *Orality and Literacy: The Technologizing of the Word.* London and New York: Methuen, 1982.

Page, Philip. "Furrowing All the Brows: Interpretation and the Transcendent in Toni Morrison's *Paradise*." *African American Review* 35.4 (Winter 2001): 637–64.

Page, Philip. *Dangerous Freedom: Fusion and Fragmentation in Toni Morrison's Novel.* Jackson: University Press of Mississippi, 1995.

Paquet-Deyris, Anne-Marie. "Toni Morrison's *Jazz* and the City." *African American Review* 35.2 (Summer 2001): 219–31.

"Parenthood Group Renamed." *New York Times* (6 March 1942): 23:7. (March 1933): 34, 110.

Pingree et al. "A Scale for Sexism." *Journal of Communication* 26 (1976): 193–200.

Plante, Ellen. *The American Kitchen, 1700 to the Present.* New York: Facts on File, 1995.

Poovey, Mary. *Uneven Developments: The Ideological Work of Gender in Mid-Victorian England.* Chicago: The University of Chicago Press, 1988.

Powell, Julia. *The Julie/Julia Project.* 2002. 1 Nov. 2007. http://blogs.salon.com/00 01399/.

Powell, Julia. *Julie and Julia: 365 Days, 524 Recipes, 1 Tiny Apartment Kitchen.* Boston and New York: Little, Brown, 2005.

Prenshaw, Peggy Whitman, ed. *Eudora Welty: Critical Essays.* Jackson: University of Mississippi, 1979.

_____. "Sex and Wreckage in the Parlor: Welty's 'Bye-Bye Brevoort.'" *The Southern Quarterly: A Journal of the Arts in the South* 33.2–3 (January 1995): 107–116.

_____. "Woman's World, Man's Place: The Fiction of Eudora Welty." Eds. Louis Dollarhide and Ann J. Abadie. *Eudora Welty: A Form of Thanks.* Jackson: University Press of Mississippi, 1979. 46–77.

Prince, Valerie Sweeney. *Burnin' Down the House: Home in African American Literature.* New York: Columbia University Press, 2005.

Proitsaki, Maria. "'Cause It's My House': African American Women and Domestic Empowerment." *Moderna Språk* 99.1 (2005): 2–11.

"Railroad Maps, 1828–1900, U.S. History." *Library of Congress's The Learning Page.* 8 January 2001. Library of Congress. 30 January 2001. *http://lcweb2.loc.gov/am mem/ndlpedu/collections/rr/history.html.*

Raper, J. R. *Without Shelter: The Early Career of Ellen Glasgow.* Baton Rouge: Louisiana State University Press, 1971.

_____. "Invisible Things: The Short Stories of Ellen Glasgow." *The Southern Literary Journal* 9 (Spring 1977): 66–90.

Rattray, Diana. *Diana's Kitchen.* October 2000. 5 October 1999. *http://www.ebi com.net/kitchen/.*

_____. *Southern U.S. Cuisine.* 15 November 2000. About.com. 5 October 1999. *http:// southernfood.about.com/food/southern food/mbody.htm.*

Reed, Julia. "The Bubba Stories." *New York Times.* 30 Nov. 1997, late ed., sec. 7: 23.

Richter, Amy. *Home on the Rails: Women, the Railroad, and the Rise of Public Do-mesticity.* Chapel Hill: The University of North Carolina Press, 2005.

Rodriguez, Denise. "'Where the Self That Had No Self Made Its Home': The Reinscription of Domestic Discourse in Toni Morrison's *Beloved.*" *Griot: Official Journal of the Southern Conference on Afro-American Studies, Inc.* 20.1 (Spring 2001): 40–51.

Romero, Channette. "Creating the Beloved Community: Religion, Race and Nation in Toni Morrison's *Paradise.*" *African American Review* 39.3 (Fall 2005): 415–30.

Romero, Lora. *Home Fronts: Domesticity and Its Critics in the Antebellum United States.* Durham: Duke University Press, 1998.

Romines, Ann. "Reading the Cakes: *Delta Wedding* and the Texts of Southern Women's Culture." *Mississippi Quarterly* 50 (1997): 601–616.

Romines, Anne. *The Home Plot: Women Writing Domestic Ritual.* Amherst: University of Massachusetts Press, 1992.

Roosa, John, and Edward Davis. *Handbook of the Anatomy and Diseases of the Eye and Ear.* Philadelphia: F. A. Davis Co., 1904.

Rothman, Barbara. "Pregnancy." *The Reader's Companion to U.S. Women's History.* Ed. Wilma Mankiller. New York: Houghton Mifflin, 1998. 468–70.

Rouse, Blair. *Letters of Ellen Glasgow.* New York: Harcourt, Brace, 1958. Routledge: New York, 1997. 1–6.

Sadker, David, and Myra Sadker. *Failing at Fairness: How Our Schools Cheat Girls.* New York: Simon & Schuster, 1994.

Scanlon, Jennifer. *Inarticulate Longings: The Ladies' Home Journal, Gender, and the Promises of Consumer Culture.* New York: Routledge, 1995.

Scarry, Elaine. *The Body in Pain: The Making and Unmaking of the World.* New York: Oxford University Press, 1985.

"Screenfridge." *Electrolux.* 18 March 1999. Electrolux. 2 October 1999. *http://www. electrolux.co.uk/screenfridge/start.htm.*

Selzer, Linda. "Race and Domesticity in *The*

Color Purple." *African American Review* 29.1 (Spring 1995): 67–82.

Smith, Lee. *Fair and Tender Ladies*. New York: G.P. Putnam's Sons, 1988.

Smith, Lee. *Oral History*. New York: Ballantine Books, 1983.

Sontag, Susan. *AIDS and Its Metaphors*. New York: Farrar, Straus and Giroux, 1988.

Sontag, Susan. *Illness as Metaphor*. New York: Farrar, Straus and Giroux, 1977.

Southern Belles Web Ring. 18 October 1998. Yahoo. 5 December 2000. *http://nav.we-bring.yahoo.com/hub?ring=belles&list*.

The Southern Kitchen. 31 August 1998. Geocities.com. 2 October 1999. *http://www.geocities.com/~angelpig/southern cookin.html*.

Squires, Rhonda. "Bug Bite Soup." *Mother Red's Southern Country Kitchen*. 1 October 2000. DB Tech Personal Pages. 3 November 2000. *http://web.dbtech.net/~sun castl/kitchen.htm*.

Steinem, Gloria. "Sex, Lies, and Advertising." *Moving Beyond Words*. New York: Simon & Schuster, 1994. 123–68.

Stepto, Robert. "Intimate Things in Place: A Conversation with Toni Morrison." *Conversations with Toni Morrison*. Jackson: University Press of Mississippi, 1994. 10–29.

Stevenson, R. Scott. *A History of Oto-Laryngology*. Edinburgh: E&S Livingstone, 1949.

Strasser, Susan. *Never Done: A History of American Housework*. New York: Henry Holt, 2000 (first published 1982).

Tate, Claudia. "Toni Morrison." *Conversations with Toni Morrison*. Jackson: University Press of Mississippi, 1994. 156–70.

Taylor, George, and Irene Neu. *The American Railroad Network, 1861–1890*. Cambridge: Harvard University Press, 1956.

Thomson, Rosmarie Garland. "Feminist Theory, the Body, and the Disabled Figure." *The Disability Studies Reader*. Ed. Lennard Davis. Routledge: New York, 1997. 279–92.

"A True Internet Appliance: Kitchen Information Center Previewed." *AllNetDevices:*

News. 7 January 1999. AllNetDevices. 2 October 1999. *http://devices.internet.com/ news_archive/q199/990107Kitchen/990107 kitchen.html*.

Tuchman, Gaye, Arlene Kaplan Daniels, and James Benét, eds. *Hearth and Home: Images of Women in the Mass Media*. New York: Oxford University, 1978.

Turkle, Sherry. "TinySex and Gender Trouble." *Border Texts*. Ed. Randall Bass. Boston: Houghton Mifflin, 1999.

Vande Kieft, Ruth M. *Eudora Welty*. Boston: Twayne, 1987.

Wagner, Linda. *Ellen Glasgow: Beyond Convention*. Austin: University of Texas Press, 1982.

Wagner-Martin, Linda. "Introduction." *Virginia*. By Ellen Glasgow. New York: Penguin Classics, 1989.

Waldron, Ann. *Eudora: A Writer's Life*. New York: Doubleday, 1998.

Walker, Nancy A. *Shaping Our Mothers' World: American Women's Magazines*. Jackson: University Press of Mississippi, 2000.

_____. "The Romance of Self-Representation: Glasgow and *The Woman Within*." *Ellen Glasgow: New Perspectives*. Ed. Dorothy Scura. Knoxville: The University of Tennessee Press, 1995.

Wardi, Anissa Janine. "A Laying on of Hands: Toni Morrison and the Materiality of *Love*." *MELUS: The Journal of the Society for the Study of the Multi-Ethnic Literature of the United States* 30.3 (Fall 2005): 201–218.

Welty, Eudora. *Delta Wedding*. New York: Harcourt, Brace, 1946.

_____. *One Writer's Beginnings*. New York: Warner Books, 1983.

_____. *The Collected Stories of Eudora Welty*. New York: Harcourt, Brace, 1980.

_____. *The Optimist's Daughter*. New York: Random House, 1969.

Wendell, Susan. "Toward a Feminist Theory of Disability." *The Disability Studies Reader*. Ed. Lennard Davis. New York: Routledge, 1997. 260–78.

Westling, Louise. *Eudora Welty*. Women Writers Series. London: Macmillan, 1989.

Westling, Louise. *Sacred Groves and Ravaged Gardens: The Fiction of Eudora Welty, Carson McCullers, and Flannery O'Connor.* Athens: University of Georgia Press, 1985.

Wiegman, Robyn. *American Anatomies: Theorizing Race and Gender (New Americanists).* Durham: Duke University Press, 1995.

Wilson, Judith. "A Conversation with Toni Morrison." *Conversations with Toni Morrison.* Jackson: University Press of Mississippi, 1994. 129–37.

Woolf, Naomi. *The Beauty Myth.* New York: W. Morrow, 1991.

Yaeger, Patricia. *Dirt and Desire: Reconstructing Southern Women's Writing, 1930–1990.* Chicago: University of Chicago Press, 2000.

Yardley, Jonathan. "Manners Make the Novelist." *The Washington Post* 3 May 1998: X03+.

Yardley, Jonathan. "Toni Morrison: An Introduction." *The Washington Post* 6 March 2006: C01.

INDEX